Under the Bed

Stories & Thoughts From a Desert Island

Under the Bed
Stories & Thoughts From a Desert Island

Robert Pierse

LITTLE PLATOON

Under the Bed: Stories & Thoughts From a Desert Island
Published in 2019 by Robert Pierse
Listowel, Co Kerry, Ireland

Copyright © Robert Pierse

ISBN 978-1-5272-3962-3

The publisher, Robert Pierse, would like to thank Maurice and Jane O'Keeffe, of Irish Life and Lore (www.irishlifeandlore.com) for allowing him to reproduce, in the attached CD, Maurice's interview with him, from the Irish Life and Lore Series, Achievers in Profile, collection.

Robert Pierse would like to thank Brendan O'Bryne of Little Platoon for supporting this publication and assisting with its promotion.

Typeset by Dominic Carroll, Ardfield, Co. Cork
Printed by SPRINT-print Ltd, Dublin
Editing and Representation by Jeremy Murphy, Editor and Literary Agent
www.jeremymurphyeditor.com

Dedicated to:
Benedict Cyril Pierse who was with us for 30 weeks
and then 20 minutes

and to
Fr Gerard Pierse RIP, who was with us for 59 years

and then to
Ranguana Caye
(In the hope it will not be washed away)

and to
Caroline and Donal
(As exciting and wonderful hosts)

to
My wife, Olive, Aislinn Gildea, Seán and Paul
(My fellow travellers to Belize)

to
Kevin Maderia
(Our multitalented fisherman and friend with a big bottom)

to
Jean
(The caye or the island's "Taker of Care")

to
Vance
(our 007)

And finally to
Harry the hare & Scruffy the dog
(Cheerful companions in a storm)

CONTENTS

ENJOY THIS, PLEASE!!

This short record is for enjoyment. Enjoy it in small bites, maybe as a light interlude in a heavy day. It is of peculiar birth and content.

This book is about something you may be familiar with:

A. Being marooned on a small desert island, which is being washed away in a storm off Central America?
B. What you do and say when marooned?
C. Being the father of ten children and a country lawyer in a small Irish town.
D. Being involved in life for over 80 years and law for almost 60 of these, enjoying them both.

If you are so familiar, do not buy this book.

If you are not so familiar maybe you should buy it and learn more about life's interesting events in 1999 for me, a humble lawyer (and I have much to be humble about!). It was largely written on toilet paper so it may be rubbish anyway.

I began my first scribblings in the back pages of that excellent, but heavy, law journal called *The Irish Jurist*. Holidays are the only time you can plough through the law's deep searchings for its own meaning. Special thanks to Maria here, who has made something of my notes.

I have avoided, these past 20 years, tackling an untidy collection of toilet paper, as well as notes on law journals and novels. Some of these were typed over the years when I got a push from my son Gearóid, to do something about it. It is mainly short stories about incidents in my life. I believe that heavy law is part of life also and there is a little of that in this book. Not everyone is so blessed or befuddled, but there are wonderful individuals everywhere.

In December 2005 Maurice O'Keeffe broadcast an hour interview he had with me on Radio Kerry. It was a light-hearted take on my life and experiences. The response rather startled me. One man said to my son Risteárd:

> I always thought that your father was an austere and unapproachable man until I heard that programme. I was amazed he could tell funny stories and laugh.

That was my public image, probably still is.

It is for those of you stuck in traffic jams far from Ranguana Caye, Belize. Drivers are often marooned in their own island of a car, so the CD might lighten a few minutes.

I hope it makes them laugh. Laughter is a morning medicine, a prelude to a delightful day. Love each day with its dawn, daylight, dusk and darkness.

> What is this life, if full of care,
> We have no time to stop and stare.
> No time to see in broad daylight,
> Stream full of stars, like skies at night,
> A poor life this is if, full of care,
> We have no time to stand and stare.

Thank you Mr WH Davis.

Pressure came on two Christmases ago, Christmas 2017, to resurrect *Under the Bed*. I suppose the fact that I have thirty-two grandchildren and twenty of their parents urging me to write my stories on my 80th birthday shows they think my time is running out. Maybe it is, but I have asked my doctor wife to keep me going for another 80 years as life is so interesting. I have so much still to learn.

We had our 50th wedding anniversary on 29th June 2013 on Valentia Island. When I said to her: 'What for the next 50 years?' She said: 'I could never manage you another 50 years.' Pessimist!

I will review the life situation after those 50 years, probably (or should it be improbably?).

I hope you enjoy the artwork which enhances this book. That great artist friend of mine, Tighe O'Donoghue Ross of Killarney, did the needful for me.

I want to thank my grandson, Fergal Pierse, whose fantastic drawings are also included. I better mention my godson, Maurice Pierse, whose far too flattering portrait of me adorns the inside back cover.

Pauline Bewick, a renowned artist, has kindly agreed to the use of one of her paintings, *South Sea Island*, which I think captures everything I loved about Ranguana Caye. Find Pauline's painting inside.

I thank all the people who helped with this book, and who gave me permission to reproduce such beautiful poetry.

I must thank Cyril Kelly and Billy Keane, both writers, and both Listowel men, who kindly agreed to launch this book. My thanks also to Joe Mannix, my friend and fellow solicitor, who read a draft of this book and made helpful suggestions.

I and some of my children (and their spouses) seem to think I am incapable of writing anything other than 'heavy' law! Let's see!

I give up making excuses, so here goes. I have thrown in a few up to date remarks in my revision process. I was going to put them in brackets but I didn't. I do not particularly like brackets and footnotes. Do you?

I particularly want to thank my editor Jeremy Murphy, who is based in Listowel.

If you have got this far and intend going on, bravo! Enjoy it!

Robert

The Kingdom of Kerry (Only so Far)

31/12/2018 and a bit of 2019 also

DAY TWO: THE BED

The Calm

Olive and I left the *Seagull* cabin and retired to the *Laughing Bird* cabin at about 9 pm. The bed was big, with an old and strong timber-frame. It was about two feet off the floor, with a 6-foot wide mattress in its latex-like frame. The *Laughing Bird* cabin was the cabin nearest the sea on the eastern side of this most beautiful, and very small, island of Ranguana Caye, Belize.

Yes, the wind was more blustery than the previous night, but there was nothing to tell us what was coming. It is January 1999 and we were in Central America. That is where Belize is. We arrived on Sunday, and we had completed (we thought!) our first peaceful day on the sandy caye.

We had left Big Creek, a large port in Belize, on the afternoon of Day One, a lovely trip out to here. It was uneventful, so I omit Day One; mostly.

Today has been good. Olive, my darling wife and friend of nigh 40 years, had set off with the others on a fishing expedition at 5:30 am. The 5s, am and pm, are the best time for fishing here. It has something to do with the light.

As I had been out on the 5 pm shift the evening before and caught two sizable tuna, I was left in bed this morning. We only fish two lines on the boat, so there is no point in too many of us going out. Caroline, *mo iníon céile* (my daughter by marriage) and I stayed on in the caye. She was expecting their first.

As the dawn was so lovely I couldn't stay on in bed. I sat on the small veranda of the *Laughing Bird* and looked around and down. This actually was my favourite past time on the caye, or 'small sand island'.

I had looked down at what I thought was silt or brown debris along the glistening white coral and sand. However, I soon realised my mistake.

Suddenly, the brown layer erupted. It was in fact a layer of sardine-sized sprat swimming in multitude. Its eruption was due to an intruder – a big, nasty, greeny blue fish that was almost invisible in its natural camouflage. It gobbled up the brown layer and disappeared.

My eye was to become more attuned to this and other natural camouflages as I looked out onto the reefs of Belize. This morning I sat calmly and sleepily enjoying the utter remoteness away from an uneasy world. The brown layer of fish was at calm again, forming a much smaller cluster.

The intruder was suddenly gone, having had breakfast on my largely vanished neighbours. Such is nature. They multiply in a few hours into a dense brown mass.

This is a warm, vibrant and colourful place. I have recently been to Russia, which is so different. A grey, cold place.

Russia

I was supposed to go to Africa, Kenya, I think, with the International Bar Association (IBA).

They (The IBA) cancelled for fear we lawyers would be endangered – or was it that the Africans did not want to bring another dangerous species to Africa? Am I wrong in thinking that lawyers can be regarded as a dangerous species? By the ill-informed only of course!

As it happened, the African trip was cancelled because there was trouble there, political unrest.

The IBA changed the venue to New York where I had been a few times. Olive had relations in New York, who come and go to us, so we come and go to them. However, the New York trip was also cancelled, so to Russia we go instead of the Big Apple.

Moscow was grey; the sky was grey, the food was grey and awful, the clothes were grey and awful, the streets were grey and awful, and the women were grey – because of abortions and lack of blood according to my medico wife.

Moscow was a disaster of a place really. We were followed around by young streetwise boys who would sell you these dolls that fit into each other for a dollar. The dollar was king.

We flew off to Georgia after a few days in Moscow, where there were very poor people – in the birthplace of Stalin! There we suffered from hunger. The only ones who had food were the communist bosses. We saw the food in a restaurant where the communist meeting was happening, but couldn't buy it. Our hotel had only black tea, black hard bread and greasy fried eggs.

We eventually got back to Leningrad (now St Petersburg) – lucky us! Passing through the airport I saw a duty-free shop decorated with shamrocks and made straight for it. Our guide said 'NO, NO', we could not go in as we were not departing Russia.

I saw an Irish man, recognised him from his T-shirt which had a shamrock on it. I called him over and explained to him the situation, our group's hunger. He was a Kerryman in fact, who was related to me through my father's people, one of the McKennas from Ballyduff. He worked in the Aer Rianta duty-free shop. We got Jacob's biscuits and Irish cheese. What a glorious feast!

The Hermitage

Then we visited the Hermitage Museum in St Petersburg, a lovely but poorly kept museum in a lovely but poorly kept city.

It used to be called the 'Venice of the North'. When we were there it was old, tired and dirty. The Hermitage was vast, on the edge of a vast square. One room was full of impressionist paintings: Renoirs, Picassos and van Goghs. Some were worth countless millions. On the parquet floor there was a bucket sitting on a sack. Why? Because the roof was leaking. There was no money to repair the roof, we were told.

Later I tried to get a print of Van Gogh's *The Red Vineyards near Arles*. No print for sale as they had no paper. That was in a city surrounded by forests. Communist planning and efficiency!

I had left Olive in the café, but when I returned I noticed the glass cup from which Olive had her tea was cracked, and on closer examination was dirty. My worst fears were realised that night, Olive got seriously ill. We needed a doctor urgently at 2 am in our hotel.

The Helping Hand

We were staying in a very large state hotel, (I do not think there were any non-state hotels) which was supposed to have a receptionist on each floor. No receptionist could be located on our floor, so I went down to the main reception desk. I rang bells, opened doors and shouted for help, but no one could be found.

Then for the first and only time in my life, I had reason to enlist the help from a most unlikely source, a prostitute!

In my desperation, I was running out to the street to get help. At the door, there was a soldier guarding the hotel. On his knee was a prostitute of doubtful age. She, however, had a basic grasp of English – a need of her old profession. She quickly understood about a medico. She disappeared into the bowels of the enormous building.

Within minutes, staff sleepily arrived. I was so angry, but a nice young doctor arrived with a grumpy 'manageress' dressed in military or police uniform.

The doctor, who spoke good English, was able to help Olive on a medical colleague basis and give her medicine to get us back to Ireland the following day.

I never saw the prostitute again, which was unfortunate as I would like to have thanked her. I assume the grumpy manageress banished her – saying no doubt such a profession does not exist in the glorious USSR. She was such a good human being. The kindness of strangers.

I went to pay the doctor but the grumpy 'manageress' informed me I was in the glorious Union of Soviet Socialist Republics and that visitors to the glorious Union of Soviet Socialists Republics did not have to pay for medical treatment, as they would have to in their capitalist states. Such twaddle, when I could read in the doctor's eyes that a few dollars would be welcome. I cannot ever remember it being otherwise anywhere in the world.

I was so grateful to this young man that I was determined to be a bad capitalist and so corrupt him with $20.

I said to Ms Grumpy that I had a male complaint that I wished to show the doctor in private in the bathroom. In we go, and I slip him $20. He told me it was the equivalent of a month's salary. He also told me he could not use the dollars really as there was so little to buy in the shops. I knew this to be true, as we had gone into a supermarket in Moscow to get food. There were only two items for sale, tired looking uncooked chickens and saucepans!

I got over the doctor's difficulty by writing my relation's name on my business card and explaining to him that Kerrymen were everywhere, including the heavenly, fully-stocked duty-free shop in Leningrad Airport.

The kind Stranger FP

I remember the following day, the day we were scheduled to go home, Olive looked badly. We were travelling up a long, straight road heading to the airport. I worried would she get through the next ten hours. I worried would we be left on to the plane. She did and we were. We arrived in Dublin. I got her to the medical centre.

When I came out through the door, I knelt down and kissed the green ground, saying to the Lord, 'thank you for getting us back to paradise'. We Irish have to go away to realise that Ireland is a paradise – well most of the time it is.

I was told our helpful doctor turned up at my Ballyduff relation's shop and got a bundle of grub. I hope he enjoyed it and lives happily ever since.

The time we were in Moscow a well-known, worldwide capitalist institution had just opened its doors there. The big M for McDonald's was shown to us by the guide in our tour of Moscow. It opened each day at 8 am. The morning we passed it (at 6:30 am) a queue of about twenty people had already formed to get their capitalist 'fix', 'The Big Mac'. I am not a fan of McDonald's – it's making young people obese. Do you notice that?

Another peculiarity I remember was that no one ever checked bus or tram tickets. It seems no one ever checked if the ticket collectors turned up for work. So they never turned up for work. I wonder how they were paid? As far as I could judge the locals, therefore, had free buses.

I'm led to believe things are much improved in Russia now, in 2019, although there are mixed views on that. They have become capitalist. Greed is a great economic motivator. Mr Putin, who I instinctively fear, is on the rise. Seeing him upsets me. That look in his eyes. I hope I am wrong.

I must go for a short walk and worry about rising wind and sea. Olive and the others are out there on the sand on the west side.

Caroline – Mo Iníon Céile

After an hour of fascination, when the brown sprat layers seemed to grow again in the sun, I moved off to have a cup of tea with Caroline, *mo iníon céile*, Donal's wife.

I did not use the term 'daughter-in-law', but the Irish expression; I say Caroline became my 'daughter by marriage'. I do not like the changing laws on marriage in Ireland. They are so damaging to family life, the core of a secure, caring and disciplined society.

Caroline is a delightful girl from middle England. Middle England is a more civilised area than London and the other urban jungles that festoon our sister island and are beginning to clutter our own Emerald Isle.

Over our Earl Grey tea on this minute island, we discussed the unusual events that brought us to Rangauna Caye, eight miles off Big Creek in the south of this small country, Belize.

After Caroline got her degree she worked in the management of a large sports complex in London. It wasn't very satisfying for her (a spirited and thoughtful young woman), as the clients were solely the pampered rich. That day, she verbalised for the first time the spiritual tug that got her to pack her bags. She was helped by a whiskey drinking, English priest who said to her to go to where you are needed and where you can do good. He needed her to go to Honduras.

She packed herself and her bags off for Honduras. There, to the dismay of her parents, she worked in an Aids hostel for the Catholic Church. She had to raise funds for the hostel and a crèche. Her father, Cyril, was sent out – you know the way wives send husbands on missions impossible – to get her to see sense and come back.

Cyril arrived. Caroline needed someone to drive a dying sailor to see the sea for the last time. It was his dying wish. Caroline handed Cyril the keys of the van. He was the new recruit. Caroline stayed in Honduras. Cyril did not, but he did stay long enough to meet Donal. They became great friends.

Donal Arrives

On one fateful (or faithful) occasion Caroline ran a garden fete to collect funds for the Aids hostel. She was having a row with the local bishop, who couldn't explain how funds allocated to the hostel were going to his own family.

Donal, my son, came to help to run the fete. His job, which he liked, was the dispensing of Guinness in the Irish stand. Donal was representing Fyffes, the company for whom he worked. Fyffes were sponsoring the stand – bananas with Guinness!

One now goes into that delicate area of who 'spotted' the other first. The best account seems to be that the lady spotted this rather large, dark-haired male dispensing Guinness. She freely admits she had not seen a large Caucasian male for four months.

Well, the lioness, a far more deadly species than the lion I am told, moved towards the lion for a pint of Guinness. She shimmered forward in her green dress. Male takes the order but takes his time, taking a good look at the contents of the green dress. Obviously, a long approving look!

Lady in green returns to base. Male busy for 10 minutes, then moves out of his lair behind the counter to the area where the green dress was last seen. The other girls, including Niamh Killalea from Galway, send out information by female bush telegraph that male wants to chat up green dress. Green dress reappears. All this leads to an Anglo-Irish Agreement. They were married in September 1998 in middle England. What a day!

Caroline claims that, shortly after their meeting, she visited all the churches in South America while on holidays there. She says she used up all her three wishes in each church on Donal, so the guy didn't have a chance. There are a lot of churches in South America due to the Spanish conquest.

I must tell you about my first meeting with Caroline. I was in Dublin on a law case – I am a solicitor. Caroline was over from the UK visiting someone. She came up to the flat in Charlemont Place where I was staying. I suddenly found I was being interviewed. She obviously wanted to see how her intended might be thirty years down the line. I found it unusually difficult to get on the same wavelength, until she laughed about all her South American churches.

I told her of my beloved St Paul. She had a deep knowledge of her religion and St Paul. Actually, women generally do not like St Paul. I do not know why, as in his letters he often sends greetings to women. St Paul realised women were the bosses then, as now, and that if the new religion was to flourish it would be through women. St Paul was smarter than most males in realising women are the bosses. I think Jesus realised that too (Martha and Mary!), but then he never wrote anything that we know of.

One can have no better description of true love than 1 Cor 13. You know the one you hear at most weddings: 'Love is gentle and love is kind.'

It always bothers me, as a lawyer, that Jesus himself never wrote anything down.

As my late mother used to say, the women outnumbered men three to one at the foot of the cross. Wise woman my mother too, and most certainly in her own way the boss of her husband and seven sons.

Actually, there is a story about my mother, a deeply religious woman. Her friends, Kitty McMahon, (our author-teacher Bryan's wife) and Peg Murphy, went to daily mass with her. These three good women were coming up from their daily mass. In Lower William, a publican with a well-developed front was at one side of the street and a butcher, also with a well-developed front, was at the other. One shouted at the other across the street as the three women approached: 'Here are the three craw thumpers, statute adorers and holy water sprinklers coming up from Mass.'

Before the other man could answer, my mother sweetly looked up and said in a loud voice: 'We outnumbered you at the foot of the cross and it's that way since.'

Actually, that particular man, the publican, was turned into the character of the Bull McCabe by John B Keane in *The Field*. It was one of the interests of the town folk in Listowel to guess who John B was portraying in his latest play.

St Paul had some other remarks about women, about how they were giddy and talkative in church. However, I'd never even mention or write that, nor could I say that St Paul would be horrified by these mobile phones. Generally speaking, a certain sex is generally speaking, I believe but daren't say it! I'll be speaking about St Paul further on so we'll be meeting him again.

My reward from that interview with Caroline was a wonderful, deep friendship; what a wonderful wife and mother she has become.

You may have noticed that this book is dedicated to, among others, Benedict, Caroline and Donal's first baby. Benedict survived only 20 minutes, as he was born in the wilds of Belize, over 100 miles from a hospital. He lies peacefully in Belize, RIP.

Wedding

I got into terrible trouble at the wedding of Caroline and Donal because I spoke for too long. You know the learned and thundering-sound type of speech to try to keep people awake. It was a wet day in the reception tent.

I tried to justify it later by saying that the guests had nothing better to do than listen to 'the Irish man'. When I saw the video I was shocked. I hadn't remembered the poet Dryden's warning:

> Words are like leaves
> And where they most abound,
> Much fruit of wisdom
> Beneath is rarely found

All weddings since have my children in a frenzy of gambling to judge how long I will be. One daughter sought to bribe me with a most sweet smile, and I had to give her a guess/estimate of my time as there was a lot of money in the pot!

Daughters know their fathers are wrapped around their little fingers! I never had a sister, so I am at a total loss with the female sex anyway.

Donal's Baptism & Some Musings

While in that church at Caroline and Donal's wedding, I remembered Donal's baptism. Donal had arrived with a Rhesus blood problem, and when I first saw him he was very jaundiced. I remember my knees getting weak. Any illness of a child affected me. When they got an injection, I would have preferred to have the sharp pain myself.

I had arrived down to St Finbarr's, Cork, with Olive's brother Fr Gearóid to baptise in a hurry. Mom, my mother-in-law (a very small woman) and my brother Michael (a very tall man) were the godparents. As Donal was in an incubator, we were told to hold a toe each through a hole in the incubator. A wholly irreverent thought occurred to me – they looked like Mutt and Jeff from the newspaper cartoon! I didn't tell that story at the wedding.

Belize: I have been walking just now. I wish the boat was further back from the shore. I see, just walking past here bent low against the wind, that the waves are getting further up the beach. The wind is getting stronger, but it is warm.

I am hopeless at weddings. I regard weddings and marriage as so hugely important, because of my own wonderful wife. At Caroline and Donal's wedding, the young people maybe thought I was a pompous old windbag, but I did strike a bit of a chord with the over 50s.

They liked my poetry and exhortations from St Paul. In fact, in middle England they seemed a bit surprised that I could spin off so much of the Bard of Avon, their romantic poets such as William Wordsworth and the New Testament.

An Irish lawyer was a new phenomenon, especially when he spoke with a Kerry accent. I really was a bit of a windbag, but lawyers tend to be.

Speaking of which, English and Northern Irish Christians, both Catholics and their Protestant friends, are much better readers of the Bible than we are in southern Ireland. I suppose it is the competitive, religious element in Northern Ireland and England.

In the south of Ireland we choose the bits of our religion we like, talk about it, pray a bit, but rarely put many Christian principles into practice. We are like people hopping on and off the bus.

I think it was GK Chesterton who said the great failure of Christianity is that it has never been practised. I believe that applies to some clerics too – I often wonder about these bishops' palaces and churches built in famine times.

Caroline's family is very Catholic. I think that bond of Faith is a good cornerstone in the life-long vocation of marriage. Then of course, Ireland contributes much to English faith. The Venerable Bede, writing in the first half of the 8th Century, said:

> At this period there were many English Nobles and lesser folk in Ireland who had left their own land during the episcopates of Bishops Finan and Colman either to pursue Religious studies or lead a life of stricter Discipline. The Irish welcomed them kindly and, without asking for any payment, provided them with books and instructions!

Belize: Look, I am off for a bit of a walk and look around. I am back. Let's continue with wedding & adventures.

The oddest thing that Donal said at the wedding was that he could not really promise Caroline much other than a life of adventure. I assumed Donal's mention of adventure referred to past sailing trips, as Donal, like myself, had sailed from the USA to Fenit. How wrong I was!

His spirit of adventure would later lead me to this night and on this island off Belize, and to a storm in our *Laughing Bird* cabin.

Three Adventures; Adventure One

Caroline has already experienced the trials of Donal's adventure programme. One week into their honeymoon he broke one of the vertebrae on his back. It happened at about 11 am in the morning, but it was 2 pm on that Saturday that I was wheeling him down the corridor of Tralee General Hospital, enclosed in metal supports.

I had just seen him being lifted off a helicopter. That time, to the minute, was a week after I saw a smiling, radiant Caroline walking up the aisle to Donal in Colwich Church, an old church that had been renovated under the guidance of her architect father, Cyril. Donal was grinning from ear to ear in the lovely old church, at the sight of Caroline.

What happened? A simple thing. Donal and Paul, our youngest, were swimming and bodyboarding on surf near Kerry Head; at a place we call 'Pierse's Island'.

In fact, it is neither Pierse's nor an island! It is a lovely, secluded strand of golden sand nestling between black cliffs, with green grass and red heather tops.

Donal saw a big wave coming and turned to warn Paul, but was caught himself by the wave. Caroline, his bride, was watching from the cliff top. The wave turned Donal upside down and his head came in contact with the sand. He felt a crack in his spine. Surprisingly, he was able to stagger out of the water and on to the beach before collapsing. Drama followed!

Paul raced a mile for help. Wonderful neighbours (Liam Casey Leen and the O'Donoghues) came. People phoned for rescue service. A helicopter was to be sent. The Ballybunion cliff rescue team arrived.

They were in a dilemma, as was Dr Stephanie O'Reilly who had come down the cliff. They felt Donal should not be moved – moving would have meant hauling him up a cliff. Still, no helicopter was coming and the tide was coming in and heading for Donal's legs with the awesome inevitability of the cruel, unthinking rhythm that is nature.

Some demarcation mix up in calling the rescue service got sorted out and a helicopter arrived, the Big Bird. It was just in time as the tide had reached his shoulders. Donal and Caroline were winched up, Donal on a special stretcher, into that Big Bird.

I was at Tralee General Hospital when the Big Bird landed. I was there to pick up Olive for lunch as she was at a medical seminar there. It was scary even for a father of ten children used to offspring creating emergencies.

Doctors stuck pins into him and his reaction was good. Surgeon Murphy, with whom we were friendly, held up a small needle sideways to me saying: 'He is so lucky, he was within that much of being paralysed for life.'

X-rays revealed a bad fracture – 1 cm more and he would have been paralysed for life. Olive, who is a doctor, was then able to stop praying, get off her knees, talk and cry with relief.

Donal got wonderful care in Tralee General Hospital. He was immobilised but was going to be OK. Caroline had her first major adventure. One she and we would have wished to avoid.

Adventure Two
After six weeks or so they went back to work in Belize, Donal all strapped up and ready to commence adventure No. Two!

They just landed before a typhoon hit Belize and Honduras. They spent days dodging falling trees, moving up, down and around mountains, sleeping on friends' floors or under their houses, before that typhoon passed.

Caroline revisited Honduras to check on work colleagues and friends. The devastation and death in Honduras was appalling. However, the pair survived. Donal's broken back survived.

I wonder about climate change, global warming versus our consumers' comfort! I did a six-month environmental law course in UCD recently. It brought home to me the damage we are doing to Mother Earth. I don't use plastics wherever possible and I have planted fifty acres of trees in Athea.

Adventure Three (This Adventure!)

So, our present adventure came about because of the need for Olive, exercising her maternal medical mandate, to go to Belize and check out Donal's back. She came here armed with his X-rays and accompanied by 'Himself' (that's me) as well as our sons Seán and Paul.

Seán brought along his delightful Dublin girlfriend, Aislinn Gildea. I see wedding bells in two sets of eyes. I just love all these new girls and boyfriends entering our lives. They are wonderful.

Off we set from Shannon in an Aeroflot plane, on a pleasant flight, after a row with a Mr Boris (whose name other than Boris I never got as he had little English) about dates.

'They' (one never finds out who 'they' are in these type of circumstances) got our flights mixed up, our seats mixed up and us mixed up. We had been told to arrive at 4 am for the 7 am flight, which was daft. We arrived pronto at 4 am.

A cemetery would have been more cheerful than Shannon Airport at 4 am.

I have an attitude problem when it comes to Russian flights, and to a large extent Russia itself – I still have.

Miami

I really must get out of my bad habit of wandering into other stories and losing you and myself. Where was I? Yes – Shannon to Miami on a Russian plane on our visit to see Donal and Caroline in Belize.

I issue you a warning. If you land in Miami, as we did, believe nothing that is said to you. We had so much hassle in getting our boarding cards to Belize that Olive got ill from the distress.

Keep away from Miami Airport is my free legal advice. We were sent from here to there in a spiritless airport that morning. Everyone was overweight and awkward. The staff had a psychological incapacity to tell the truth. They had seriously overbooked our plane.

Public bribery had to follow to get us on a plane to Belize. This ended up with six people getting $100 pocket money and a free night in a hotel to remain until the following day. The backpackers were delighted. One said to me: 'We know the flights that will be overbooked, so we head for those. There can be a nice few bucks if you get the really badly overbooked ones. You just hold out until the money is right – it can go up to $200.00!!'

This anxiety, useless rushing, queuing and the upset severely affected Olive later – hours of tension about gates, flights, tickets, passes, is not good for a mother worried about her son and his back. She always called Donal 'Dotey Pettums'. I do not know why mothers do these sorts of things.

Another thing I detested about Miami was the way they treated South Americans and Mexicans – boy were they third-class people!

The mention of Miami reminds me of a true story about a case in Florida in 1901. A Mr JB Brown had been convicted of murder. When he was standing on the gallows, still protesting his innocence with the rope around his neck, it was discovered that the death warrant bore the name of the foreman of the jury instead of Mr Brown. Brown was reprieved and his sentence commuted to life imprisonment. Two years later another man confessed to the murder and Brown was set free. Who says the law is not an ass?

It is true stories like that and the 'Birmingham Six' that show what frail vessels of potential injustice courts can be. It's the main reason I am against the death penalty. Courts do make terrible mistakes, as we all do. Juries often get carried away in the wave of emotion hyped up by the media and fake news.

I always find it difficult to know what is the truth. Indeed, isn't it difficult to know if you know anything? In 'knowing' information what have you in this world where the catchphrase is 'everything', (such as 'knowledge is everything')? Wasn't it Socrates who said the secret of all wisdom was knowing thyself?

Lawyers have always had difficulty with knowledge, fact, truth, guilt, innocence and reality. What do these words mean?

I am reading Richard Ellmann's classic book on James Joyce at the moment. Joyce had an avid interest in words and their meaning, and in the law. He attended many trials in Dublin, as can be seen in his thoughts on Thursday 16th June 1904, as recounted in *Ulysses*.

Ellmann's book is a difficult read and his interpretation of *Ulysses* differs from Joyce's own. Joyce said of his most famous novel: 'In *Ulysses* I tried to keep close to the fact ... to reality which always triumphs in the end.'

I humbly disagree that reality always triumphs in the end, particularly in modern democratic politics. Most law cases are presentations of two perceived sets of realities, neither of which the judge may see as reality. Am I being complex?

Joyce's unwise father wanted his son to be a barrister. I think in fact he did go to some lectures in law at Trinity but quickly changed to try medicine, but gave that up quickly as well'.

Gosh, I've wandered from America. I will take a break. Do not get me wrong, I like America and have some great friends there. In fact Listowel, my hometown, is twinned to a delightful town called Shawnee in Kansas. Now there is a hospitable place, especially on St Patrick's Day! We visited it some years ago. Dogs with green fur, leprechauns all over the place, wonderful parade where we actual Irish walked along.

I also love New York, it is so informal and it has great book stores. This is despite the fact the humidity was so bad one day that I had only walked 200 yards from Olive's cousin's house to a bus stop when I wanted to go back for a cold shower.

I also love Washington. A city without poles or electrical wires, at least in the centre. Wonderful architecture in both cities.

Belize

We did however arrive at Belize from Miami. It is off the Belize coast that I pen these notes. It was a great joy to find the newlyweds still in the land of bliss – long may they remain so is my prayer.

We headed in a jeep for Big Creek where they live. The 'good roads' ended after about forty miles. The muddy, potholed track we drove in was bad for Donal's back, and they lasted for the next hundred miles.

Yes, Belize was formerly British Honduras! It is there in underdeveloped Central America – you know that bit between North America and South America that looks like a shoehorn, or a funnel.

It is very beautiful and is beginning to develop a tourist trade. Donal works here for Fyffes, the fruit company. Big Creek in Placencia is where millions of bananas are shipped weekly to the USA and Europe by Fyffes.

Listowel in Belize
On the way to Big Creek we stopped in Belize's Listowel. Listowel, Ireland is my hometown. I have lived almost all my life there. One of the joys of leaving it is the joy of coming back to it. It is full of rural character and characters. It has all one needs.

> Ó áit go háit ba bhreá mo shiúl,
> Is dob ard mo léim ar bharr an tsléibh,'
> I long 's i mbád ba mhór mo dhúil,
> 'S ba bheo mo chroí i lár mo chléibh.
> Mar chois an ghiorria a bhí mo chos,

Mar iarann gach alt is féith,
Bhí an sonas romham, thall is abhus
Sa ghleann 'nar tógadh mé.

Thank you Mr First Irish President, Douglas Hyde. Roughly translated, President Hyde was saying poetically that the glen where one was born was great. Listowel in Kerry has its own 'Gleann' (Glen) football team, and the street where my office is situated is called *Glean a Phuca*, or 'The Glen of the Fairies'. I also remember the stanza about the fairies from *The Fairies*, by William Allingham:

Up the airy mountain, down the rushy glen,
We daren't go a-hunting for fear of little men
Wee folk, good folk, trooping all together,
Green jacket, red cap and white owl's feather

William Allingham was a customs officer, just like our own great, North Kerry writer, Maurice Walsh. Maurice wrote some great novels, such as *The Blackcock's Feather* and *The Key Above the Door*. His birthplace is a house with a large key above its door. My father would say he recognised many of the characters in Maurice's books.

People were afraid of the fairies, the wee folk, when I was young. Actually, a farmer who was a bit of a character played a trick on the town during Lent. He had a greyhound that would run from one end of the town to the other in darkness to get home.

What the farmer did was dress the black greyhound in a white sheet that flapped noisily as the dog ran through the town heading home at about 11:10 pm. This was the time the somewhat drunken 'boyos' of the town would be leaving by the back doors of the pubs. It is said that many of them gave up drink for the rest of Lent, believing that a ghost was about town. The wives played it up, of course, getting out the holy water and rosary beads – to beat the banshee who heralded death!

I heard the banshee when my brother, baby Maurice, died, RIP. It was a long, lonesome lament. My brother Gerard and I were awakened by its haunting sound, at the exact time Maurice died in Tralee hospital.

In Belize, as we drove up a long hill of greenery, there was a big signpost pointing to 'Listowel'. This led us up a dusty road towards what turned out to be a disused boys' orphanage *cum* reformatory school and other buildings. This was set up about one hundred years ago by the then Lord Listowel.

He was in the British Colonial Service in what was then British Honduras. The school was closed down about ten years ago – lack of funds, or to use a modern political catchphrase, 'under-resourced'.

We gathered later from a policeman, in his USA supplied, anti-drug police car, that it had been taken over by the druggies. They had an informal airstrip in the sports-field. The policeman was casual about it all. It seemed to be a way of life in these parts, the drug export business.

Lord Listowel drew rents from my hometown during all of my earlier legal life. These were ground rents mainly on the town business. He also collected cattle tolls at the corner of the Square on fair days. My father and others refused to pay them. The tolls are gone now for some years. Many solicitors' letters were written, but my father and the farmers won.

Actually, there is another Listowel in Canada – I have not gone there.

Going back to the rents payable to Lord Listowel, I think some ground rents are still payable to Lloyds Bank, the trustee of the Lord's estate. I believe there is still a landlord around somewhere in South Africa, but I gather the rents are so devalued by inflation they are not worth collecting. There is legislation that enables you to buy out by paying a multiplier of the rent.

I was an apprentice solicitor in the 1950s in Matthew J Byrne and Co, the office that collected the rents for Lord Listowel/Lloyds Bank. That office bore the name of a very learned lawyer and Latin scholar. He died before my time. He is gone, as is his successor, James Raymond. The office is gone too. We all go, to where we do not know.

I have a copy of Matthew J Byrne's translation of Don Philip O'Sullivan Beare's book *Ireland under Elizabeth: Chapters towards the History of Ireland in the reign of Elizabeth*, written in the early 1600s. A book Byrne translated in 1903.

Interestingly, I live on the same farm Matthew J Byrne lived on.

His book came with an interesting map, made by John Norden and preserved to this day in the Public Records Office, London.

Lixnaw, (spelt Licksnaw) appeared to be the most prominent town in North Kerry; the dominant families were the Browns and the O'Connors of Kerry. The Lixnaw spelling is close to the Irish name, *lough snámha* or lack snámha, which means a place for swimming, or the swimming stone; which isn't surprising, as the river Brick is close to Lixnaw.

The map isn't very accurate, even the mouth of the Shannon is called the bay of Tralee (spelt Tryle). One intriguing detail is the name given to a certain hill, 'Knock Patrick', which it locates near modern-day Glin, in Co Limerick.

Intriguing because, according to a historian I once met, St Patrick never came to Kerry. St Patrick came to West Limerick by boat, went up a hill, and blessed Kerry, which was to the west in the setting sun

Listowel isn't even shown on the map at all. This is probably because the Lord of Kerry's castle had been taken and destroyed by crown forces about ten years before. The remains of the castle in Listowel, as well as the nearby museum, are well worth a visit.

Getting back to that other topic, where we go when we are gone. I do believe there is a 'where' or possibly a 'what' when it comes to where our spirits go to. The notion of an original Creator is central in my thoughts about the meaning of our existence. I believe the universe, our world, did not happen by chance. The Creator, in a way our puny minds cannot understand, was the uncaused caused. It, the Creator, did not create the condition for our evolution for no good reason, it must have had a purpose. At least I so reason, believe (faith), and hope in. Without a Creator, there would be nothing. The Swiss psychoanalyst and psychiatrist Karl Jung wrote: 'The lack of meaning in life is a soul sickness, whose full extent and full impact our age has yet to comprehend.'

Then we discussed that book of Victor Frankl, *Man's Search for Meaning*. That book of hope and meaning in the Holocaust, in which his parents, wife and brother were gassed. When Frankl was told it was a bestseller, he said it was, 'an expression of the misery of our times'. He found meaning in our existence.

Am I getting preachy?

These thoughts come from a discussion we had in the jeep as we left Listowel, Belize. Gosh was it hot – no air conditioning!

Ranguana Caye & Big Creek

Let me come back to the here and now.

We listened to the weather forecast when we arrived in Big Creek on Day One – it was good. 'Light chop to choppy,' which was interpreted to mean the sea was to be calm. Slightly rough would be 'choppy, chop, chop'. Donal says that is the same one every day. How wrong they were, we did not suspect!

Big Creek lived up to its name – big ships taking freight were being loaded there. Mostly bananas and other fruit destined for USA and Europe. These ships are refrigerated to keep the fruit from ripening too quickly. Listowel gets the best fruit just at the right time and taste – up Fyffes!

The big tourist event of our trip was to get to the picture-postcard, remote tropical island of Ranguana Caye.

Yes, we made it here yesterday (Day One).

It was all we were led to believe it would be: blue sky, clean seas, white coral and isolation, with just enough civilisation for frugal comfort. It has reefs with fabulous fish on colourful coral, situated a few minutes snorkelling out from the sparkling sandy beaches. Belize's reefs rival the Great Barrier Reef off Cairns on the east coast of Australia.

If you get to Cairns, Australia, as I did, visit the eco-friendly Kilroy Island. I have to go back to this miniature paradise before it is destroyed by global warming and local exploitation.

If you get down to the east coast of Australia go to Heron Island. It has 40,000 birds on forty acres, and magnificent fish life on its colourful coral. And the turtles! Their babies trying to get down to the sea is a sight to behold! Only one in ten survive because of seagulls gobbling them up on the beach.

Do it soon before the great coral reef of which it is part dies – 70% of the reef was dead or dying when I was there. If water temperatures rise a further two degrees (just 2°!) it is predicted that the whole reef will die. Will generations to come deem our generation environmental vandals and barbarians if we murder these great natural wonders? They rightly will and how I hate plastic! We will poison everything, and indeed ourselves, at the rate we are going.

However, my thoughts have strayed again. Sorry, back to the here and now – Day One was yesterday.

We could not, and did not, ask for anything more when we arrived on this caye. We got more that first evening on this caye than we had been led to expect. There were even a dog and a hare, of all creatures, on the island. Scruffy is the dog's name, but Kevin insists it's Scrappy. He is a quiet dog and makes no protest. The hare's name is Harry. They have low expectations and seem to live in harmony.

Expectations not realised are the basis of difficulties in ourselves and in Irish society. Look, I am not going to be political or anti-political. Dogs and hares seem not to be politicians.

Gone Fishing
On Day One we had a wonderful trip to a lobster fishing area.

The sea was as Keats described it in his *On the Sea:*

> Often 'tis in such gentle temper found
> That scarcely will the smallest shell
> Be moved for days from where it sometimes fell
> When last the winds of Heaven were unbound

Here in the clear shallow sea near the caye, Kevin Madeira, our guide, boatman, fisherman, cook and boss, showed us his extraordinary ability to swim almost better than any fish.

My abiding memory of Day One is of watching him when diving. I peered from on high in the boat. Down about twenty-five feet to and around a large coral rock Kevin swam with gaff in hand. He found a hole in the rock, in goes the gaff, a struggle follows, and out comes the gaff with a crawfish.

Incredibly Kevin stayed down and actually went partially into the hole. I saw only his large backside ('big bottom' per Paul) and his flippers waving. Then, which seemed to me a lifetime later, out he comes with lobster/crawfish number two in one hand, and gaff with impaled crawfish in the other. What a performance!

I could not clap as I held the oars, but I did shout 'congratulations' as his head appeared.

We swam around spiking fish and catching two more crawfish. They are called lobsters here, as the Spanish do, but being coloured red they are more like our crawfish than our blue (before boiling) lobster. They have small claws.

Kevin was very good at teaching the lads (Seán and Paul) but they were only allowed spearfish we could eat. Kevin is a natural conservationist with great respect for creation and creatures. He is an environmentalist amid the capitalists, many of whom were beginning to exploit Belize, although some have good intentions.

Two hours more were spent swimming in the balmy, clear water, and watching the blues, greens, whites, browns, yellows of the living, growing and waving coral, and the multi-coloured fish. Then we went back to 'home' to the caye.

I noticed the sky filling and that we were not catching tuna, as we had earlier. We discussed why it is that fish do not bite when there is thunder around. Sensible fish go down deep. We had our catch at the bottom of the boat, still alive.

We landed on our small island. Kevin gets out his formidable array of knives and the fish chopping business begins. We then retire to the largest cabin, *The Seagull* cabin, which was HQ. We eat royally, noticing the odd flash of lightning in the southern sky and the loud whispering, hissing northern wind rolling up the surf.

No problem, just another tropical storm per Kevin. We chatted long after about families in great companionship at the end of the Day Two, our first full day on this tiny strip of sand in the vast sea.

Lobster Recipe
I have a great interest in lobsters always. I like fishing for and eating them. My families for generations have caught them on the north side of Kerry Head on the shores of:

> Oh, the rough, the rude Atlantic, the thunderous, the wide,
> Whose kiss is like a soldier's kiss, that cannot be denied.
> *Fontonoy, 1748,* Emily Lawless

This haven or heaven in Kerry Head in the west coast of Ireland lies about 3000 miles east of this caye, which itself is on the east side of Belize.

I used my grandmother's recipe last night which Kevin loved. Maybe you should have that recipe, in case you catch a lobster on your desert island or just buy one. The recipe is good.

A. Boil your live lobster for 10 minutes (15 if the lobster is very big). Let him cool in the water for 60 minutes.

B. De-shell the 'meat', the tail and claws have most 'meat' (fish actually) but you will find some in the body. Break the meat into half-inch portions.

C. Put the meat in a saucepan. Add 1 pint of milk and 2 slices of white pan bread crumbled into breadcrumb form, without the crusts. Add a large knob of Irish butter – Kerrygold!

D. Slowly bring to almost the boil. Add a very good pinch of salt and a very small pinch of pepper.

E. When you have it just at the boil turn off the heat – or take it off the open fire as we did last night on the beach.

F. Then carefully add 2 tablespoons of white vinegar.

G. Serve in a bowl and dunk in your buttered, thick slices of shop bread.

You will enjoy it – I guarantee.

There you have my grandmother's recipe, still used one hundred and fifty years later. The milk and breadcrumbs give it bulk so it feeds more. The Pierses always had big families. I sometimes say when God said 'increase, multiply and fill the earth,' a Pierse was listening in. Result, I have ten children and have (in 2018) thirty-two grandchildren. Thank you Olive and God.

I like lobsters also as I made my courting money from selling them. On my first big date with Olive in 1958, I sold 3 dozen lobsters at 5 /- each, which amounted to €14.20 in today's money. I bought a big meal, a box of chocolates, 2 dance tickets, minerals and some petrol for my father's car with that. What value I got. My best investment, I still call Olive!

How the price of lobsters has changed!

Fortunately, Olive is still wonderfully unchanged. I had a tough time explaining to my fellow fisherman where his one third share of the £9 for the 36 lobsters went. I came home with only £2, but it was the best investment I ever made.

At that time I was not entitled to all the proceeds from the 36 lobsters (£9). My friend and co-fisherman, Patty (Farmer) O'Connor was entitled to one third and my father as boat owner to another third. I had to go to my post office account to get funds to pay Patty and my father.

Patty was in the courting business himself so he had been tolerant of my extravagance of 'blowing' most of the £9. The rest of that summer I worked hard catching lobsters, picking carrageen, dillisk and blackberries, before selling them as necessary courting money. Busy summer!

Olive had come as an in-house medical student to St Catherine's Hospital, Tralee. I was wonderfully smitten – still am!

I was one of seven sons and had no sister to teach me how a girl expected to be treated. I therefore obeyed my mother's views on this matter: that men were put into the world to look after women!

I find the modern custom of the lady paying for herself strange. My mother claimed, and trained her seven sons accordingly, that it was the male's privilege to pay for all the females. Tough woman my mother? Not really, she just believed men and women were that different.

You should have heard her about the women libbers! Such a waste of money burning good bras. She also possessed a wooden spoon to keep the seven sons in order. Olive says she did a good job on me! Maybe I will come back to our romance later.

My six brothers were all taught that women were different. She, our mother, celebrated the difference. She would have liked what Brigitte Bardot said: '*Vive la différence*.'

Still, she could wield a wooden spoon with deadly effect on her sons. The Collins temper – she was Michael Collins' eldest niece. Indeed, the men ran too if she got cross and came out the brown backdoor with her large, black and brown wooden spoon. She got particularly angry if one of my father's greyhounds killed one of her hens – we all ran when she appeared with the wooden spoon. Our workman Tom James (now RIP) ran with us. Sorry Nana!

The Storm

At 9 pm last night Olive and I headed off to the *Laughing Bird* cabin, our sleeping cabin at the other side of the caye.

We dined in the *Seagull* before chatting in candlelight with the others in the *Man of War* cabin. Olive and I are odd in Irish society, in that we believe, along with farmers, in the old maxim:

Early to bed, early to rise,
Makes a person healthy, wealthy and wise

This practice of early to bed has been commented on by my brother, Frank, as the reason we have ten children. As Olive and I enjoy our first of many hours of sleep, he is probably in John B Keane's pub, playing cards or bridge.

Result: he has that nice suburban type of modern family, a son and daughter. This is an amateur performance family-wise in our view. It takes all sorts.

I still think 'one crowded hour of glorious love is worth an age without a name'. Olive says she had the children, and I had the shared momentary hour of glorious love.

The others are in the relatively big *Man of War* cabin, the real social cabin. They stayed chatting as we left. Olive arranged for Aislinn to sleep in the hammock outside. That is where her mother would like for her single daughter to be, according to Olive!

When Olive said anything about domestic matters it became a rule – she always claimed to have ten votes in the home. The rest of us had only one each. That is domestic democracy in the O'Donoghue/Pierse home.

In our *Laughing Bird* cabin there was a fine, solid, box-like timber bed. We got in and said our Rosary in thanks. We headed into sleep, the innocent sleep, the death of each day's night: we were wrapping up the ravelled sleeve of care with sleep, sweet nature's balm! A good night's rest was expected. Our expectations were wrong.

The big storm was heading for us. Olive wanted to leave the cabin door open so that we could hear the sea; Yeats' 'lake water lapping with low sounds by the shore'. I felt a few drops of rain before we came in the door so I closed it. I closed the windows too.

Lucky me, as an hour later the storm howled down on our island. The cabin creaked. It was made of timber, even the seven windows were timber with vents for ventilation. Now they shuddered, rattled and howled. Bang! The crash of wild waves. The cabin swayed a bit, then a lot.

The sense of the 'terrible beauty' of irate nature, glimpsed among the flashes of lightning, turned to gradual fear as the cabin shook. The sea thundered and the sky thundered like terrorist bombs. The sheets of lightning lit our cabin through the slits in the side of the cabin. *Laughing Bird* cabin was frightening the two of us birds in its bed nest.

There was a lull after an hour. The peals of thunder were farther away. You know the trick of counting between flashes of lightning and the peal? Every second is reckoned as a mile in the distance the lightning is away!

We felt slightly more secure with the windows closed even if we could not sleep. We felt the storm must blow out quickly. The heavens surely could not remain that angry for long! They did.

Thank you, dear reader, for making it this far. I hope you are reading this on a warm day on the beach.

Robert.

DAY THREE: MONDAY'S WRITINGS

The Gust

It was that gust that shook the northern wall of *Laughing Bird* at 5:30 am of Day Three on the caye that finally galvanised me into action.

The Northern wall shook under that bulldozing gust. I was thinking another blast like that and that wall of timber board could come on top of us in our bed. Enough!

The thunder roared rather than clapped. The whole of our cabin vibrated continuously. The thunder rolled on and on without a break. It was here, not there. Light from lightning seeped in through the slats in the windows as if pushed in by the wind.

I could hear the sea, the strong, strident sound of the swish and snarl of the surf heading straight up the sand.

I wondered would it reach the stilts of the *Laughing Bird* and would it sweep the sandy foundations away. Do not build your house on sand the Bible says. There was nothing else here to build it on and little enough of that sand too.

I was suddenly fearful the timber cabin was going to collapse on top of us. I had to take action. It was obviously impossible to leave the cabin in the dark and storm. We had only a small torch, as there is no electricity on the caye. The island had a contraption working from two solar panels for heating water.

I reckoned that last gust was eighty mph. The storm was intensifying, the wild wind was stronger, the great gusts were frequently frantic, and the roars of the sky and the sea louder. The sheet that covered me in the bed was lifted by wind bursting in through the window slits. I must take action. I know Olive's head was close to that wall, the wall that was taking the force of the hurricane.

What could one do in a 15ft by 15ft cabin on stilts in the sand? Action? Yes. GET US UNDER THE BED, as it was a strong wooden frame and would protect us from flying boards. I thought the roof was loosening. It sure was rattling and screeching.

Under the Bed

I got out of my side of the bed and found the torch by feeling around on the floor – if we could call the candle-like bulb on it a torch. It had been knocked off the table by the storm. It was working.

Strange thing to think of at that moment but I felt the sky itself might fall on our *Laughing Bird* – we certainly were not laughing. So, I move into action. I shout to Olive 'UNDER THE BED!' – that sturdy frame would be over us.

We pulled the big mattress off the wooden structure, a strong cradle bed of timber. We pushed and shoved as the gales screamed at us in our shaking shelter.

We got the mattress under the bed. Oh, but a bit was sticking out in the centre of the cabin, I do not know why. I felt it was best to put our feet there so that we could evacuate out quickly.

There under the bed, Olive slept, uneasily for a short time, while I conceived the idea of noting events for the days I felt were to come. When Olive was awake I told her of my plan and started telling stories to pass the time. This was about 4 hours into the storm and it was showing no sign of abating – somewhat less thunder, less lightning but still much wind. We survived and so did the others.

In 1980, when sailing across the Atlantic, I had been caught in a storm at sea which went on for six or seven days (now that's another story!). I wondered how long this would go for – we were only supposed to be here for three days. Mother Nature can be a dour, dark and dangerous foe.

I could not write at night so I resolved that every morning I would put together what paper that I could and exercise the mighty pen. I ended up putting notes all over my law books, on the back of novels, and on toilet paper as it turned out.

I am now turning this into a book, so many years later.

Four hours passed, and the mighty storm passed but not fully. We came out from under the bed. We bent low in the strong wind as we moved across to the *Seagull*. It was late morning when we headed for breakfast – all the others thought it was a thrilling night!

However, I saw no sign of Scruffy, the resident dog of the caye, or Harry the hare. Presumably, they had gone under their beds too.

A Man With a Cap
(Important note on pronunciation: 'Men' plural is pronounced 'min', as in the 'min with the caps'.)

There is a joke in the countryside at home about keeping cash under the bed. This was done out of fear of the nosy pension officer, the worst of all these revenue men (and women too, lots of them), would learn you had money.

'The Lord between us and all harm, if the revenue found out that you had money you would be ruined. You would get nothing from the government. They would want to take stuff off you, bad luck to that Dublin crowd', said a small farmer to me one time.

He was a bachelor with a cap. He never took the cap off except to kneel on it outside Ballybunion Church at mass. He also had the Sunday paper to read during the sermon. He had been robbed by 'a bunch of tinkers', as he called them, of his money under the bed in the tin box.

I advised solemnly that banks were the place to keep money. He said he did not trust banks – he had a rich uncle in the USA in the 1930s who had lost all his money in a bank that went wallop.

You cannot win when dealing with these wise men (or 'min'!) with the caps – or maybe he is right. I could understand him about the bank.

While under the bed, Olive began telling stories about her uncle Flor.

Olive's uncle Flor was a taxi driver in New York. He picked up two men one day in Wall Street. He heard them talking about a financial crash. When he went home that Saturday he decided to take his money out of his trustee bank and put it under the bed.

He went down to the bank early that Monday morning. The bank never opened. He had lost all his savings. He and his wife had $200 and four children in a rented flat! He got through it, but never trusted a bank or banker ever again.

He came to Ireland in the 1970s. He insisted on driving my car – he was still a taxi man. He gave me a bad fright one day when we came around a corner in Tarbert and he automatically went to the right; which was the wrong side of the road here, but the right side in the USA.

I saw a big Kerry Co-Op lorry heading towards us. I yanked the wheel to get up to the left, and correct, side of the road. Horns blared but we survived.

Come to think of it, the sight that excited Flor most was that of men making wynns of hay! Memories! He told me he had gone to America with only £5.10 (less than €10) in his pocket. He survived, married and got lonely to see the old country so many years later.

I think we trust our banks too much. I cannot understand what money is. I know it is good to have and bad to be without.

This is one of the stories I will tell tonight, after the storm.

Book

Could I put these stories into a book? The idea, germinated under the bed, grew through the enforced idleness and confinement that began on Day Three.

My son, Gearóid, had been 'at' me for a long time to put pen to paper about the stories I told him and my other children over the years. I knew I should have done it a long time ago, but I did not.

Will I be able to get away from serious law? I am supposed to be a serious man, no fun in me, a lawyer and a father of ten. You see I have written two serious law books, one on road traffic law and the other about damages for personal injuries. Neither could be described as compulsive bedtime reading.

So, that is how this book began – from a night awake under the bed. I hope you like it and that Gearóid will enjoy it. I was sorry he was not here. He is an accountant, who is an SAP (Sophisticated Accountancy Systems) expert. He also has a large number of languages.

I remember how he learnt Italian. He had met a nice Italian girl on a train in Europe. He was in his backpacking university days. He wanted to keep up the connection with her. He liked girls, as most boys do. You know the type, those who believe girls were made to love and kiss.

So when he went back to Galway University he joined the Italian course. He passed the exam with flying colours. He has English, Irish, French, German, Italian, Spanish and possibly others. He is currently in Hong Kong, where he is learning Chinese. He always enjoys the physical, even though bright with the metaphysical.

Paul, Seán and Donal, his brothers who are also on the island, think I am daft sitting out a storm writing away, using up paper and biros. They prefer fishing with Kevin, even in the storm.

While they fish along the more sheltered side of the caye, I decide to have a stab at writing a non-lawyer type book – to show we lawyers are human after all!

The trouble is that people often group us lawyers as sharks, but then say they like us individually. It is just the law is so complicated a solicitor can rarely give a simple and clear answer to a straight question. Not that there are straight questions, not in life or law.

You know, I think I will go outside for a breath of air – too dangerous to go walking in this wild, western wind.

Sharks

That air was nice. You know the story about the shipwrecked solicitor?

There were three survivors of a shipwreck in the Pacific. A lawyer, a priest and a doctor. They saw an island from their raft. They decided to check it out for cannibals. However, they saw sharks around. They drew lots as to who would go to investigate. The priest drew the short straw. He blessed himself, said 'the sharks will respect the man of the cloth' and jumped in. They didn't – must have been non-Catholic sharks.

The doctor went next saying, 'everyone, even sharks, know doctors are good'. Unfortunately, these sharks didn't – exit medico.

The lawyer jumped in. The shark population swam aside and waved him on to the islands. Their valuable motto was, 'sharks do not eat sharks'.

I didn't tell Olive that story under the bed – she being a medic!

Canon Brennan

Speaking of priests, we had a great and hardworking, if controversial, parish priest growing up – a Canon Brennan. He was a Fine Gael man, as his father had been pro-Treaty in 1922.

At the other end of the town was a Father O'Connor, the much feared and disliked principal of St Michael's College. He was a de Valera man – Fianna Fáil. I think Dev stayed in his house during one election. When Dev was going to the Square to speak that night, I remember they gave him a guard of honour, a torchlight procession that started at the top of Church Street, near Fr O'Connor's house.

Dev's speech was poorly delivered, compared to the one James Dillon, the Fine Gael Minister for Agriculture, delivered a few nights later.

When I was young, Dev was a political 'Saint' to a large portion of the populace.

Whenever an election was on, the Fine Gale canon made sure to give his sermons the correct political hints. Fr O'Connor was not allowed say a public mass during an election, as he might commit political heresy!

The mothers of Listowel sent us off to confess on Saturday evenings to get us out of the house. There could be forty of us lined up outside the confessional. The canon would come out, look at us and say: 'Sure you lot do not know about sin, but I will give you general absolution to make sure you will not burn in hell!'

Sometimes he gave an altar boy in the group a shilling (6c) to buy gobstoppers for us at Lena Mullally's shop next to Bryan MacMahon's house.

The story goes a man went to Canon Brennan to confess. After the preliminaries, he confessed he hated another man. The canon said: 'Now my son you will have to give up that. It is as simple as that, very serious.' The man said: 'I've tried and cannot. I just hate him.'

The canon, very serious, said: 'Tell me, who is this man you hate?' The man said 'de Valera'. The canon said: 'That's no sin, I cannot stand that man too. God bless you.' He shut the shutter. Of course, it was the penitent who told the story to his wife – that is how it got out. Half the town loved it.

And they said we were priest-ridden! The Dublin crowd, especially their peculiar writer set, just do not understand the subtleties of country life. Things are not what they seem among the 'min' with the caps.

Of course, confession is gone out the window for most so called Catholics nowadays, as is the notion of sin. The state and politicians always see the values promoted by religion as rivals to, or limits on, their power.

We in Ireland do not value our freedoms, including religious freedom, enough. We seem not to understand the value of basic values and the need to maintain and nurture tried and tested values. Ireland is being overly influenced by consumerism, TV and media. We follow USA, UK, EU values rather than our own traditions and culture.

Politically, bureaucratic Europe is invading our fragile democracy with over-regulation. I say 'fragile democracy', as pressure groups with single issues may produce here a 'packocracy' rather than clear, strong and principled governments. We have of course left one empire, but I wonder have we joined another?

I wonder can I get a debate going on that tonight? Probably not, as the kids want stories rather than 'deep' subjects.

Then my father fell out with Canon Brennan over the national school.

The canon was in charge of the school and it was a disgrace – an open sewer.

At a meeting, my father told the canon he was shilly-shallying in not demanding the school be closed. It worked! The canon could not take criticism, so the friendship ended.

The canon also made a bad judgment about an unmarried mother, which turned the town largely against him.

We forget how weak some priests are, that they are human beings with our own weaknesses and strengths.

We wrongly forget the message in condemning the messenger. That is becoming more common now as the 'message' sets unwanted limitations on our conduct. Religion is no longer 'cool'. It's very much an inconvenient truth or a set of uncomfortable values.

The Storm Continues?
Gosh! I have my times mixed up. I should not get side-tracked by all these stories. I will have to go back a bit as I seem to have gone forward a bit.

The storm was again gaining momentum, instead of abating as it had slightly some hours previous. Darkness, with its mystery, makes the sounds worse. It was 4:30 am when we scurried back under the bed.

I wondered about the animals on the island. Where were they hiding? My thoughts went back to my own interest in animals and the law relating to them.

This is a subject of much contention in my rural practice. Memory rose like a cork as my thoughts turned to Ireland, my home, and my law.

There wasn't enough light to read by, due to dark clouds pouring lashing rain, so here are random bits of recollections and stories about animals I thought of last night.

I try to reproduce some of these now while huddled in the more sheltered side of our *Laughing Bird* cabin. No laughing birds here today. They must have gone to another island. The pages I am writing my thoughts on are going out of sequence. Ah! There is the light of dawn – so sudden in 5 or 10 minutes. I will come back to animals later as I must go out to have a look around (as well as other natural relief).

Now there are the pelicans. I have been fascinated by these and the cycle of nature all around me. The sardines were massed again like brown rubbish under the tree. I first thought they were debris again. They washed in and out with each wave. They multiplied in the sun. Then a variety of big fish, eels, bluish fish with big eyes, and green fish with big mouths, moved amongst them, gobbled up those who could not scatter.

Then the big jackfish moved excitedly in – the water boils as they get into a frenzy of an eating orgy. The pelican stood still in the water but suddenly he darted his beak into the sea and it emerged with a struggling jackfish in its last movements and moments.

It's an old saying; big fleas have little fleas on their backs to bite them. With fish it is the opposite – big fish eat small fish. Sounds like an economic law.

Supermarkets and big shops close down small shops. Big business eats up and takes over successful small business. Often the business with no ideas buys out the people with the new ideas – you know 'to develop them,' or, in other words, to close them down.

The Duke

Why was the first person I thought about for a story, 'The Duke'? Maybe it was because I usually met him at times of disaster.

I do not know why he was called 'The Duke' but that is what he was to us locals. In fact, I cannot remember his Christian name now. In Listowel, if you were called an appropriate (or inappropriate) nickname it stuck with you. Remind me to tell you about our 'Jessie James' sometime.

The Duke was single and he used to say 'free'. He lived in the old cottage which Olive and I had rented at £1 a week when we first were married in 1963. That is where Olive's wedding dress got mouldy in the damp mass-concrete cottage.

When the Duke went in there first, he bought a table with one broken leg, or a 'three-legged table' as he liked to call it. He decided to sell it. He put it outside the front wall on the side of the Tarbert Road with a sign on it: 'For Sale – Fit to kill a pig on.' The missing leg was replaced by the wall.

The wise farmers of North Kerry did not buy that table, as they considered it necessary to have a four-legged table for the important business of chopping up pigs. The Duke eventually chopped the table up for firewood. I will not digress here about pig killing but see below.

The Duke was 'a man with a cap' and a bachelor. Poor man, never to be bossed (sorry, I meant blessed) with a woman! In the morning the cap would be peak front. However, by pub closing time in Listowel – usually then about 2 hours after legal closing time – the cap would be back to front. Beware of a man with his cap back to front. He is not a wise man with a cap.

Then the Duke had his accident. We had two public court appearances as a result.

The facts, or should I say as a lawyer, the alleged facts, were briefly that a motorist, Mr O, a cattle dealer from east Kerry, was proceeding along a wide road (the old coach road from Limerick to Tralee on which the Liberator Daniel O'Connell travelled in his coach) when controversially he knocked down the Duke.

The motorist Mr O claimed the Duke staggered out suddenly and drunkenly, which is non-legal language for under the influence of intoxicating liquor to such an extent so as to endanger his own or the safety of others.

The Gardaí unfortunately seemed to agree with the driver, though the Duke protested his innocence loudly. He said he was as sober as a judge, which was a totally unhelpful comparison in the area at the time.

I never found out if his cap was peak front or peak back at the time of the accident – maybe just as well. I suspect it was peak back, which was a bad sign when it came to intoxicating liquor.

So, the Duke and driver were summoned to the district court. The charge against the Duke was being drunk and incapable on a public road. The charge against the driver was driving without due care and attention.

Mr O's evidence of the events was a bit unclear. On cross-examination by me, he was vague on his speed and on what lights he had on. I asked had he had a few drinks. He couldn't remember. Was he a bit tired? He didn't know. It was a wide road, why had he not seen my unfortunate client?

I thought I had the sympathy of the court for 'my client'. I pleaded that he was badly injured and so does not really know what happened. It is a type of defence that fortunately works sometimes when you have no better one.

The prosecution case finished lamely, so I said I did not propose taking up the time of the court calling a defendant who really did not know what happened due to his appalling injuries. The poor man had been rendered unconscious, and the situation had been totally misinterpreted by the driver and the guards as intoxication.

The judge was nodding, he sympathised with my interpretation of events, and seemed to agree with me that it was hard to say conclusively whether the Duke was drunk or not.

I could see the words 'the Probation Act' coming from his mind to his lips. However, they never got there.

Up stands the Duke at the back of the court and says (to my horror)

'I want my say; I want to say my say'. I turned to him and said, 'you have nothing to say'. He shouts back, 'I have and I want to say it'.

The District Justice said: 'Mr Pierse, he is obviously a man who does not believe in the old motto, 'If you have a dog you should let him do your barking'. So, let him up.'

Up goes the Duke to the witness box – impressing his supporters sitting behind him in court. He is sworn. The justice said to him: 'Now, my good man will you tell me why you were walking in the middle of the road?' To which he got the shattering reply (the Duke having turned around to his audience at the back of the courtroom): 'Well, you do not think it is in the middle of the f****** ditch that I should be walking?' There was a stunned silence and a nervous titter at the back of the court. I sunk into my seat trying to hide behind my law books and files.

Then the explosion occurred. The red-faced district justice said: 'Get down you blackguard. I have a good mind to send you to jail. I am fining you £10 and if I ever see you here again I will give you 3 months to put manners on you.' End of case Number One.

The Duke's Second Case

I had issued a civil bill claiming compensation early on for the Duke as he had fairly nasty injuries. I was now stuck with it. I decided to proceed – like Macbeth, it was as easy to go on as to go back. I warned my client to behave, and no drink under any circumstances until the court was over.

The civil bill came before the Listowel Circuit Court a few months after Case One. Fortunately, it came in late in a long list on a Friday.

Fridays are the 'settling' day, and it's a major advantage if the case is near the bottom of the case list. You see the counsel, insurance men and judges were mostly down from Dublin, as usual. We cute, poor Kerry lawyers knew that they wanted to get back to the rich city early on Friday. Therefore, cases settle more quickly and easily on Fridays.

Anyway, the Duke and I met our counsel at 9:30 am. He didn't think much of the Duke's chances, but 'we'll see'. He was the late William Binchy BL of Trinity College, the father of Maeve, the writer, and that wonderful pro-life lawyer William Binchy.

William said to me, on the quiet, that he was acting in a large equity case about drains and rights-of-way, which were always protracted and fully fought, so we could hold tough. On that day, thank God, the equity case was listed early on. This delay, I hoped, might lead to the defence offering me something.

The defence was huffing and puffing about this outrageous case and the cheek of us after what had happened in the district court! I played cool. The equity case started. It went on all morning.

My good friend, Dermot Kinlen SC, then BL, and later High Court judge (now gone to the God he loved) acting for the defence in the Duke's case, approached me just before lunch.

He said his insurance man might give us a small figure to buy us off so everyone could go home. This was the first wobble, so I explained how serious my unfortunate client had been injured by his reckless driver – the usual!

He had a great twinkle in his eye. Dermot Kinlen was an honorary Kerryman by decent and inclination, so it was '*aithníonn ciaróg, ciaróg eile*' (or, in the language of the English, 'one earwig knows another earwig'). So, work that out!

Then he said: 'Well look, I'll give you our offer of £250 and talk to your man.' I hop out to the Duke and say we have an offer of £250. Thank God for a Friday and the long equity case. I explained to him that we would have to take that offer if I couldn't do better as his case was poor and he agreed. I explained that if the equity case didn't settle over lunch – and those cases between neighbours rarely did – that I'd play tough until about 2:30 pm. Then it would be psychologically best to settle, otherwise it might be adjourned to the next law term.

I warned the Duke to keep what I said private and no drink. He agreed, but as usual he didn't take any notice of my warning. He was a good fan of Mr Guinness – 'a martyr to the drink the poor man', as 'they' still say in feigned charity!

So, I was back in the bar room in the courthouse on that 2 pm. In gloomy tones, I said to the defence lawyers that £250 was really an insulting offer, but my seriously injured client would oblige them by taking £300.

I remember Dermot Kinlen's merry laugh so well. He took me by the arm and maneuvered me out into the courtyard. He said: 'Robert I'll tell you a little story. About ten minutes ago my client, Mr O, the car driver, went into the men's toilet at the back. Your client was there and was somewhat the worse of wear after a liquid lunch. He didn't recognise my client the defendant driver and said to him: "What are you doing here?" My client, Mr O, plays tough (this didn't surprise me, he was a cute cattle jobber and farmer!) and says: "Yerra, I'm just hanging around about a case, what are you here about yourself sir?" Your client then tells my client: "Well I'm here in a bad old case; I was knocked down one night when I had a good few in. To tell you the truth my solicitor got an offer of £250 before lunch and we're delighted. My man is in there trying to knock another few pounds out of that Dublin crowd."'

So, Dermot Kinlen, BL said to me, 'Robert, you have five minutes to take the £250 or it's withdrawn'. I ran around to find the Duke. Yes, he was 'three sheets in the wind'. No he could not remember what exactly he said to the nice man in the men's toilet but, 'sure, he was a nice man and he listened to me'. I had enough. I ran back in and took the £250 with my tail a bit between my legs. Clients can spoil the fun sometimes in our lawyers' little games!

As it happens, the poor Duke died some years later in another accident; RIP.

Black Puddings

I must tell you about pig killing – without the Duke's three-legged table! Almost all families in the 1940s, even into the 1950s, kept a pig in the back shed – the one nearest the backway. The pigs were largely fed on the leftovers from the family.

My father, Eddie Leahy, Eddie Scanlan and Patsy Walsh (all neighbours) arranged the killing of the pigs, usually one every two to three months. This was done by Mr Costello, from O'Connell's Avenue, with his big knife. Mostly he worked for 'Colonel' Murphy (why he was called 'Colonel' no one ever knew) in Murphy's butcher shop.

My father, a vet, was the meat inspector for North Kerry. This meant he was able to arrange the pig killing rotation. The pig killing was always done, for some reason, at about 4 pm, just after school. We all watched – well most of the girls didn't. I believe my brother (later a priest) used to charge 'outsiders' a penny (or was it a halfpenny?) to watch the two-hour ritual.

I will not go into the details of the squealing pig, the throat cutting, the basins of blood (to be made into black puddings), as I am too delicate for that! The chopping of the pig for division among the neighbours on a 'coring' (reciprocal) basis was a community exercise.

The art of black pudding making was a matter of great pride among the ladies of Market Street. We always thought our mother was the best! She was a Clonakilty woman where there was, and still is, a tradition of black pudding makers.

There was a famous black pudding maker in Listowel, John Joe Kenny of the Square. They came from far and near for his pudding. Even when we were in University, John and I used to get John Joe's black pudding posted up to us. Two rings once a day was the treat. We spread it on our bread. Smashing!

Heavens, I am straying from what is going on here. The wind is still strong. I am going to head out to see the fishing and whether Scruffy and Harry have survived – strange companions. Scruffy has never been told that he is supposed to chase the hare and Harry has never been told he is supposed to be afraid of Scruffy! Interesting!

The Blaskets

I am back. The lads are having a great time with Kevin fishing out over the surf at the somewhat sheltered east-side. Scruffy has emerged and is barking with excitement. No sign of Harry.

I mentioned also last night the value of shifting the peak of the cap in the Blasket's tradition. Apparently in bleak winter on that bleak island, the women wore nightcaps, large woolly ones. The men kept their caps, the ones with the peak, on their heads.

It is said that when on certain bed business the peak to the front produced a boy, but peak to the back a girl – or maybe it was *vice versa*. If you are in that business don't take that bit of information as gospel!

Ah, the 'min' with the caps!

I was once called to make a man's will in Listowel hospital. He had his cap on in bed. The nurses told me he never took it off even when having a bath. Those guys loved their caps.

I had a great law case involving the Blaskets but, as they say, *sin scéal eile,* (that's another story). It went on for fifty days in the High Court.

Cogito, Ergo Sum

I went for a walk in the wind. I am back writing on the back of the *Irish Jurist* – an excellent legal production.

Now enough of these old stories. What else did we talk about last evening and today in the HQ cabin? We were told about what happened in the *Man of War* hut (named after a jellyfish that has a type of sail built into its top) during the storm. We told about what happened in the *Laughing Bird*, the shaking and swaying, and getting under the bed. The other cabins swayed and rattled but survived. Two more lines of Keats' *On the Sea:*

> Oh ye! whose ears are dinned with uproar rude,
> Or fed too much with cloying melody.

It didn't actually come in on top of us while under the bed as I had feared, but the hut was wet underneath. Well, of course, the fact that I am writing shows that I am not dead. You know how the famous philosopher Descartes said to prove he existed, *cogito, ergo sum* ('I think, therefore I am'). I am saying I write therefore as proof that I wasn't killed by a collapsing *Laughing Bird* cabin or swamped under a surging sea!

I heard a better tale about a philosophy student in Maynooth recently, about whom it was said he had no Latin. This philosophy student was having difficulty with that Frenchman's *cogito,* so he said: 'Well, I didn't know why the French guy had so much trouble proving to himself that he existed. I have a pain in my stomach this morning, so I know that I exist.' Maybe he was more of a realist than Descartes.

Talking about realists, do you know there is a school of legal thinking in the USA called the realist jurists? They say, don't mind what the law book says, what is important is what the judge does. That great American judge Oliver Wendell Holmes Jr was very much in that school. Therefore they, the US lawyers, study the judge's history – family background, schools, his wife, his religion, and the clubs he belongs to. They pitch their arguments according to this profile. I think one of John Grisham's books had that type of approach by the tobacco industry's lawyers and judges. It did not work with the jury.

Juries are usually great. They bring common sense, that rare commodity in this technical age to the law. You have to be careful though. Since women came on juries I think one has to be very cautious in sexual crimes.

I remember one alleged rape case I was in. The trial was in June – a very hot day. We had a jury of seven men and five women. I remember the women had short sleeves and open neck light tops on the first day. The woman gave her evidence – she was dressed so demurely one would think butter wouldn't melt in her mouth. She cried during cross-examination when we put to her that she and the defendant were rotten drunk, that she had slept with the defendant several times before, so how was he to know that she was not consenting?

When I came in on the second day I said to my counsel, 'we're gone'. 'Why?' he said. I replied: 'Look at the tops – up to the neck, sleeves to the wrist and all dark colours.' I was right. The jury convicted and the judge gave a prison sentence of three years. The court of appeal reduced it to a year and left my man out.

I met the foreman of the jury a year after and said to him: 'Tom, why did you convict?' He told me the women all wanted to convict while he and many of the men didn't. Finally, the women said: 'We'll keep you here all night until you convict.' Tom said: 'What could we do, three of us were farmers and wanted to get home to milk our cows.'

Later again a witness came to my office (too late) who told me the true story. The men were right. It was a 'hell hath no fury like a woman scorned' story.

It taught me a lesson in sex cases! On the other hand, older women on a jury have a great understanding of human nature. I remember a jury leaving off a client who had clearly shoplifted. I remember the judge being furious at the 'not guilty' verdict.

I met Ann, who was on that jury, later. I said: 'Ann, why did you leave Mrs O'Brien off?' Her reply was, 'well, she only took food and children's clothes'. The jury did not like the judge's attitude and said: 'What good would come of her going to jail?' One of the men on the jury knew her family and said they were OK. It was done out of necessity, not badness.

I think it was Thomas Aquinas who said, 'don't talk philosophy to a hungry man, give him bread'.

Ten Children

Well, of course, we spent much of the night in our shaking and swaying cabin, the *Laughing Bird*, talking about the kids who are no longer kids (our ten children!).

I have just said to Olive I am writing something about the children and she says don't. She says no one would be interested. However, I wonder how many of you have had ten children? It has been an interesting experience rearing them in a small country town.

I refer to our small country town in a praiseworthy way because Listowel has been a great place to rear a family in (1964 to date). Yes, our eldest Risteárd is 35 this year, married to Majella Cooney from Fermoy and they have presented us with three grandsons so far, Daniel James, Keelan and Simon.

More recently they have presented us all with a wonderful granddaughter, Sophie Mai. Sophie Mai has Down syndrome. Olive's reaction to her birth was wonderful. She said to Risteárd when he rang with the news: 'It's a great time for her to be born, during the Special Olympics. She will be a treasure.' And so she is. She is a right toughie contending with three older brothers, who are mad about her.

My own reaction was: 'She is a lucky child to be born into a family that can and will look after her.' We do! Speaking of looking after her, huge credit must go to the Children's Hospital, Crumlin, as well as her parents and siblings.

I heard a very sad story recently about a young Irish girl who found herself pregnant while working in England. There was a scan done. Some idiot of a doctor told her the child was Down syndrome. She was advised to have an abortion. She waited, and then two months later, against all her instincts, and having had no support, she went ahead. She then learnt the baby was not Down syndrome. They had killed a perfect little girl. The mother got a bad nervous breakdown and has not recovered.

A German Wedding

I went out for a chat there now. I am back.

I often wondered how Risteárd managed to get his first named after 'Danny Jim', his Fianna Fail grandfather for whom he had great affection, and it was so reciprocated. I remember how my father-in-law referred to Risteárd as his 'daughter's child' and another grandchild as 'another woman's child'! Of course, fathers are mad about daughters while they are quietly proud of their sons.

I hope that, as I write here, Risteárd is toiling away across the Atlantic 3,000 miles away, in his solicitor's office in Tralee, keeping the show on the road. Yes, he is a lawyer son in whom I am well pleased. As I am with my other lawyer son, Riobárd, who no doubt is beavering away in Listowel, as I sit here in this hut on this storm-torn caye. I am also well pleased in Riobárd, as I am in all our children. I am well pleased with all our children.

I had better move quickly to my daughter Máire, having said, as I am, that fathers are mad about all daughters. I have two others, Carina and Eilín, whom you will read about if you read on.

Máire was a great mystery and beauty at birth time. I had no sister so when this little doll, even though she was squawking and red-faced, was first presented to me I had a rush of paternal protection feeling that has never left. I think your children never stop being your children even if your relationship changes, naturally changes a lot with the years. When Máire got the croup cough as a child I held her in my arms and said to Olive, 'if anything happens to her, I'll lose my life'. Well, fortunately, she has gone on to be a great mother herself. She is married in Germany to a gentle and kind man, Jürgen Kolb, and we are regular visitors there.

I suppose we have had to make our 'about face' when it comes to the Germans. I grew up on a diet of anti-German comics – *The Rover*, *The Victor* and so on.

In 1988 Máire met this young man while studying hotel management in Switzerland, and we had to rethink our attitude.

Jürgen was a trainee chef in one of these big lakeside hotels in Montreux. Máire had a puncture in her bike. Jürgen fixed it and it went from there. I always thought it significant that Helene's (Helene is Jürgen's mother) question, almost the first, to Máire was: 'Are you a Catholic?' When two years later Máire and Jürgen married in Listowel we had the reception in the house. This was to show off Ireland and its food, so ably presented by John O'Connor, a local chef.

A part of my lengthy wedding speech (and you are free to criticise me as longwinded too) dealt with the common bond of understanding that arose from our shared Faith – our common set of values. I delivered the part on marriage and its meaning in German for about ten minutes, even though I had to learn it off by heart.

The only bit I remember and still quote is 'Ich höre immer auf die frauen' (I always obey women). That little truism (or was it a 'Freudian slip'?) was greeted with a hoot of derision from Mrs Kathleen Guina, my able personal assistant. She said in response, 'don't believe a word of it'.

My speech in Irish, German, and English went off well. They have three delightful children: Sofia, Brendan, and Miriam. We hope to go over for Helene Kolb's 60th birthday in a few months' time and meet them all.

A Walk with Scruffy

Oh dear, Olive wants to go for a walk – around the 800 yards long caye, and is talking about needing a swim. It's sticky hot despite the storm winds. The storm is still blowing, the sea still surging and surfing, and the palm trees swaying, so we can't go swimming.

I know what we'll do to clean us. I see a plastic bucket over there with stones in it, so we'll put on our togs and throw buckets of water over each other. I put a rope on the bucket to prevent it from getting caught in the waves.

Scruffy the dog watches with great interest and barks encouragement. Harry the hare is in there – he just emerged mysteriously under the near tree washing his face with his paws.

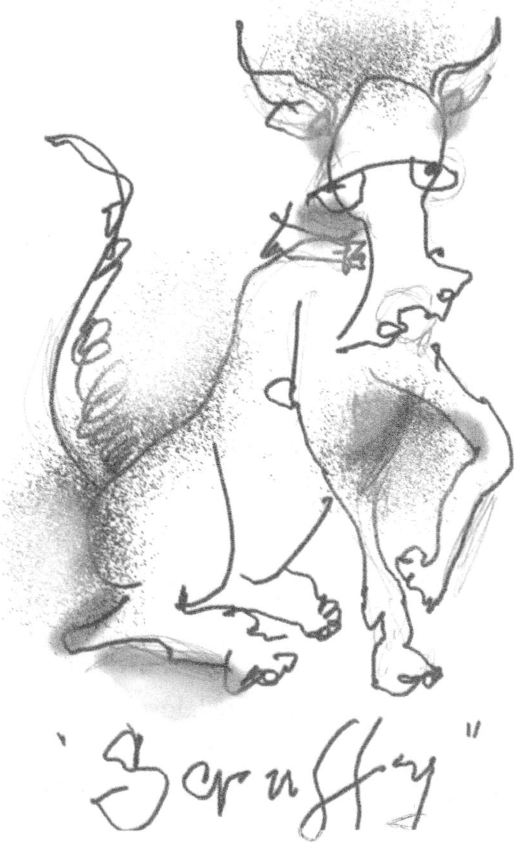

Sorry, I have not really introduced you to these two before now. Scruffy's real name, according to Kevin, is 'Crappy' or 'Scrappy' because of his colour. And Harry! How extraordinary to have a hare here. He seems to live under the cluster of trees. Scruffy and he coexist in peace. Harry is really a beautiful specimen.

My father, a vet and coursing enthusiast, would have had him chased. I am not a fan of coursing though I recognise its social value in the countryside. Coursing has got much more acceptable since the dogs were muzzled.

We are daft to be here, even if it's beautiful and thrilling in its own way. Worst of all is Caroline and Donal are expecting their first. My old protective instincts as a father are to the front. Donal is our third child and gets much mention as it is he who has us here.

We are back from our buckets of water 'swim' before we decided on a short jog around the diminishing island.

Update: Gearóid is in Hong Kong again at present. He got married to lovely Linda Rothwell from Bunclody. They have their third child almost – that will be our 26th, (or was it 27th?) grandchild, hoping all goes well.

New update: They have moved to Caragh in Nass.

Micheál is safely studying commerce in Galway and doing well.

Update: He is in France having been in Australia – big and handsome per his mother. Still single. He is a ship's captain. Olive feels he needs the guidance of a sound woman. Mothers do!

Further update: He has got one! Katrin! And in 2018 they have their second child, Seán. Enya was there first in 2016.

Seán, our son, is here with Aislinn, his girlfriend. I think that is a marriage in contemplation.

Update 2018: Yes, married with five wonderful kids to the good. They live near Crosshaven. Seán had a bad accident in 2017 but is recovering – thanks to God, the medical staff of Cork University Hospital and an astoundingly wonderful wife, Aislinn. Such love!

Carina and Eilín, our other two daughters, who I mention here and there, are spoiled by their father, at least according to their brothers! I do not believe them.

Carina is the daughter who sat on my knee when she was three and lisped: 'Daddy, me gorgeous, say yes!' Daddy still says 'yes'.

She is a physio married in Tipperary to William Smyth and in 2013 produced the exquisite Bláthin. William is from a strong Fianna Fail dynasty, a great and kind man. I am still saying yes to Gorgeous and now to Gorgeous Óg.

Eilín would have made a wonderful vet but did not get the points. She has that great affinity with animals – they simply obey her. She is like my late father in this regard.

She got married in July 2010 to our next-door neighbour Darren Enright, and their third child has arrived in late 2015. Darren was in an out of our house so much with the lads when they were all young. He is a stonemason and sculptor who produces great stuff.

Paul is here – the youngest. It is a thrilling experience he says; could not have been organised better. His father sees bits of the island disappearing in the waves. I express a differing view, but fathers are never right with teenagers. That is one certainty of parenthood. It's part of the challenge that enlivens and frustrates.

Updates: Paul is married to the delightful Aisling O'Sullivan from Cork. My mother, who was a Cork woman, always said Cork women were the best.

Paul and Aisling are now expecting their third – actually arrived in April! Anna Mae! Paul is a law teacher and mediator.

It is so great that all these wonderful people and families are now linked into us.

So, what more stories to tell? Paul wants the leprechaun stories. So, what stories to tell tonight?

A Crock of Gold

A leprechaun was asleep in a hole above *Poul Na Glocha* (the Hole with the Stones), the place where rainbows end.

He was spotted by Swag O'Connor, so called because he had a swagger when he returned from America with a pot of money!

Swag knew this Kerry leprechaun has a pot of gold under his yellow and green waistcoat. However, the Swag also knew it would be difficult to get the gold from the little man with the red hat and the white owl feathers stuck in it.

So, he went back to his village to get help from people experienced in the leprechaun business. He recruited Big Billst, the oldest man in the village and someone who knew all about the business.

Back they went to the hole in the top of the cliff.

Big Billst said: 'Catch his lapels and stare at him in the eyes for four minutes without blinking; then the gold is yours.'

The Swag crept up, caught the little man by the lapels of his coat and stared without blinking into the leprechaun's eyes when they opened. One minute passed and then the second minute.

The leprechaun said: 'Will you, kind sir, grant me one last request before I give you the gold as I will never be able to go home when it's gone?'

'What's the request?' the Swag replied.

'One last smoke of my pipe,' the leprechaun said.

The Swag was a kind hearted man and a smoker. He said, 'OK'.

The leprechaun took out the pipe and lit it up. 'Isn't the smell of that tobacco lovely?' the Swag said.

It was now three minutes into the staring match, with only one minute to go.

'To get the proper smell you would want to come nearer to the top of the pipe,' the leprechaun said.

The Swag, not taking his eyes off the little man, brought his nose down to the top of the pipe. What did the leprechaun do? Only blow hard into his pipe, and up flew the hot tobacco into the Swag's eyes. The Swag was forced to turn away. The leprechaun escaped, never to be caught again.

So, when you find a leprechaun at the end of a rainbow, you know what to do and what not to do.

The King of the Fishes

The Esk is a small inlet at the end of Con's small farm at Meenogahane. The rock at the western side was a good rock to fish from, and Con spent a lot of time fishing there.

He was supposed to catch dinner for Friday, a day when Catholics abstained from meat – I am not sure why. It is probably because of Good Friday, which was really Bad Friday.

However, the wise in the locality would say the only reason Con spent so much time there was his wife was a 'hairpin' – a tall, hard and thin woman.

She had a hard voice, a bitter tongue and was usually shouting. She was also a greedy, grasping woman – a 'hairpin' of a woman!

Late on a Wednesday, when Con and Alice (the wife) were saving hay, it began to rain. Con fled down to the Esk to get away from all the giving out.

Out he threw his fishing line with a big worm on the hook. Almost immediately, he caught the biggest fish he had ever seen.

He pulled it up onto the rock and noticed it had a bright collar around its head, and its scales were golden. To Con's amazement, the big fish spoke up and said: 'I am the King of the Fishes and I have magic powers.'

'What are they?' Asked Con.

The Fish King replies: 'If you put me back into the sea, I'll come back here every Wednesday at this time and I'll grant you anything you'll ask of me.' Con replied 'fine' and put him back into the sea.

Before he swam away, the Fish King warned that there was one request that would break the magic spell and warned Con never to ask for it. 'Be careful what you wish for.'

Con went home puzzled and told Alice, the wife, about the event. She spent the whole week thinking.

As the weather improved, Con and Alice spent time out in the clean air saving the hay with their son Tom. Wednesday came and she sent Con down to the Esk with a request.

Con goes down and up comes the King of the Fishes dead on time.

Con said what he had been told to say: 'Oh King of the fishes, Alice my wife, the plague of my life, has asked a boon of thee.'

'What is it?' said the Fish King.

'Double the size of our 25-acre farm.'

'Granted,' replied the Fish King, before disappearing. Con took a long time to get home as the fields were twice as long.

Over the next week, Alice mused on her next request and sent Con off on Wednesday.

When Con arrived, up pops the King of the Fishes.

Con said: 'Oh King of the Fishes, Alice my wife, the plague of my life, has asked a boon of thee.'

'What is it,' asks the Fish King.

'She wants a big motorcar like the one the Bishop had at Tom's confirmation and that Tom knows how to drive it.'

'Granted,' replied the Fish King, 'but remember Con,' he continued, 'there is one thing that if asked for, everything comes to an end.'

He then disappeared into the waves.

When Con returned home he saw Tom in his big, shiny motorcar.

Con said: 'We have enough. We won't ask for anything more. The Fish King warned me again that we could lose everything if I ask for the wrong thing.'

However, Alice and Tom were whispering to each other all the week.

Wednesday came. The rain was back and there was thunder and lightning. Alice and Tom decided they wanted another thing, so they demanded Con return to the Esk and meet the Fish King.

Poor Con went down and stands at the rock. Up pops the King of the Fishes on time.

Con said: 'Alice my wife, the plague of my life, has asked a boon of thee.'

'What is it?' the King asks politely.

Con said, slowly, 'to make Tom the Pope'.

With that, there was a big flash of lightning and a loud roar of thunder.

The King of the Fishes jumped up onto the rock and said: 'I can't do that, I warned you. All is at an end.' He jumps back into the sea and is never seen again.

Con hurries home, but when he arrives he notices the fields are small again and there is no car in the yard.

Con just said, 'we were too greedy'.

Fathers

I was musing just there about the role of fathers. So much credit goes, justifiably, to mothers, but some must go to fathers too.

Call me old-fashioned, but I believe that rearing children in a loving and secure home is the most important job there is.

A father's role is to support the mother when the children are young. When they start school, especially from age eight onwards, the father must come to the fore and get them to deal with the outside world; before that it is simply kicking a ball around, teaching them to cycle, swim and so forth. Giving them time in a different way.

Then, in the second decade, it is particularly important to get very much involved. I took them to sport and dancing classes, and discussed living in the community and politics with them. Praise and exhortations to do your best each day are very important. You lead by example of course.

A father is a powerful word, being a father all of your child's young life. A father must remain close to his wife and child. You don't want to be domineering.

This closeness is captured in St Paul's writings on love, his call to be 'patient and kind'. Do not store up bitterness.

I discovered a great way to teach our children values, while I was teaching them to drive.

We would drive to a farm in Athea before school. This would give us an hour alone in the car, with radio programmes like *Morning Ireland* on. I would ask him or her, while he or she was driving, 'what is your view on that matter'? These discussions helped a lot.

I would slip in advice about not always believing what you hear; learn to think about the solution, and listen to and think about every difficult dilemma; do not go by appearances alone; be independent as best you can, although in reality we are interdependent; that each person is valued because we should care and love each other, and we all need protection and support from each other; that life is good but it can be tough.

A father's role is about leading, but remember the Latin *éduce* means education is about leading out a family.

I remember we used to discuss what is right and wrong, honesty, truth, and trust: What are they? How do you recognise goodness and badness? What values should guide you and where do we get them from? I hate catchphrases and quick apparent solutions.

You have to talk about money and property with children in their teens, about planning a future life. In relationships, sexual included, how does one know who to trust? I always emphasised the value of work to my kids; the importance of working in what interests you; and why you should think out each important move in advance. How many people and groups of people do not think and are misled, especially by their leaders and politicians?

I suppose that religion and morality provoked difficult debates.

I soon learnt that each child was different. One of the most common words I used was 'respect'. Each person must have great respect for others and must maintain respect from others. True love is based on that. Being so happily married, I pointed out the enduring value of that marriage to them.

Looking around me and listening as a lawyer to young husbands and fathers, a common complaint is they feel they are treated like a second-class parent. Indeed, one man thought he came in after the dog and the cat. That, of course, is a view imported from the USA and is incorrect. Unfortunately, a lot of judges, wrongly in many cases, accept that view.

Divorce creates a lot of difficulties. I often wonder should there be a council for the rights and duties of parents and dealing with the proper roles of mother and father?

Both Olive and I were lucky as we both did marriage counselling and training, which taught us the importance of the first five years. In addition to giving the child security and a home, there is a 24 hour need for love. And love includes tough love, always the balance in care.

This is a quote from Lebanese poet Kahil Gibran's *The Prophet*, what do you think?

> You may give them your love but not your thoughts,
> For they have their own thoughts.
> You may house their bodies but not their souls,
> For their souls dwell in the house of tomorrow,
> Which you cannot visit, not even in your dreams.
> You may strive to be like them,but seek not to make them like you.
> For life goes not backward nor tarries with yesterday.

I think this is lovely, but my view is that a father can and should help formulate his children's values, and influence their way of thinking about and seeing life. Later, they may accept or reject your influence.

All fathers should read the following poem; *Walk a Little Slower Daddy*:

> Walk a little slower, Daddy,
> Said a little boy so frail.
> I'm following in your footsteps,
> And I don't want to fail.
> Sometimes your steps are very fast,
> Sometimes they are hard to see,
> So walk a little slower, Daddy,
> For you are leading me.

I know that once you walked this way
Many years ago,
And what you did along the way,
I'd really like to know.
For sometimes when I am tempted,
I don't know what to do.
So walk a little slower, Daddy,
For I must follow you.

Someday when I'm grown up,
You are like I want to be.
Then I will have a little boy,
Who will want to follow me.
And I would want to lead him right,
And help him to be true.
So walk a little slower, Daddy.
For we must follow you.

For me, these are the most important keywords when it comes to fatherhood:

Example: Most powerful! Do as you say, and read that poem above.
Interest: Be always interested.
Respect: Listen and discuss calmly; no shouting
Love: The most powerful of weapons, and one men are shy in using.
Honour: Honour your wife and always have a united front.
Security: Provide a sense of security in the home.

Now, add three other words that are of use to you as a parent:

1. ____
2. ____
3. ____

Remember the *Desiderata*. It was written by Max Ehrman in 1927, but it gained wider recognition when Reverend Frederick Kates distributed copies of it in his church, St Paul's in Baltimore. The *Desiderata*:

GO PLACIDLY amid the noise and the haste, and remember what peace there may be in silence. As far as possible, without surrender, be on good terms with all persons.

Speak your truth quietly and clearly; and listen to others ... Enjoy your achievements as well as your plans. Keep interested in your own career ... With all its sham, drudgery and broken dreams, it is still a beautiful world. Be cheerful. Strive to be happy.

A Peaceful Death

I learnt much from my own father and can only echo what Bryan MacMahon wrote in his obituary:

> He was a personality in North Kerry. Not in a namby-pamby way for he was human, original, wise, frank to the point of turbulence, impish, blunt, knowledgeable, and warm hearted.

I know he rests in peace. Bryan also wrote:

> Together too we went to college in St Michael's Listowel in the 1920's when civil war raged in Kerry. There were guns in a classroom – the bigger lads went off and took different sides in the bitter struggle.

In fairness my father never spoke of those times beyond saying they were terrible, setting brother against brother and neighbour against neighbour.

Bryan was writing about after my father's death. I felt it was a wonderful way to go, the way he died. In his own way my father was a religious man, but in a very different way to my mother. I think all men are more silent about their religious views, especially on emotional ritualism.

My father used to say the Stations of the Cross most days, two stations for each of his sons. He got cancer. He was down in the Bons in Cork, and they stuck drips and tubes into him eventually. He wasn't sleeping. I said to him: 'Grandy, what are you doing here? Let's take you home to Listowel so that you can die with dignity.' 'Right,' he said, 'but while you have the bigger car send John down as he is the eldest.'

So, it was arranged. My father kept asking John: 'Are we in Kerry yet?' When John said, 'we are in Kerry now,' my father fell asleep.

His good friend Sr Peter in Listowel's small local hospital welcomed him. He had helped her with money to do up the hospital chapel. She said: 'Dick, you're not going to die, stop that nonsense.' She had him back on his then shaky feet within three weeks. He was able to walk with a stick to his veterinary surgery.

One day I was coming out of my front door, just as he was passing, and he said to me: 'Look at Joe over there looking at me, wondering will I die soon. I won't die until he pays us the £30 he owes, we should never have let him run up a bill like that.'

A few months later he had gone down a lot and was confined to bed. We used to take turns at night to go down to Convent Cross to help my mother look after him. One night, while I was 'on duty', he fixed me with his beady eye and said, 'Robert, you always give it to me straight'. I responded, 'listen to who's talking'!

'What I want to know is there something there when I die?' You know that's an awkward question to answer. 'Well,' I began, 'I can't say I ever shook hands with God directly, or met him walking down Market St, but isn't there enough evidence that it is more than likely that there is a Creator? If so he or she had a purpose surely.'

We then went on to discuss concepts such as beauty (there was a beautiful rose on the dressing table), love, truth, faith, justice and the wonders of nature. I told him that I could never understand electricity, but I knew others did and people could make things hot and cold with it.

We then went on to discuss his power to 'devine' (not divine) things, including lost bodies which he could not explain. I think the unusual power he had really got through to him that night. We agreed it was nothing material, but that it was there.

At that, he was getting tired and said: 'You've given me enough to think about, go away to Olive and your family. I'll sleep on it.'

The next night I was on duty he said: 'Do you remember Wednesday night and what we spoke about?' I said, 'yes'. 'Well,' he said 'I have decided you're right, so I am going to go straight up to heaven.' 'How did you reach that conclusion?' 'Well,' he replied, 'I wouldn't like the other place.'

Some days later he seemed to lapse into a coma or unconsciousness. We all gathered around the bed except for my brother Fr Gerard who sat on a small stool in the corner contemplating. I don't think Gerard really approved of all the prayers out loud. Later we started the Rosary, my mother's favourite prayer. During which, when we were young, we giggled at and, worse still, our father was known to be infected by our giggling.

Olive was holding Grandy's hand and feeling his faint pulse. Around went the decades of the Joyful Mysteries, then the Sorrowful. I noticed Grandy's eyelids seemed to flutter during the Sorrowful Mysteries, he never liked saying them.

Then my mother began saying the first decade of the Glorious Mysteries, The Resurrection. My father's face lit up at the sound of her voice and then relaxed and he smiled. Olive said 'he's gone', and I added 'to Heaven', as I remembered his wish and certainty. That was why he smiled.

Dachau

A lot of what I am writing here in gas light has been talked about for the past three hours. I do not venture out in the darkness which comes suddenly, just as if someone pulled a curtain over the sinking sun.

I suppose being a prisoner of sorts on this island reminds me of a recent visit to Dachau concentration camp. I was over visiting our daughter, Máire, in Germany. I remember her in-laws didn't approve of me going to a death camp. There is a 'brush it under the carpet' mentality there.

I remember, as a young fella, looking at a newspaper picture of the living skeletons found by the American soldiers. I was about eight, it was 1945. My mother snatched the paper from me to protect me.

She didn't succeed, as that picture is burned into my mind and it is still there. It causes me horror still. I went to the camp – call it fatal fascination or a desire to understand how a historically cultured and mainly Christian people could do these terrible deeds.

What always bothers me as a lawyer is, what is law? In the camp, I saw the rules – camp 'law' decreed by the minions of Hitler and others. One rule said that if you damaged any property, such as a cup or knife, your punishment was hanging by your thumbs for six hours. Usually, you were dead or your thumbs had left your hands long before the six hours were up.

I met a German law student there. We were equally shocked at the apparent lawfulness of it all, the mass murder and torture. Dachau had ovens too. The student said to me that something like that could not happen in Germany today. I reminded him that there was abortion in Germany; the bodies of the innocent unborn thrown into furnaces.

It is a dreadful place. A visit every five years should be mandatory for all political leaders and lawmakers. What right have such rules to be called 'law'? How could human beings make such 'laws'? What are 'laws'? I think Thomas Aquinas had it right when he wrote that laws were ordinances based on reason (that divine faculty of man) for the common good and enforceable. Of course, the weasel words of 'reason' and 'common good' can be twisted by the twisted. That visit confirmed my view that abortion is an equal horror.

As for man's reason, Shakespeare said, if I remember correctly, somewhere in *Hamlet*:

> What is a man,
> If the chief good and market of his time
> Be but to sleep and feed?
> A beast no more.
> Sure, he that made us with such large discourse,
> Looking before and after,
> Gave us not that capability and god-like reason to
> Fust in us unused.

I hope that quote is right as it is important for us to recognise that we have God-like reason. The Bard of Avon was one of the wise men of history.

Another memory I have of that war was when a big British ship was sunk in the North Sea by the Germans. I remember standing with my mother at our front door in Pound Lane when these women in shawls, who were going down to the church, stopped in front of us.

They said to her: 'Mrs Pierse, will you pray that my son was not on that ship?' They all knew my mother to be a prayerful woman and daily mass goer. My mother took out her rosary beads and every woman, or man, joined with her in a decade of the Rosary. Actually, no one from town died on the ship, but two or three north Kerry men did apparently.

I remember one man quoting Pádraig Pearse: 'War is an evil thing.'

The Centre

Having seen the breakdown of the Weimer Republic, one must reflect on where Ireland is going politically. None of the Irish political parties have a principled programme. Surely it is fair to ask, what are we drifting into? It might be timely to quote the first stanza of Yeats' *The Second Coming:*

> Turning and turning in the widening gyre
> The falcon cannot hear the falconer;
> Things fall apart; the centre cannot hold;
> Mere anarchy is loosed upon the world,
> The blood-dimmed tide is loosed, and everywhere
> The ceremony of innocence is drowned;
> The best lack all conviction, while the worst
> Are full of passionate intensity

I often wonder is this actually happening in Ireland – the centre 'falling part' in face of 'passionate intensity'. It certainly fell apart in Northern Ireland. And as I said to the young law student in Dachau, the Germans are now exterminating children: 'The blood-dimmed tide is loosed.'

Min with Caps go to Germany

On a lighter note about post-war Germany, two Dublin min with caps, bachelors of course, went to Berlin in 1947 to rebuild the city under the Marshall Plan.

They had no work at home. They were well paid. 'Where's all this money coming from?' asked one. The reply from the pal, who had lifted his cap, was: 'The Marshall Plan, them Yanks beat the Germans, flattened Berlin and now pay us to rebuild it.'

The other man lifted his cap, scratched his head and said: 'Funny crowd them Yanks, maybe we should go to war with them in Ireland so they would pay us to rebuild Dublin.' More cap lifting and scratching produced the immortal thought, 'no good, what if we won, we would have to rebuild America.'

Just Law

When I look at the carry-on of so called Christians in Northern Ireland, what went on in old Yugoslavia, and the Jews and Muslims at each other's throats, I just wonder why no one listens to history?

One thing I am sure of is that the concept of 'just law', a law based on justice and reason, is still a vague dream in international thought and action. Is the notion of law as just rules and regulations to control people and situations just a myth? There is a school of jurists who regard law as nothing more than a tool for social engineering, a plaything for politicians. I wonder are they right?

In this context and in that of the substitute democracies we live in, it is imperative we all think and about these matters. After all Mr Adolf Hitler rubbed his hands together in glee saying, 'what luck for the rulers that the people do not think'. Someone recently remarked to me that what is even worse is when the rulers do not think.

Remember the words of that great Irish parliamentarian of the British Parliament, Edmund Burke, who said: 'All that is necessary for evil to prosper is that good men do nothing.'

We in Ireland are mentally lazy when it comes to politics. This is particularly so in the 'educated' middle class. They think politics is beneath them. The 'I'm alright Jack' syndrome!

We can all do our bit. I am planting over fifty acres of trees to clean up the air a bit. It is my children and grandchildren who will reap the rewards of clean air, clean water and fertile land. Let's not waste these treasures.

Gosh, I am getting writer's cramp and cramps in my flat feet. My children will say I am also getting 'preachy' and getting on my hobbyhorse about the decay of practical patriotism. A walk in the wind will blow away these thoughts. I also need to see what parts of our sandy cove the sea has invaded.

Update: I was right about the non-thinking Irish electorate in 2007 and since. How could they have been such fools? How could the politicians be so greedy? Our country was only restored by patriotic self-sacrifice over a long-sustained period. We lost our senses.

We have now left the Troika, but where are we going? In 2018, are we able to look after the homeless? The sick? Do we cherish the children equally?

2019: We are still massive polluters. Ireland has one of the worst records in Europe. We are heading off the environmental cliff.

Are we only interested in, 'fumbling in the greasy till, and adding the half pence to the pence (apologies to WBY)'?

A Walk with Scruffy & Harry

I left as I was getting writer's cramp

I am back. Had a cup of tea and a few biscuits. Told the lads and ladies what I am writing about. I promised to recount to them tonight. Other than ourselves, they are a few humans on the island – a caretaker, her husband (Eddie) and their child (who we never see).

So, I am about to leave you again to go for a walk with 'Scruffy' and get some paper to write on – the island is about 800 yards, or maybe 500 yards wide on a good day.

I think he would be a good dog in a fight. He must like the name Scruffy as he is now friendlier to me than Kevin. Dogs know where they stand with you by the tone of your voice.

My father believed you could know the character of the people in the house by the dog. Friendly dog friendly people; snappy dog snappy people.

I pat Scruffy on the head – oddly he is not into petting much. I think he is of the small, strong silent type. I have asked him about his relation-ship with Harry, but there is no bark of a reply.

Harry the hare here is a beautiful specimen. I instantly thought of the mountainy hares I hunted on Sundays with 'the lads' in Dunmanway forty years ago. I started my legal career in Dunmanway in 1960. We went hunting up the airy mountain and down the rushy glen.

Dark brown and thick fur covers Harry's back as he sat up and boxed the sand out of his paws. He disappeared during the storm. Where to, I did not find out, as of course hares do not go into burrows.

Maybe Scruffy does not know Harry is to be chased or swallowed up by a dog.

There was always a dilemma about dogs and hares in our house. It is an odd friendship here in animal terms. No one explained to Scrappy that

Harry was supposed to be an enemy. I wonder what Mr Darwin would think?

I ponder this. Shows what the environment may do – peace through ignorance of war.

Pity the world's new imperial power, the USA, wouldn't learn the lesson of the dog and hare here (that peaceful co-existence is a win-win situation!). Maybe China, a rapidly emerging superpower, will learn too. It is hard to be that optimistic about either country.

Power is a strange thing! It is said power corrupts, absolute power corrupts absolutely.

The difference between dog and man according to the 'min with the caps': a dog is taller sitting than standing, a man is vice versa. Thinking about it now so is a hare. Actually, a hare sitting up with his ears alert is a beautiful sight. Observant people these chaps with the caps – especially when they sit on the fence and advise the passer-by!

Toby Tells the News

My late father RIP was a great man for greyhounds. We always had a number of them. I remember one time he had a very good dog, 'Berkie B', called after a friend of his. My father got an offer of €1,000 for the dog, which was big money to the father of 7 sons at that time.

As 'Berkie B' was a good-natured pet to all of us there was outrage at the thought of him been sold – and to an Englishman at that, which was worse our mother said. My father must have talked sense into our mother.

A few Sundays later Ma took all seven sons to Ballybunion. We should have been suspicious as our father did not go. We not only got ice-cream, but also a bottle of lemonade and biscuits.

Peter, the youngest, kept blocking the mouth of the bottle of lemonade with the biscuits! He would then get cross and red in the face when the lemonade would not come out! That time (early fifties) we only got lemonade at Christmas. To cut the story short, home we come to find Berkie B was gone.

For this treachery my father received the combined frozen silence of his seven sons – difficult for us because he was a great pal of ours as well as our father. He was a cute man too. Within days a fluffy sheepdog pup, Toby, arrived. Toby was great fun so the Berkie B sale faded. Father came back in favour.

Toby was great with tricks – sitting, lying down, giving the paw; the usual with intelligent dogs. However, one of the tricks he performed brought all of my school friends into the house. My father taught him to go down for the newspaper. He would bring it up in his mouth, usually followed by a few school children.

My father would stand the newspaper, folded in half, up against a jug on the table with the main headline up, while Toby would sit on my father's chair with his paws on the table. My father would take off his glasses and put them on Toby's nose. 'Toby is the news good or bad?' he would say to the dog. If Toby gave one bark, my father would say, 'good news today so'. If Toby would give two barks; 'that is bad news'.

The mention of Berkie B, the man whose name the greyhound got, brought another story to mind. When that man's father died there was one of the great 'wakes' in town, according to folklore.

Mr B Senior was in hospital for some time. The nuns and doctors said he could not get alcohol. However, the women, family and neighbours didn't agree. It wouldn't do, the poor man couldn't die of alcohol abstinence. It wouldn't be a fitting end and so on. So, the first trial 'wake' began.

So every day Mr B received three items: a teapot full of the type of tea he liked (whiskey based); a bottle of apparent Lucozade (poitín coloured with a dozen tea leaves); and a large trifle (a few bits of spongy cakes floating on a very liquid jelly port). Even his visitors left well inebriated. That lasted three weeks.

Mr B died. The second wake began. Folklore has it that during the famous three day wake even some of the nuns lost their balance. Mr B was buried with whiskey, brandy and two half crowns, the latter being the fare for the boatman on the ferry over the Styx. I wonder what the fare is in 2018?

I mentioned the dilemma of greyhounds versus hares. Well, it was really about chickens in our house. My father was a great man for the coursing – even though he always advocated that the greyhounds should be muzzled, which they weren't in the 1950s.

He went on the *Late Late Show* one night for Gay Byrne. He was attacked by the city audience but held his own. I remember he said to one woman once: 'What would you do if there was a rat in your house? Would you say nice ratty and here is a bit of bread?'

He was on the *Late Late* another night with Jack Benny, the US comedian. They were great fun. Loyal locals said afterwards he got the better of Benny!

My mother was totally against greyhound coursing but would never publicly admit it. My father learnt not to say how many hares were killed at a coursing meeting. My father was cuter about women that I am, as he had three sisters. His poor sons were ignoramuses in matters relating to the gentler sex, having no sister – some would say we still are.

Was there not some Greek philosopher (Aristotle?) who said the two things he could not understand were the motion of the tides and the mind of a woman!

Maybe the moon has something to do with these puzzles. We understand the tides now, but I certainly have made little progress in Aristotle's second problem.

There were, of course, a few parrots and sea birds on the trees in the caye. They squawked at 4 am on Sunday morning so loudly that I got up. Even on the mornings of the storm I could hear them, no matter how the wind and pounding waves raised the decibel level.

They were welcoming the dawn even before we could see it. Wonderful colours. The sea birds were off on their business, the things birds do daily even in storms. I cannot figure out what the parrots survive on here.

Animals & The Law

The law in relation to animals changed a lot in my lifetime. The motorist has won out on the roads. The over-protected *homo urbanus* has taken away that one bite from the dog that he, the dog, was entitled to in law in my early days.

In my early practice days, the dog's owner was not responsible for the dog's first bite. It was only for later bites, when he knew his dog was vicious.

That rule came from the old Roman legal principle of '*scienter*' (knowledge) where the owner only got knowledge of the dog's tendency to bite humans when the dog had had his first human bite. That is changed now – no free bites really.

The Cow

As a young fellow one of my jobs was to drive a cow on foot (driver with a bike) from Listowel out to our seaside home in Meenogahane, about fifteen miles away. That seems like a long journey, but when you had a trained old cow it was not so long.

The older cows always knew where they were going and they would head off out the road themselves. I just cycled behind them. Meenogahane had the good sweet grass of good land.

Bringing them back was the job, they hated coming back into town. As the grass on the farm near our seaside home was much better, they did not want to go back to the confines of a small urban field. They, of course, do not like the restriction of being kept in a stall during the winter. The older cows, therefore, made it extremely difficult to bring them back.

Cows are smarter than you think! It would take three people to get through the first three miles back to Listowel – an exhausting three miles for cow and boys.

We had great fellow feeling with the cow. Being back in Listowel meant the end of the holidays, the end of the summer freedom, and the beginning of school routine.

Nervy Nellie

The trouble with us humans is we do not really credit animals, particularly cows, with much intelligence. In fact, animals often have tremendous memory, witness cow story above. Horses have a better memory, and of course dogs are legendary.

When I came back home in 1954 from hospital, where I had been away for a year and a half in bed with TB, I had to redevelop my muscles. At that time there was no such thing as physiotherapy or anything like that, for 'consumptives' anyway. I therefore had to take up a walking programme.

My father had a greyhound bitch called, 'Nervy Nellie'. As an excuse to get me walking, he had me take her for a four-mile training walk every day.

We went by the Bog Road, beloved of my late friend John B Keane. The bitch became very devoted to me. In fact, when she had pups I was the only one who would be allowed handle them.

When I went off to university, Nervy Nelly had an extraordinary ability to know when I was coming home. My mother used to say that when I would be within two miles of Listowel, the bitch would run up and start pawing the kitchen door. When my mother heard the pawing, she would say to my father, 'Robert is coming home'. I could never explain the phenomenon. Could dogs have ESP (Extra Sensory Perception)?

We know so little about Creation! Think about the structure and order of an anthill. How come?

I do believe in ESP in humans, from experience. There was a solicitor in Abbeyfeale, Dick Woulfe, who I knew well and did a lot of business with. I would ring him and say, 'Dick I am ringing you about such and such a case'. Only for him to respond, 'no Robert, it is I ringing you about that case'! We both would have taken out our files five minutes earlier. That happened so often that it could not be a coincidence. Then, of course, my father was a water diviner.

I am sure that as science advances and we learn more about consciousness, phenomena such as the transmission of thoughts through invisible rays, we will have a greater understanding of God's greatest creation – the human mind.

In a way, computers and mobile phones reflect the greatness of the human mind, its Creator.

The Greedy World

When I was growing up as a young fellow during and immediately after the Second World War, petrol was almost non-existent, therefore my father used to do a lot of his veterinary calls in the horse and trap. When we were on holidays in Meenogahane, our old family farm, it used to be horse and trap all the time and a grey mare.

My father often told a story about me as an innocent youth. I was going along in the horse and trap and there was this blackbird singing on the hedge. I turned to my father and said, 'Daddy, even the birds know me out here'. I believed the bird was saying hello to me. I am still fairly innocent like that!

Indeed, talking about the war, I remember often my father getting butter, eggs and petrol as part of his fee, as these were limited in their availability due to rationing.

You see money isn't much use if there is nothing to buy with it. Indeed, money is always a bit of a mystery to me. It is the oil of the exchange system. All I know is that it is normally a good thing for a father of ten to have money and a bad thing to be without it. I would never like to have too much of it, as it kills initiative and makes people greedy for much more.

My experience, as a lawyer, is it is the fuel of greed, the great corruptor.

A great friend of mine, Ralph Sutton SC (RIP) used to ask me: 'Have you Robert enough to get by?' I would say yes. He would say enough is enough, more than enough is more than enough. Think about that in this greedy world.

I remember a famous back-to-back trap and a chestnut mare of my father's. There would always be a race out from Mass in Causeway to try to be first on the road home; leather and brass dancing and sparkling in the muted excitement of competition. All the local farmers took great pride in their horses and traps. No greed there, just fun and rivalry.

At that time there were of course agricultural shows. If your horse won a prize, people would come to congratulate you. Community interest is high in small towns, some even call it 'the squinting windows' syndrome. The city people do not understand us rustics and our simple fun.

Adventures in The Hague

That reminds me of an incident I had many years later in the late 1950s. I got a scholarship to study international law in The Hague. I was going over with two Irish girls. We took off from Dublin, crossed the sea to England and crossed England by train. We boarded a ship going (I think!) from Harwich to the Hook of Holland. When we got on the ship we were rather tired and hungry, so we were told to go down for a meal.

We all tucked in with great gusto into this red rare roast beef. However, I was very suspicious of the colour of the beef. When we came up from the meal, the ship had moved out into the North Sea. It was getting a bit rough. We were sea-sawing around a bit.

'You know that was a nice bit of meat, wasn't it?' I remember saying to the two girls. They said 'yes'. 'I am pretty sure it was the old grey mare we used to have in Meenogahane that we sold last month,' I said. The next thing that I saw was the two of them leaning over the side of the boat, bottoms raised. The grey mare, if it was the grey mare, was disappearing into the North Sea.

It took several days before I was back in their good books, and then only because they needed an escort to their digs at night. They needed someone to protect their virtue in The Hague.

It was my first time leaving Ireland. I would say it was 1959. In Holland, memories of the war were very ripe. My landlady would not permit a German to come into her house. I saw people spitting after Volkswagen and Mercedes cars. Common market my eye!

My two Irish lasses, young and lovely, had to be escorted home each night because of prowling Germans and other 'foreigners'. This meant a three mile walk every night as none of us could afford a taxi.

The first week there was an eye opener. I had to pay ƒ2 (two Dutch Guilders), which was about 10 p or 13 cent, to go on the beach.

We 'escaped' our lectures on international law on fine days by signing in to get our credits, taking our lecture scripts to read, before climbing out the toilet window. It was a female toilet we had to use as its window was bigger.

It was also a shock initially to have to pay four times at mass and to get four receipts for each payment – apparently tax deductible! All this was very tough on a poor Kerryman! The kids here on the caye thought all this was very funny last night when I was telling them.

Paris

When we got married in 1963, Olive and I went to Paris on our honeymoon. When we arrived we were fairly hungry. We were sitting in one of these wayside cafés in the *Champs-Élysées*.

Feeling it was a very important occasion, we ordered two steaks. I gave a look at the two steaks and I said to Olive, 'cheval'. 'I wonder is it the old grey mare they pulled out of storage?' I said. She absolutely refused to eat, so I had the two steaks.

Cheval or no cheval a Kerryman does not pay for two steaks and allow them go uneaten, especially at French prices. Olive claims that it was an opportunity for her to lay down certain markers in relation to conversation at the table. I just enjoyed my steaks, grey mare or otherwise. I have been firmly under the thumb since, in these matters anyway.

Paris was a delight, even if it still traumatized by its capture by the Germans about 17 years before. We stayed in a small, old-fashioned French hotel where the proprietress had her little dog all dressed up with bows the colour of the French national flag. She wore a scarf with the same colours.

We were made to feel very welcome, she even gave us extra coffee and croissants when she saw our green Irish passports – we weren't Krauts! I wonder will this common market stay together? I suppose money and the necessity of peace should win out. One never knows.

I always remember the old song: 'Money talks, it don't sing and dance, but it sure talks.'

The Facts of Life

My father was a vet, so I grew up around and was reared with animals. Indeed, my mother attributed my survival in childhood to the care lavished on me by a black Labrador dog, 'Bruce'. Whenever I cried, he jumped into my playpen. Then, he would curl himself around me in the playpen to keep me warm.

My father not only influenced my attitude towards animals, but passed it on to my daughter, Eilín, who is doing agricultural science in UCD now. She has always had a collection of canaries, cats (three), dogs (in large numbers), a couple of horses (sorry, increased to five this year), a rabbit, and about twenty bullocks. As part of her agricultural degree training she worked on a pig farm. She says pigs are very smart animals.

Update: She now owns the farm, and has two degrees in agricultural science. She is married to the ever-helpful Darren and they have three children – delightful.

She is a very courageous horse woman and frightens the life out of me when I go to shows with her. But as we say in the Kingdom, 'breeding beats feeding'. My father was mad about her too – showed her plants to pick for her canary, the right way to groom a horse, and when to 'worm' the dogs.

I remember the embarrassment one day I felt when driving her out to Hannon's Strand near Ballybunion. We were taking 'Bunny', her favourite horse and a gelding, and 'Betsy', her mare donkey, to the beach for a run. She was about 14 years old at the time and an equally young pal was with her.

They began an intimate and detailed discussion on how they might get 'Betsy' in foal. The various jackasses, their known sexual abilities and offspring were discussed. A red-faced father in front concentrated on his driving as he found himself tongue-tied, a rare condition in a lawyer! As I told Olive later, I was relieved of my parental duty to explain the facts of life to Eilín.

The following summer several jackasses visited Betsy, but to no avail. Betsy was eventually stolen by a 'knacker of the worst type' according to the females of our family.

That reminds me of another story about 'the facts of life'. We fathers of Listowel used to go to an annual retreat weekend to the Redemptorists in Limerick. Part of the weekend was how to deal with teenagers when it came to drink and sex. We would learn from each other and, in many ways, some of us set the standards for local family life.

I remember one solicitor colleague's account of a familiar ordeal, talking to his eldest son about *les girls*. He was a man of rigid views and he was the Fishery Board's prosecuting solicitor, so we were all wary of him. He was pushed into this job by his wife after attending a retreat where he was supposed to have learnt it all.

He made a few notes preparing for the ordeal. He and his fifteen year-old son sat down. He said to the son: 'I want to talk to you about a difficult matter. It is about being a young man, dealing with girls and how to respect each other. What happens when you get married and so on.'

He paused, somewhat red faced. 'Dad, is this about the facts of life?' the son said. 'Yes,' said father. Son says, 'I know all about that from a book a pal gave me'. 'What is the book?' 'It is called *Lady Chatterley's Lover.*' Father replied, 'that is banned, I will have to burn it'.

In fairness, those retreats provided us with good resolutions. Some of these did not last. There was the story of three pals who took the pledge at one session. Whatever went wrong their car, on their way back to Listowel, stalled at Punch's pub. It took the car two days to get to Listowel. Their local publican breathed a sigh of relief. The natural order of his clientele was restored.

Knackers

Do you know there is officially such a thing as a 'knacker'? The Act providing for the regulation of 'knackeries' is the Protection of Animals Act 1911 (1 & 2 Geo. 5.c27). Section 4 (1) reads:

> Every person who shall carry on, or assist in carrying on, the trade or business of a knacker shall observe and conform to the regulations set out in the first schedule to this Act.

While Section 15 (2) reads:

> The expression of 'knacker' means a person whose trade or business it is to kill any cattle not killed for the purpose of the flesh being used as butcher's meat.

I got these pieces of information from the 1915 *The Irish Justice of the Peace* by James O'Connor, which comes in two large volumes. It was used so frequently in the district courts of the 1960s that I paid £100 for it in 1965, which was about 20% of my profit for the year – probably the equivalent of €1,500 now.

I am now, as I was then, a 'sucker' for books and knowledge. Irish law books were in very short supply back then. Nowadays we have a great supply. As I get older, I buy more and more of them as I realise I know less and less about anything, and especially the law. *Ancora imparo* (I am still learning) as Michelangelo said.

In case I did not know it, my children keep reminding me of my ignorance of modern life, especially of those dreadful mobile phones. They, the phones not the children, should be banned on trains and buses.

Maybe that 'Knackers Act' is repealed – it's hard to know what acts are not repealed or in force now. We used to get a government publication on that once, but it has been discontinued. Helping lawyers to find the law does not get many votes.

TB Cows

In the times that I grew up, namely during and after the Second World War, farmers did pretty well. They began to recover from the earlier economic wars with England that de Valera had launched about land annuities and so on. That was about paying rents to landlords.

Animals were valuable and well cared for, despite the scourge of tuberculosis. Much money has and is being spent on trying to get rid of TB in cattle – with little enough success initially due to badgers and a few 'rogue' farmers.

Talking about TB cows, my late father was a veterinary inspector for the Department of Agriculture. One of his jobs was to kill cows diagnosed with TB. He claimed he was a better diagnostician than doctors, as the cows could not tell him their symptoms.

When a cow had TB, it was killed by a humane killer gun by my father.

The TB cows became 'Roscrea cows'. Their lungs were sent to the Department in a labelled rubber bag by train – yes I remember the steam trains and then the diesel trains from Listowel. The remaining carcasses of the animals, minus the lungs, were sent to a factory in Roscrea, Co Tipperary, to be turned into 'meat and bone' feed for animals.

I suppose that was why my father was so shocked when an X-ray showed I had TB. I wasn't shot, but I was sent off to a sanatorium in Dun Laoghaire. It is now the National Rehabilitation Hospital.

I also remember the train load of live cattle leaving Listowel during and after the Second World War. We were rationed on what we could get, but there was a good barter system going. England needed milk, beef and other agricultural products. However, the barter scheme worked well, so Ireland prospered. Ration books continued in use after the war for years.

Cattle Dealers

I remember an old cattle dealer friend of my family called Jack Keane, now with his Creator, telling me a couple of the stories about his early years as a cattle dealer, the time of the Economic War included. A friend of mine from Dingle told me Jack was known in West Kerry as, *O Catháin Na Shean Ba* ('Keane of the Old Cows'). The stories illustrate the times and ingenuity of these men. They were natural psychologists.

During the Economic War, times were so bad that cattle were being sold for £1 (€1.27) or less. Jack remembered a man approaching him at a fair once to tell him he had not been able to sell his cow and would Jack ever give him £1 for it. Jack said no, that he had no market for the cow. The man replied he had to pay 12s 6p for his Land Commission annuity the following week or he would be evicted. The year had been very bad.

Eventually Jack told the man he would give him 12s 6p (62 ½ p or 80 cent now) and if he accepted, leave the cow into Jack's field that evening. If not, he can take the cow home. When Jack got to his field that evening the cow was there; things were bad!

As a young fella, I remember one summer where it rained constantly. The Ferris brothers from Rattoo tried to cut our corn in Meenogahane with their reaper-binder machine. Almost all the corn rotted. My job was to carry, up and down, overcoats and hats to them every hour; to keep them dry.

The Land Commission annuity was a payment to the government in lieu of the old rack rents to landlords. I sometimes think our taxation system is akin to the old landlords' extracting rack rents from us, especially as our government seems to operate on a spend and hope for tomorrow's taxes basis. But then I do not understand money, particularly public money and debt: Do you?

1998 was as bad for many farmers. I have a small bit of land myself (well, it is Olive's actually). I took fourteen weanlings to a mart in the autumn of 1998 and could not get even £60 each. They would have made £300 each three years before. Imagine the political uproar if a publican had to suddenly reduce the price of a pint by four-fifths! Prices were still bad in 1999.

I know my urban reader will not believe all this but it is true. Small farmers are disappearing under the strange EU and Irish bureaucratic policies. The cheque in the post is their only real income. We see their numbers diminishing under the programme of enlarging farms. That is a pity as they are such decent and hard-working people. We will end up with EU subsidised ranches here.

On the subject of the ownership of the farm, when we bought it I put it in Olive's name. When an old farmer neighbour heard about it he disapproved, saying that I am giving the woman too much power. That attitude has changed a lot in the last twenty-five years, thank God.

There is also the World Trade Organisation. While it may do some good, it is often an economic vehicle for the rich economies to buy cheaply from the poor farmers of the world and bring down the farmers in the western world to part-time farming.

Politicians are allowing cities to enlarge to concentrate voters. Securing votes and winning a seat in the next election are what preoccupies politicians as far as I can see. Enough of this cynicism!

The Luck Penny

Another story Jack Keane (the cattle dealer) told me, and one he took great pleasure in, dated from the World War itself. He made a deal with a relation of a man who had been a very bad landlord's agent – the worst type!

Memories of landlords were still very much alive. These farmer gentry, imaginary 'gentlemen' really, clubbed together in a particular bar, the Horseshoe Bar, in town. On the evening of the fair they usually drank a fair amount of whiskey.

At that time there was a campaign by the government to buy old TB cows to try and get rid of TB – something that has not been fully achieved sixty years later! These TB cows were only making £1 to £5 at most, whereas good cows were making £15 to £25. The war created a demand for beef for 'our boys at the front'. Bullocks were fetching £10.

Jack bought the old TB cow from a 'gentleman farmer', Mr Sandes, for 25 shillings (£1.12p or €2). He did not pay this man at a particular time. He waited until the evening when they, the self-styled gentry, were having whiskey inside the Horseshoe Bar. Jack went in, touched his hat said, 'sir, I want to pay you for the cow'.

This particular gentleman farmer, Mr Sandes, did not want his pals to know that he had old TB cows making only 25 shillings. He said, 'Mr Keane we will go outside now about that'.

He went out, collected his 25 shillings. He then went back into the bar. About five minutes later Jack came back in, touched him in the arm again and said, 'oh, Mr Sandes, you did not give me any luck penny out of that fine cow'. All his pals said, 'how much did you get for the cow?' Sandes hesitated, and Jack said, 'oh, 25'. His pals said to Sandes, 'oh God, that was a remarkable price, £25'.

You see, Sandes could not deny it. His cronies said to Mr Sandes, 'you had better give Mr Keane a good luck penny'. Mr Sandes had to put his hand in his pocket and give Jack a 10-shilling note, which was almost half the price. So Mr Sandes ended up with only 15 shillings (90c) for his cow! Jack was always particularly proud of that manoeuvre. The Sandes family had a hard name in North Kerry.

A local village in North Kerry was called Newtownsandes after that Sandes' family. It has now been changed to Moyvane.

One of the family was the author of a rather good criminal law book, now out of print. It was I believe the first Irish Free State book on criminal practice and procedure. Many years ago, someone asked me to find out more about that author as some relative was going to rewrite it. Pity he did not then. However, we now have replacements that fit the bill to some extent. Criminal law changes so rapidly that a book is out of print as soon as it is printed.

There is now so much criminal law we probably need an encyclopaedia. It has become a huge problem for lawyers to know what the law is. We have a tsunami of laws, rules, regulations, statutory instruments, bylaws, directives, decisions and case law from the wretched EEC/EU/EC Parliament, ministers, county councils, 'authorities' and the like on top of our own lot.

Someone told me that each working day the EU produced four times more law than one could read in that day. You would be three days behind in attempting to read it the following day.

When you have the necessary presumption, I suppose, that everyone knows the law, it is no wonder the law is regularly portrayed as an ass. We are swamped with these rules called 'laws'. What do you think about it? Or do you? My audience last night got bored when I mentioned law. Farmers I know are being driven mad by these rules. Unknown law is bad law in my book.

Update: The situation has got worse in the law, despite technological advances. Now we have Brexit adding to the confusion.

If you ever get a chance to get a hold of Fr Tony Gaughan's book (a parish priest near Monkstown, Dublin) about Listowel, you will find all about that Mr Sandes. You will also discover what an interesting place Listowel is. I always say all human life is here.

Another member of the Sandes family had a very bad reputation as a landlord's agent – mean and vicious; an evictor and womaniser.

He achieved local fame for his criminal exploits. He was a middle landlord who had a big house in the Square. He was well off and always had two servant girls in the house. They were young and innocent until they suffered the advances of Mr S.

I heard a story once about one of Sandes' tenants who had fallen badly into arrears and, as he had many children, he was forced to give his daughter into service to Sandes (free of charge!) to pay off the rent. When the poor child became pregnant Mr S married her off to the gardener's son! Do things change?

The House of Lords

When I started practising law in 1960 the law on animals was governed by an English case called *Searle v Wallbank* (1947), which had been decided in the House of Lords during the war. It dealt with the problem of straying animals and this new-fangled motorcar, both of which seemed to be in regular collision during the blackout.

This was a time of many commonages in Ireland and England. The collision in question happened in a commonage in England during the War at night. The motorist could not have his headlights on due to blackout regulations, as the lights might attract a bomb from a German plane.

The House of Lords decided that there was no duty on farmers to fence in their animals. If animals strayed on the road, it was the duty of the motorist to keep out of their way. Adding that this was founded on: 'Our ancient social conditions suitable to the robust conditions of the English countryside.'

The House of Lords traced the history of the law of animals back to 1649 in that case. That seemed sensible law then, animals being there long before these wretched automobiles.

I am tired of writing. I am going for a bit of a jog or walk along the caye while it is nice and bright even if still very blustery.

Maybe you, dear reader, are tired too and should put this aside until the morrow.

The Sergeant's Car

I am back – nice walk. Dropped into *The Seagull* cabin which is the head-quarters really. Had a cup of juice and a large coco nut, island grown, which was knocked in the storm. I told them some stories I was writing. I was told to continue and tell them tonight, the funny ones only!

Reasonably early in my career, I had an opportunity of using *Searle v Wallbank* in a very interesting case. It was before that late, great jurist, Judge Barra O'Briain.

I had appeared at Causeway District Court for a farmer who was charged by the guards under some bylaw or other – I think the Road Traffic General By-laws 1964 – for allowing his animals to wander on the road.

What had happened was that a horse had got on the road some way or other. The animal then jumped up on top of the local garda sergeant's car. The horse put his hoof through the roof. The horse picked the wrong roof!

I quoted *Searle v Wallbank* and other cases with youthful legal enthusi-asm. I remember the district justice saying, 'Mr Pierse, what has the House of Lords got to do with Causeway District Court'? I said 'everything' in principle. He said 'nothing' in fact. He was the kind of judge who felt he was 'The Law'.

The district justice, knowing the sergeant well, held against the farmer and fined him £2 despite my reference to House of Lords, as well as rights in common law jurisdictions such as Canada. He never thought I would have the gall to appeal a fine of £2.00. I had.

What was bothering me was the fine would probably result in the farmer paying compensation for the roof. The farmer had no insurance. I therefore advised the farmer to appeal. We did.

I remember our day of appeal in Listowel Circuit Court well. District court appeals were dealt with first, as they are usually extremely short. On that day there was a big case coming on, it concerned a fire in a local ballroom. It was a malicious injury claim and everybody seemed to be disputing it. I remember there were several senior counsels involved. Included the late Dermot Kinlen SC and Paddy McKenzie SC, as well as Tony Kennedy SC. All three went on to become judges. I just realised that now!

They were appearing that day for the County Council, the ballroom owner and an insurance company respectively. There were of course joined by three junior counsel, with three solicitors in the wings.

Anyway, my district court appeal came on. I remember Judge Barra O'Briain looking down at me, over his glasses, as I spoke. He said, 'Mr Pierse, a £2 fine on a point of principle'? 'Yes, very much so,' I replied.

We took off. I produced a whole lot of authorities, including *Searle v Wallbank* and a Canadian case I had come across, to the effect that it must be proved that the farmer deliberately or carelessly left the gate open to make him liable. I had a new book on animal law by a famous English jurist, Granville Williams. The judge and I passed up and down the authorities to each other, and as a result we spent the whole morning on the case.

The state seemed to have been unusually anxious to get the conviction affirmed. State solicitors and Gardaí sergeants work together you know, and they have to be watched. Just before lunch the judge decided in my favour, dismissed the state's case and allowed my client's appeal.

I will never forget Paddy McKenzie, SC coming over to me, in the presence of my client, and saying: 'It may have been about £2, but there was more law here in Listowel Circuit Court this morning than you would often hear in a couple of days in the Supreme Court.'

My client felt he had got good value for the £20 he had paid me for the appeal. It always annoys me that it's virtually impossible to get costs against the state. So much for equality before the law! The civil case never went ahead.

Fair dues, the sergeant never held it against me and he became a client of mine later. There is often a difficult relationship between lawyers and the Gardaí you know. He was a fine man the sergeant and got the Scott Medal for bravery. Generally, garda sergeants deserve their stripes in my experience.

How did he earn the Scott Medal? He and my lobster-fishing pal Patty O'Connor of Meenogahane carried out a daring rescue many years ago. A small yacht had gone aground on Birds' Island, about three miles from Meenogahane pier. These two brave men rowed Pat's currach in bad weather and rescued the crew off Birds' Island.

They deserved the Scott Medal.

A currach, or a naomhóg, as they are often called in Kerry, is a flimsy boat made of timber strips or laths covered in canvas, which is covered in layers of tar to make it waterproof. It is a smaller version of the boat that great Kerryman, St Brendan, used to find America.

A Thirsty Bullock

One of the cases I used in that case about the sergeant's car was an interesting one about a bullock that ran out of Kingsbridge (now Heuston) Railway Station in 1923 while being unloaded.

The bullock ran down towards the Guinness's brewery. It was probably thirsty and heard, as we students had heard, that all visitors got a free pint. Unfortunately, on this excursion to relieve thirst, the bullock did not succeed in getting to the brewery. It headed off down Winetavern Street and into Lord Edward Street.

There it knocked down and injured the plaintiff, one Ita Howard. The case came before Johnston J and a Dublin jury. This case dates from the early days of Saorstat Éireann, when the Irish legal system was seeking to distance itself from English law. In the court report reference was made to Mosaic Law (see Exodus XX1 28, 29); ancient Greek law in Athens; Roman law with its distinction between animals *ferae naturae* (wild animals) and animals *mansuetae naturae* (domestic animals); the French code Napoleon; Scottish law; and the Brehon law.

The Brehon law tract referred to was entitled *Judgement of Co-Tenancy* in *Ancient Laws of Ireland*, Vol. IV Pg103. The penalties incurred by the owners of 'gorers and fierce cattle' are detailed with great particularity. The author of the Brehon law tract then adds:

> These are their Judgements here, unless the calf has never been known before as a gorer; but if he had been known as such ... let the man whose property he has taken, take the flesh of the calf, and his neighbour shall give him another calf.

The *Book of Aicill* differentiates between the compensation payable in the case of a bull's first trespass and any subsequent ones. It also draws a distinction between injuries done by a small animal of 'first offence' or 'an animal of first trespass', and 'a habitually wicked animal'.

You know I often wonder about that sort of Brehon law. It reflects the Roman law view of 'first bite/no compensation'. I think St Patrick, who was the son of a Roman officer, brought more than Christianity to Ireland. I wonder, I wonder!

The result, in a twenty eight page law report, was Ita Howard got an award of £250 from the jury. An appeal to the Supreme Court resulted in three judges holding for Ms Howard, so she kept her award of £250.

It firmly established a principle in the new state that if you bring animals on the road or allow them to escape on to a public road, you must pay up.

However, it was limited to cases where the animals are brought onto the road or allowed to escape through the negligence of the owner. I hope you are intrigued by all that, including the bullock who wanted a pint.

However, the law continued to leave the position of straying animals, as opposed to those brought on deliberately, unchanged. These are the subtle distinctions that abound in 'the lawless science of the law'.

I suppose I should give you the whole of the quote from which I took those six words. The 'lawless science of the law' as I remember it off the top of my head:

> Mastering the lawless science of our law,
> That codeless myriad of precedent,
> That wilderness of single instances.
> Through which a few, by wit or fortune led,
> May beat a pathway out to wealth and fame.

I actually used that quote from Tennyson's *Alymer's Field* in a recent contribution I made to the 200th anniversary book (*Then and Now*) on the foundation of the world wide law publishers, Sweet and Maxwell. I was the 'Irish contributor' to this commemorative collection of essays.

However, I refused to attend its massive launch in the Lord Mayor's Hall in London. I was invited, but alone. Is that how the English treat marriage? I said I do not attend such functions without my wife. No budge by Sweet and Maxwell on that – no Robert to London therefore.

I still remember the amazement of the executive when I told her of my decision. Thank God we still have a family protection clause in the Irish constitution.

Did you know the present Irish Constitution came into operation two days before myself, on the 29/12/1937? Now those were two important events happening in the last days of 1937 I suppose. It is only me who supposes, as the rest of you did not know!

The Hairdresser

Talking about Causeway court, that was an unusual courtroom. It was in a small little room about twenty feet square. Overhead there was a hairdresser in a similar small little room. The open stairs to her emporium went up through the court room. She conducted her business throughout the court, her clients coming up and down as the lawyers, myself included, presented their cases.

I noticed the hair colour improved as they came back down.

She, the hairdresser, also had a wash hand basin. She let the water out of it often. It used to rattle down through a tin pipe on the side of the courtroom wall, just behind the district judge.

When it was rattling down everybody had to stop talking, as you could not hear what was going on. And everybody included the district judge, Gardaí, solicitors, litigants and the curious public. Generally the door had to be left open, except in the winter. There was no such thing as central heating.

When a litigant was outside and his case was called the word was passed out to him to come in. The district court clerk would shout out the door 'small guard's cases first' at the beginning of the court. These cases concerned offences like no lights on bikes, noxious weeds offenses and so on. Later came the serious crime, like being in the pub after hours.

The Wayward Ass
Talking about Causeway court, I remember another extremely interesting case I had about animals there. I told this last night in *The Seagull* cabin at our fishy evening meal.

In reality I was appearing for a misbehaving donkey. An old friend of mine, Tommy Diggins (known always as Tommy Fox) was summonsed for allowing his donkey to wander onto the road in very unusual circumstances.

Tommy had a very intelligent, and normally well-behaved, donkey (Hilda), who was a half a sister of a famous, local TV donkey. Tommy Fox also had an even more intelligent, and also normally well-behaved, male sheepdog called Shep.

They, the dog Shep and Hilda the donkey, had been going to the creamery for so many years that Tommy Fox was able to let them go off on their own. There was one dangerous crossroad, the Lodge Cross, between his home and the creamery a mile away.

Shep would guide the donkey through that crossroad with canine cuteness. Shep would run up to the crossroad ahead of Hilda and cart, and look right and left. Shep would give one warning bark if Hilda was not to go forward, and give two or more barks if it was OK for her to go through the cross. One bark was to stop. Two or more barks was the all clear signal, no traffic and no danger.

One day, when they were returning from the creamery, they came to the crossroad. Shep the dog went forward, but instead of looking for cars he got totally distracted by a bitch. Apparently, the bitch was 'in heat' (fertile condition) which is of course a very distracting thing for a poor male dog. Shep got wildly excited and barked too much. As a result, the donkey proceeded through the cross believing there was nothing coming. Alas, there was! A van came on and there was a crash.

Tommy Fox got a summons for allowing his ass, Hilda, to wander or permitting it to wander on the public highway, or something like that. I would say the guards had a puzzle in preparing that summons. I should have kept the summons. I headed eventually to Causeway court to defend Tommy, the dog and the ass from the wrath of the law.

There was learned argument in the district court before that most amusing, learned and wisest of district judges, the late Dick Johnson (father of the retired High Court president, Richard Johnson SC).

I argued the point on *mens rea*. *Mens rea* is a mental element that must be present in crime. I remember questioning the guard on whether he alleged *mens rea* against the donkey or against the dog or against the absent owner.

I also pointed out that a sister (or half-sister) of this donkey was a TV star, until its demise two years before. The erring ass had big potential. Hilda was going to be a star. Her career might be affected. A conviction might spoil her chances of fame and fortune if she had a criminal record.

In any event the district judge dismissed the case, blaming the bitch and not the distracted male dog, the donkey or the absent owner.

That caught the headlines. I remember a client of mine in Boston sending me an extract about it from the *Boston Globe*. The case had been picked up by that US paper. A somewhat different version of the case appears as follows:

IRISH EYES ARE SMILING:
Donkey Makes an Ass of Itself
Because his papers were not in order, King Puck 'got the goat' of an immigration official in New York and was refused entry into the United States. His Royal Highness had to hightail it back

to Ireland on the Irish Airline jet, where his travel documents were rectified. Then he victoriously returned and now, thanks be to God, he is safely here this time. If not a wild goose but a wild goat, King Puck himself, The King of Killorglin. He is going to act as a special mascot for the Annapolis class of 1927 at their 40th renewal at this year's army-navy game. Let's hope our American eagle will not resent King Puck's presence. Otherwise Irish American relations might be affected adversely ...

A donkey training to be a television performer made an ass of itself recently in a row with a dog. Sounds confusing but it is true. The donkey belonged to Thomas Diggins of Drumnacurra, Causeway, Co. Kerry. The dog also belongs to Mr Diggins. The donkey's stepsister who recently passed away appeared on television several times and performed some clever tricks to the command of the family dog.

It was hoped that the young step-sister would also become a performer. One morning at the creamery, Mr. Diggins went inside and left the donkey and the dog practising their parts on the roadway. Artistic temperament came to a boiling point however and the donkey kicked the dog aside and took off with the cart attached. She was found later by a policeman who arrested 'her'. When the hurried and worried Mr. Diggins showed up he was promptly charged with allowing the donkey to wander on the public road. In due time he had to appear in court to answer the charges (this time he left the donkey and the dog at home). A considerate judge listened to the attorney for the defence. He asked for 'leniency for the vagaries of an aspiring TV star, even if it is a donkey'. The judge was lenient and applied the Probation Act, adding that he hoped that the happy donkey dog relationship had been resumed and that rehearsals would continue as this type of act would be superior to some of the asinine things seen on TV today. A dog gone nice judge!

Those of you who are unfamiliar with the strange goings on about a goat in Killorglin, should visit the drinking session known as Puck Fair.

You risk life and limb and motorcar at times in so doing. It is a throwback to pagan days, where the veneer of modern civilisation recedes *in vino veritas*.

Well, at least it is good to know that the goat has almost as much trouble getting in to the United States as an Irish man or woman has nowadays.

I must go out for a bit of relief – the natural type – and a walk or trot.

Insure Your Cows

I hope the stories about animals are of interest, as we need animals. *Homo Sapiens* is too dominant and is destroying much of nature and wildlife. There have of course been considerable changes in the law of animals as the power of the motorist took over. One of the difficulties in these cases is that farmers, certainly in my earlier practice days, never had insurance.

I remember one man coming in to me, whose cows had run out onto the road. He didn't have time to close the gate. An unsuspecting Tipperary motorist on the north road to Ballyduff had crashed into his cows and damaged her car.

My poor Kerry client got a long and threatening solicitor's letter about all the damages. I knew him quite well. He had no insurance. I also knew his small farm was not in his own name, as his father had died without a will.

I told him he might win a law case but it would cost a lot one way or the other. I got him to write a nice letter back in his own handwriting, which I drafted, to the Tipperary solicitor, saying that he did not own the farm, it belonged to his five brothers and sisters and himself. That it was a small farm, he had nothing out of it, and he could not pay anybody. He was sorry for what happened to that nice Tipperary woman.

That is the last he heard of it. He was a bit indignant when I charged him £2 for the advice, saying he wrote the letter himself!

The Mad Goat

A few other clients of mine had bad experiences with animals and could not get anything. A neighbour of mine, a very precise Englishman, was on his way to catch the Shannon ferry when he was attacked by a mad Clare goat, who jumped right up in front of his soft-topped roof. The goat fell down through it and got stuck.

The client's statement on that case was a very funny description. It described the motorist looking out at the goat, whose head was on the windscreen, and the goat looking through the windscreen at the motorist. No insurance, so therefore no law case and compensation; tough luck!

Sorry, I am off for a few rounds of the island with Scruffy, who is a good listener, and to have a chat with the other two-legged inhabitants. I am telling them these stories first before I return to my wind-battered hut. We have a few hours of eating, talking and card playing for match sticks after dusk! Night comes suddenly here. My yellow pad of paper is running out.

Harry the hare never listens to anyone.

The Stallion

It's still bad out there; heavy clouds and the wind must be about gale force eight. Spray everywhere. Lads fishing. Ladies reading and chatting in *The Seagull* hut.

Let's resume on animals – the Creator's gift to us. Another not so funny incident was of a young lady who was travelling along one day when a mare in heat, looking for a stallion, jumped out over a fence right down on her. He injured her quite nastily, damaging her eye and face.

I had to advise her she would not succeed because of the way the law was at that time. It was governed by the old case of *Searle v Wallbank* I mentioned earlier. This type of law has been largely changed by the Animals Act of 1985. That Act basically overturned the case of *Searle v Wallbank*. It made farmers normally liable for negligence if their animals were left in an unsafe situation, such as gates left open and poor fences.

Most of you are motorists now, so maybe you are interested in the wording of the actual section. Isn't this a handy way to learn a bit of law? Section 2 of the 1985 Act reads:

2 (1) So much of the Rules of the common law relating to liability

for negligence as excludes or restricts the duty which a person might owe to others to take such care as is reasonable to see that damage is not caused by an animal straying on to a public road is hereby abolished.

I believe the subsection (2), which deals with unfenced land, or land by custom unfenced, was put in for places like the Curragh in its pre-motorway days.

Shortly after that Act was passed, I know that a judge of the High Court, Judge Johnson, gave a decision to the effect that he would presume that a farmer left the gate open or had poor fences if the animals were wandering around the road. It was up to the farmer to prove otherwise.

I was explaining this one night at a farmers' meeting in Ballybunion. I remember at the end of the meeting an old farmer saying: 'Ha, that judge fellow, his mother Annie was a Shortis from Ballybunion and tis many a gate that fellow, when courting around here, left open! He should not be picking on us the poor farmers.'

You can't beat the 'min with the caps'.

Annie Shortis' brother was killed in the GPO in the 1916 rising. She was Judge Johnson's mother. She remained a republican all her life, and was married to the first district justice appointed by the Free State.

Most farmers now are wise enough to insure.

Why not listen to music now. What a great gift music is? I would love to have an hour of classical music here – as the storm is not music. Although the rhythm of the sea outside the cabin is music of its own type.

I am off to the toilet for two purposes, one being to collect writing paper as my yellow pad has run out. You work out the other one.

Your Home is your Castle

As I said above, in the old days there was a law that every dog was entitled to his bite. It was known as the doctrine of *scienter* (Latin word for knowledge) and it meant that the owner had to know the dog was vicious. That law is gone now and that creates a problem.

Lots of my clients, the older ones in particular, are very anxious to have a dog for home protection, especially those in the country. Man's best friend can often be his worst enemy by biting someone when protecting his owner.

However, I do remember when I was building my new house being at one of these shows for modern homes exhibitions. The Gardaí had a stand at it about protecting yourself and your home.

I started talking to a young garda. He asked me where I was living. I said in the country outside the town. He said buy a couple of dogs, that is the best protection you can have.

This is an example of the difficulty in balancing rights in law. The householder wants to be protected. Postmen (who dogs seem to dislike) and other visitors who are attacked want to be compensated. I must confess myself I take the view that the householder should be allowed to guard his house more or less as his castle. I think if you put up a sign 'beware of dogs' or something like that, you may be exempt from civil liability.

I am told the reason dogs attack postmen is because the dog never sees its owner leaving the postman into the house.

There is an Occupiers Liability Act, but it is too complicated. You can buy plastic notices to stick up on the entrance of your property. However, in these cases the result sometimes depends on whether you have a city-bred judge or a judge reared in the country. Knowing the judge is often more useful to a solicitor than knowing the law.

I am sure I am blatantly biased in thinking that country judges are more sensible. A solicitor should not pass a comment like that – so don't tell a judge.

Scruffy is scratching the door. We must go for our walk of the far end. The island has been badly damaged in the middle. So, we may be reduced to 500 meters by 600. I am building a relationship with the dog. I'm back.

Talking about a man's home being his castle, I saw a sticker on a fridge recently, it said: 'A man's home is his castle ... until his queen arrives.'

I inherited that view about a person's home being his castle from my mother. She was Michael Collins' oldest niece. She experienced the British forces and the 'Black and Tans' burning down her home at Sam's Cross, near Clonakilty.

Towards the end of her days she charged me with keeping her in her own home. It hurt me deeply that we had to put her in a home eventually on medical advice as she had broken her hips. She was well looked after there by wonderful nuns and nurses.

The problem of old age is a serious problem in this country, especially now with the breakdown of the family caring structure. Care of the old is becoming a time bomb.

The Min with the Caps Again!

As to old age, the 'min with the caps' would say, 'everyone wishes to have a long life, but no one wants to be old'. I am beginning to find that myself a bit now as I am a grandfather several times over. Actually, I came across a rather cynical view of life in the magazine I bought while hanging around that dreadful airport in Miami on the way out. I must go up to *Laughing Bird* to find that page.

Right! I am back. This is it.

On the first day, God created a dog and said:

'Sit all day by the door of your house and bark at anyone who comes in or walks past. For this, I will give you a life span of twenty years.'

The dog said: 'That's a long time to be barking. How about only ten years and I will give you back the other ten?'

So, God agreed.

On the second day, God created the monkey and said: 'Entertain people, do tricks, and make them laugh. For this, I'll give you a twenty-year life span.'

The monkey said: 'Monkey tricks for twenty years? That's a pretty long time to perform. How about I give you back ten like the dog did?'

And God agreed.

On the third day, God created the cow and said: 'You must go into the field with the farmer all day long and suffer under the sun, have calves and give milk to support the farmer's family. For this, I will give you a life span of sixty years.'

The cow said: 'That's kind of a tough life you want me to live for sixty years. How about twenty and I'll give you back the other forty?'

And God agreed again.

On the fourth day, God created man and said: 'Eat, sleep, play and enjoy your life. For this I'll give you twenty years.'

But man said: 'Only twenty years? Could you possibly give me the sixty extra years, that is the forty the cow gave back, the ten the monkey gave back, and the ten the dog gave back? That makes eighty, okay?'

God agreed.

'And you must give me a companion to marry', said man.

'Okay,' said God. 'You asked for it.' My God you did!

So, that is why the first twenty years we eat, sleep, play and enjoy ourselves. For the next forty years we slave in the sun to support our government and family. For the next ten years we do monkey tricks to entertain the grandchildren, and for the last ten years we sit on the front porch and bark at everyone.

For a much nicer description of the seven stages of your life, see Shakespeare's *As You Like It*. It starts off with the infant mewling and puking in the nurse's arms. Then, the whining schoolboy with his satchel, and shining morning face creeping like a snail unwillingly to school; then, the lover sighing like a furnace.

I can't remember the rest of it. Except that, at the end, Shakespeare says we descend into 'second childishness' and 'mere oblivion': 'Sans teeth, sans eyes, sans taste, sans everything.' Not nice.

Life has now been explained to you as observed by the man with his cap.

I prefer Karl Jung, the psychoanalyst's, view. He said: 'You spend the first half of your life following your ambitions, and the second half searching for meaning.'

Unfortunately, in Ireland, I see many of my elderly clients shoved into a nursing home for their last ten years. They are primed to look like zombies – medicine!

Expensive Grass

There was another animal case I remember in Ballybunion District Court. It involved a farmer whose land had been 'invaded' by fifteen goats for two weeks. These goats belonged to an itinerant.

The farmer issued a civil process for damages for trespass as the itinerant was a semi-settled itinerant, one who lived in a house in Listowel in the winter but was off to the fresh air in the summer.

Having heard the case the justice ordered damages of two shillings a day per goat. The itinerant was a regular customer of his, this justice, and was 'defending' himself. 'How much is all that? He said to the judge. The justice and court clerk got the pens going and said, '£21.00 and £6 costs'. The Itinerant said: 'My God Judge, it is a good job they weren't there for a few more days or you would have made the man a millionaire.'

Witchcraft

The day of the itinerant's goat case in Ballybunion produced another unusual case. Ballybunion court was, in the 1960s, a red corrugated iron shed at the side of the garda barracks. It was formerly a crossroads dancehall.

In the summer it was like an oven, in the winter everybody wore overcoats, long underwear and gloves.

If by any chance, and there often was, hailstone, proceedings were suspended because of the symphony on the roof. Feet were stamped and fingers blown to get the circulation going.

One of the cases that cold day was a claim under a long-forgotten Act dealing with witchcraft. It seemed that Joe Ambrose, the very learned district court clerk, had dug it up. I regret I didn't get a copy of the summons at the time. Ballybunion court and its records are long gone.

In goes the plaintiff, Mr X, to the witness box, with the help of his white stick. His testimony was lengthy. He was complaining that a neighbour, Mr Y, had prevented him getting the blind pension. This was done by the neighbour putting a pin in a voodoo doll of the witness Mr X on the day he was being examined by Dr O'Donnell, the eye specialist.

Mr X described in detail how he would arrive at Dr O'Donnell's door with his white stick, totally blind, but when the doctor's door opened Mr X could see perfectly. This had happened several times. He was cross examined by an old colleague of mine, a man without any sense of humour, Mr Z. Mr Z questioned him on whether he had seen this doll. A neighbour had apparently noticed it on the window of Mr Y.

Mr X was told by another neighbour that Mr Y put spells on people and practised the black arts. Then, came the vital question: on what dates did this occur? 'Hold on,' said Mr X, as he poked around in his coat pocket to produce a small diary. Mr X read through the diary, and read aloud several dates. By this stage the court was laughing. The solicitor did not see the contradiction, so tried to continue his cross-examination. After a few questions, the justice had recovered from his laughter. He said to Mr Z, the solicitor, 'you have won your case, I am dismissing the case'. More laughter broke out when Mr Z said, 'I'm sorry about that as I have many more questions'.

The Mobile Phone

Talking about the 'min with the caps', what about the money and the phones?

I saw my daughter in law recently putting her mobile phone into our fridge. This intrigued me – well women and their manoeuvres do. I asked why into the fridge? 'So that I would not forget the smoked salmon that Olive is giving us,' she said.

The male mind was still puzzled – not unusual in yours truly, but then I never had a sister. So, I asked how does a phone in a fridge remind you to take the salmon away? The mystery was solved by the following answer:

'Well I never leave the house without my phone or the car keys. I can't find my car keys, so I put my phone into the fridge, so that when I am going I take the stew and smoked salmon.'

When leaving a few hours later she used my landline to ring her phone to find it in the fridge, where she also found the salmon and the stew. She sent my son to find her keys! All ended well!

I am very suspicious of these new phones. Last year, I was inside a massive stone building, the Four Courts. I had to ring a witness in the USA. I got through clearly. When I finished the call, I looked at the instrument and said to myself: 'If you can send out rays that travel 3,000 miles, what are you doing to my poor brain?'

Well enough! I hope you are enjoying this, even if I tend to ramble? Enjoy it in small bites, that's how you eat an elephant. I think, in all modesty, the audience last night enjoyed these stories even though Kevin doesn't have a Kerry sense of humour. Alas!

My First Kerry Court

Before I finish about Causeway court, I should write a little memorial to my first court client in Kerry. I had set up on my own in 1962 (5th of February) in what had been my mother's sitting room.

The late Francie Browne and I knocked a window in the front wall into a door. We divided the sitting room into an outer office for a secretary and a room for myself. I could not afford a waiting room for potential clients. So, I had two chairs in the secretary's area. That wasn't such a problem as I could not pay a secretary.

No clients arrived in the first six weeks, which was a bit unnerving. My mother prayed and I read law books. The adventure of setting up had become a bit of a nightmare.

One in the legal profession then could not advertise and I had no legal connections. I just had a foolish desire to be my own man in my own town.

As it happened, a good, kindly and learned colleague, the late Gerald Bailey of Tralee, rang me on my little used phone, Listowel 169. My father's had been Listowel 27. There were only 142 new telephones in Listowel and its surrounding area in thirty years. Gerald told me I should get introduced to court in Causeway the following week. That way I would get my name in the paper, that local Gospel, *The Kerryman*. He would do the introducing.

You see Causeway was considered my native territory. My grandfather had been a farmer in the townland of Meenogahane. It is pronounced '*Mín – ná – Guthán*', which means 'Plain of the Echoes'. The Irish version of a townland is so descriptive!

Back to getting my name in *The Kerryman* through Causeway court. Out I went, getting a lift from the garda superintendent as I had no car of my own. I did not get a car until I married Olive, and her eight year-old somewhat rusty Volkswagen. The VW Beetle rusted a lot during its stay on Valentia Island – salt does that to cars.

I arrived in Causeway early as the super had to check cases with the Gardaí. I stood between the two Harty pubs, one at each side of the street, waiting. A man appeared, looked at me and said: 'Are you by any chance a solicitor?' I readily acknowledged my qualification. This man, the late Will Young, says to me:

'Look, I am having a bad time with my rates. They go up faster than I can pay them. The Council are after me again today. They are looking for £27 this year and I haven't got it. You have to get me six months to pay, as they'd send out the sheriff to me last year. All I can pay now is £15.'

'Fine. Let's look at the summons,' I said.

I, all my life, like to look at the summons. That is training from that very careful District Justice Crotty in my year and a half down in Dunmanway. He would look at you and say: 'What is the law Mr Pierse?' I learnt to look up the law.

I did not like the look of the summons for £27 rates entitled: 'The County Council of Kerry -v- William Young.' I had no books or rules with me but Justice Crotty's training surfaced. I marched into court with the precious summons near my fast beating heart and knew I was going to chance my arm.

Fair dues to Gerald Bailey, solicitor, he introduced me with style and surprised me by trotting out my exam results in my LLB degree. I had obtained first prize and first-class honours. I shared this accolade with the now very well-known Dublin Solicitor, Maurice Curran. The UCD authorities found in the overall result that there was one mark between us.

They gave each of us a first prize and first-class honours.

I gave the cheque, I think it was £75, to my father who got many months of pleasure out if it showing it to people, in the way parents do about their offspring! I understand his actions much better now. I admit to myself that I take immense pride and pleasure from the doings of our offspring, more than I would publicly admit.

Robert, stop wandering and get back to that rates summons!

To stop wandering, I go back to Causeway court, interrupted by the hairdresser's ablations and rattling pipes.

Rate summonses were an early item in the court books. Michael Foley was the rate collector. He was sworn in and thumbed through the sheaf of copy summonses, giving evidence of default. His decree had ten shillings and six pence (52 ½ p or 75c) costs for each case.

Andrew McCarthy, the court clerk, called out: 'The Council -v- William Young.' Up I got and said, 'I appear for Mr Young, Justice'. Surprise! Persons who got rates summonses couldn't afford a solicitor, even of the most juvenile type! Worse still, this juvenile said, 'I wish to object to the summons'. Shock! Unheard of! 'What may I ask, Mr Pierse, is your objection?' District Justice Johnson asked, pushing up his spectacles on his forehead and fixing his beady eye on me.

I launched into the wording of the summons and how it, in a single document, claimed rates on three different hereditament (or rateable premises). I stated that there should be three summonses, one for each valid hereditament. I argued that each rate amount was a separate debt on a different property. Each might be open to challenge and so should be separated. Michael Foley said he never heard that before. The district judge pulled down his glasses, looked at the summons and said:

> 'I have not heard of it either, but there could be something in it, as they are separate hereditaments on your evidence. I think I will adjourn it Mr Foley for you to get the County Council's law agent to look into it.'

What was most helpful was of course the additional remark he then made: 'You know, Mr Foley, if Mr Pierse is right we will be in big trouble.

I have given you hundreds of decrees like this over the past two months. If he is right, they will be wrong. I think you should settle with Mr Pierse after the court.'

The court lasted another hour, occupied by crimes such as not cutting weeds under the Noxious Weeds Acts, being found without a light on your bike or everyone's favourite, being caught after hours in the local hospitality venue!

Fines for these heinous acts ranged from 2/6 (12½ /18c) to Justice Johnson's mysterious 'half a guinea'. Well what is 'half a guinea'? It was 10 shillings and six pence old money. Probably 65 or 70c in this miserable euro stuff!

A good local assault case, of course, always increased local attendance.

So out I got after court. I thank Gerald Baily as he heads off. I ask the superintendent from Listowel to wait a few minutes to give me a chance to make a deal. I stand across the road in front of Sonny Harty's pub. Will Young, who is next to me, says: 'What will we do now?' 'We will wait and see,' I reply.

Mike Foley, the rate collector, was over across the road in front of Michael Harty's pub, putting his rate books and summonses into his car. He put them in on the road side with his back to me, pointedly ignoring me. This was a good sign, as it meant he was thinking out how to deal with me. Sure enough, the mating dance of bargaining was about to begin.

I told my client to go to the other side of the street. Mr Foley turns around, comes across and shakes my hand. He said it was nice to meet a new solicitor, and he had known my father, a decent man, and not a man who would not pay his rates.

'You aren't serious about the summons are you?' he said.

'I was and I am,' I replied.

I said it was nice to meet him, and while I would be very sorry if his summonses and decrees were declared invalid, I was very, very serious.

I said that my poor client couldn't pay this huge demand, creating an opening for a bargaining. Eventually he said: 'Well what would you pay, so that we would all go home friends?' 'Well, I will have to consult with my client about paying anything, but I would like to know what you would take?' I replied. He muttered, eventually, that he would accept half (£13-10-00) if Mr Young paid on that day.

I crossed over to my client, told him of the offer and asked, 'well'? 'Well done, I have £15 here,' Will said. 'Hold on now for the moment,' I replied.

I went back to Mike Foley, leaving Will Young a bit away. I said to Mike Foley: 'We have a problem. Will is prepared to give you a fiver to cover the rates, and pay my fee. I think what we should do is you get a fiver and I get a fiver.'

Mike Foley gulped and said the council would not take it. I warned him that this will end up in the High Court on a point of law, and I will knock great costs out of the council when I win!

Well, to cut this long story short I had to give Mike Foley £10 and I only had £5 for myself!

Will Young, fair dues, gave me as much business as he could for the rest of his life and spread the word, which was more important. Do you know that a US survey showed that when a lawyer sends away a satisfied client, that client is likely to send in three new clients? If however the client is dissatisfied he will tell ten prospective clients not to go near you.

So, I left Causeway that day with £5, one twelfth of my first year's private practice earnings. Thank God I am earning a bit more now! On the way home Superintendent Burns asked me how I got on. He of course told me some of his anti-lawyer jokes.

I made great friends in William Young and his wife Bridie, both gone to God now, as Bridie was a fierce woman for the religion. We were both stuck in the pro-life campaign in 1983.

Garda Jokes

Bill Burns, the super, was in fact a great friend of my then fiancée's family, having been a sergeant in Killarney and next door neighbour of hers. The jokes went something like this as far as I remember:

A labourer who had been awarded a £100 by Judge Barra O'Briain in a workman's compensation case comes into his solicitor, to collect his money. (Mr Moran, the solicitor, lived next door to my father's house in Pound Lane.)

The labourer gets a long speech about the difficulties of the case, the barrister's fees, the court costs and the miserable job being a solicitor was.

His solicitor (Mr Moran) makes out a cheque, the client looks at it and says: 'Mr Moran, is it you, the barrister or me who was knocked off the ladder and broke his leg?' The Cheque was for £50.00!

Solicitor (showing an opposing witness a photo) asks a question:
        'Is that you?'
Witness – 'Yes sir.'
Solicitor – 'Were you present when that picture was taken?'

I said to the super, 'that is an American cop joke'. So, he gave me a poem about lawyers from an American book:

In the heels of the haggling lawyers,
Too many slippery 'ifs' and 'buts' and 'howevers',
Too many 'hereinbefores' provided, 'whereases',
Too many doors to go in and go out of,
When the lawyers are through
What is there left – a cent?
Can a mouse nibble at it,
And find enough to fasten a tooth in it.

Well, the super had the car and I hadn't, so I said no more. 'A shut mouth catches no flies,' according to 'the min with the caps'.

Burying a Solicitor

Well, what is a 'guinea'? If you know you are showing your age or you are a barrister. One guinea was £1-1-0 (€1.40 approx.) and that is how barristers charged up to relatively recently. They now do it in large amounts of little euros!

If you ever see a barrister gown you will see a little pocket at the back. Traditionally (a tradition long gone) his fee in golden guineas was slipped into that pocket. Nowadays that pocket is sown up. A small piece of paper known as a cheque or bill of exchange, and one with a good figure on it, will never be seen soiling the barrister's hands. Guineas were then of course, not now!

Well talking about guineas, here is an old story about an Irish judge in the 18th Century. A poor Dublin solicitor died, and a collection was made to bury him. The then Lord Chief Justice of Orbury was asked to donate. He gave a shilling.

The collector thanked him, and said that was enough to bury the poor man in a pauper's grave. 'Oh is it,' said the judge, 'if so here is a pound (20 shillings), go and bury twenty more of them!' Nasty judge! Such creatures do exist.

Well, I keep wandering off mentally, if not physically. It is difficult, here in the *Laughing Bird,* not to let one's thoughts float in this torrid, tormented air tearing through the three trees near me, and taking my solid thoughts with it.

Darkness

The sun, which we did not actually see much of today, is gone on its eternal round – or isn't it the world that has spun around the sun? Was that not the great discovery of Copernicus? Movement, design and gravity are great mysteries of creation. Why doesn't water and everything else fall off in Australia?

Thanks Creator for holding it together. The Creator who put us all together was gifted beyond our comprehension. I regard this essence or energy that created substance and gave it the potential to develop and change as God. As we cannot understand such a Being (the uncaused cause) we have to be humble and accept the evidence of the Creator of substance and potential. Why is there something, anything? The First Mover! I must discuss these mysteries tonight.

The trouble with faith is it is difficult to have the humility to say I cannot understand. To admit our total failure to understand why there is a creation at all. Science is pulling back layer after layer, but we are still in theory; and is not faith the ultimate theory?

Darkness falls like a curtain across the sky here, excluding the light in minutes. No, 'now fades the glimmering landscape' on this caye off Belize.

I am called to grub (more fish) at our HQ, the *Seagull* cabin. Scruffy is on the move also with his nose twitching. He looked back as me as if to say it will be all gone if we do not hurry. Scruffy has a great understanding of the priorities of surviving.

We will tell more stories, and hopefully I will find some paper to write on tomorrow. We are scheduled to leave tomorrow but I doubt it. The howl of the wind and hiss of the waves are as loud as ever.

The light is gone anyway and you are probably glad of a break too.

I must say, I have done a power of writing today. 'Sleep, sweet nature's balm,' should come quickly, once the tummy is full.

As it turned out, Olive and I did not stay after the meal. We therefore never got around to solving the Creator!

DAY FOUR: WE REMAIN, STORM REMAINS

Fishing for the Big One

Dawn came late. We had planned last night, provided the sea had calmed down, to set off at 4.30 am this Wednesday (Day Four) morning to 'The Spot', a fisherman's paradise fourteen miles east the caye. We wanted to get to where the sun was rising, to get 'The Big One'.

Yesterday evening, Kevin predicted the storm would blow itself out and would be gone by the night, and the fish would be hungry! He was wrong. The storm remained, shaking the *Laughing Bird*. We were again under the bed; the fish remained safe from us today, even though hungry.

When we had arrived on this island on Saturday (or was it Sunday?) we received some very exciting news; Kevin had caught The Big One the night before. The Big One was is 40 lb. tuna. The biggest Donal had caught was a 23 lb. one, and man was that a 35-minute ordeal of muscle strain and vein bulging effort to land him. So, the race began for the 'Big Big One'.

We fished almost continuously on Saturday from pre-dawn to post dusk on Day One. Kevin and Donal were the fanatics. They talked endlessly about light, bait, strain weight (of the lines), and of battles with big ones.

Alas, all is abandoned this am. We abandoned our plans to go by boat to the spot where The Big One is, and abandoned our plans to leave for the mainland tonight. Is this fisherman's dream of the 'Big Big One' worldwide?

Let's get back to today! The wind did its almighty best just about an hour after dawn today, Day Four. We were still under the bed. The cabin shook something underneath the floor as one burst really got in under the cabin. We thought the whole thing might take flight. The *Laughing Bird* shook and jerked under that burst but held its ground, it remained. The storm remains. We remained, at least for now.

Then the wind seemed to blow itself out of strength a bit. We were going to be able to fish from the western shore of the island.

The fishing began this am here on the island – no Big One though. The jumping jacks are jumping again on the bigger western strand. We rush out from our porridge for breakfast. Kevin has, by some instinct, realised the fish are back and biting. He, Donal, and Caroline had caught ones earlier.

They are out in the less stormy shore. It's brighter than thirty minutes ago. We rush to the gear, the younger ones win, the reels whistle. Donal shouts 'oh boy!', but the line seems to fail as the fish run in to shore and then turn to try and break the line. It doesn't break. The struggle and the language (Olive not hearing this fortunately) ran parallel, but finally, after a wait, the fish is landed!!

He is big but not the 'Big One', let alone the 'Big, Big One'. He is gutted and stripped into nice steaks for breakfast. Back to the *Seagull* cabin we go.

I write this for you as I wait amid the smells, the clatter of the wind on the sides of the cabin, and the clatter of plates. Kevin continues preparing for a late breakfast. He is making savoury pancakes of the fish. He (Kevin) gives some fish to Jean, the almost unseen caretaker on the caye.

It was all very interesting, but it was the last night we had the big feast. The big feast during the big storm.

Oh! Heavens above, we just had another episode of fish. We had come back in from round two of the conquest of jumping jacks. They were bigger fish than Saturday's, although Saturday's fishermen were slow to agree.

Aislinn stayed behind. Aislinn rushes in for the camera as Paul has a real monster on the line. Paul has to exhaust the fish, or maybe it is the fish exhausting Paul. Aislinn expects Paul to win, so she got the camera. We all rush to the south end of our island. Paul wins. Photo taken.

Excitement swells again as the jacks are jumping on the two sides of the island. Breakfast is forgotten. This time the men are standing out in the sea, armed with lines, (we cannot put out the boats). Very dangerous but fishing mania prevails.

The angle of the wind changes suddenly. The boats are pulled up further. The waves are getting further up. Some of us have sense to stop fishing; reels whine in.

Kevin says 'oh shit', as he loses a reel, and says 'oh fuck' in Belize English as he stumbles in the wave. I said to Olive he said 'oh damn', as she does not like the other expressions. Standards are to be kept up, and she says so to Kevin later. I do not know if Kevin blushes, as he is brown-skinned and bearded – a Belizean Othello.

Hey gang, it is 12 o'clock so let's get to finish breakfast – yes, the fishing was really good. The fish is so fresh that it is delicious even to those among us who do not normally eat fish. We tuck in with gusto and without may-onnaise. The Yanks drown the taste of fish with mayo!!

The storm still howls around us, but is somewhat less stormy. It is not as bad as it was, but the winds are still 45 – 50 mph according to the radio. We discover the uncommunicative caretakers have a battery-operated tran-sistor. Actually, we never saw Jean's companions once – a man and child apparently. We are not too pleased with the forecasters but they do have a difficult job.

The main town in this part of Belize is Placencia. The marine port of Big Creek is the centre for exporting bananas. Placencia, I think, means quietness. There is no storm there – or at least Donal hopes not. He is getting worried about his banana crop.

They get four crops a year and are harvesting one at present. Last week they sent out a big shipment, and another ship is due in to Big Creek tomorrow. However, it will get delayed by the storm.

It looks as if we will not get out of here today. Olive, who is a doctor as well as mother of ten, is laying down that law because of Caroline's pregnant condition. No banging up and down in waves is the law for her. The sea is mad and beautiful, the white at the top of its deep, blue wavy hillocks sweep in and burst on our bit of sand. I must go to look at the brown fish.

I am glad to report the tide of brown sardines is bigger. The weather is protecting them, I think, as the big fish are afraid they might get thrown up on the sand in a wave, or maybe a coconut might fall on them!

A good lot of coconuts have fallen already, some on to the bobbing sea. We watch out for our heads on land. Scruffy guides me.

We wonder now when we are going to get off – this storm should have finished hours ago according to the radio. We are all thinking of Mitch, the hurricane that hit Honduras a little over a month ago and caused such devastation. It had been heading for Belize but side-tracked to Honduras. I am a strong believer in climate change. It is going to cause many, bigger storms! Yikes!

Belize was of course formerly known as British Honduras. Belize is now independent and politically finding its feet. It has improved noticeably (roads particularly) since I was here two and a half years ago.

I notice a lot of Irish connections, probably from Irish soldiers being here in the British colonial days.

Our guide's Christian name is Kevin, Kevin Madeira.

One of the interesting fish we saw yesterday was called Ballyhoo, it is a fish that skips along the top of the water in skips of about a foot in length. We also saw the flying fish. They are something else – they fly about 100 yards at great speed when pursued.

There was a whale shark around near our boat. Whale sharks are big, a real big type of shark as the name suggests. The one near our boat was surrounded by smaller fish. It seems they help each other to find food. The small fish live off the whale shark's back. There is some type of sea lice they clean off the whale shark's back. It seems like big fleas and little fleas again.

The sea is really a fascinating place, because we know so little about it. The sea here is ripe with crops of various fish. One of my great pleasures on any coral reef is to swim slowly so that I can pick out the fish in the coral – the browns, blues, yellows, silvers, pinks, greens are all a reflection of the coral.

It helps one to believe in a Benevolent Creator. We do not understand him/her/it, but a Creator must exist. You cannot understand without the Creator how something, indeed all things, can come from nothing. What we cannot understand is this uncaused cause. No scientist can convince me of that.

Although, I do have one heretical thought. Why are we told or how do we know, that God/the Creator is perfect? What is 'perfection'? I better not say that tonight.

Robert you are getting 'preachy' again? Is that wrong?

Anyway, let's protect the oceans. We need to. There is a lot of pollution and overfishing.

Believe it or not the wind is getting stronger again. We have been asked to leave the *Laughing Bird* cabin by the caretaker as other guests are scheduled to arrive. Fat chance. They would be mad to come out in my view, but then again there are a lot of crazy people around. Is it possible we are in that group?

Police?

We had odd visitors last night just as we were heading in to the *Seagull* cabin. There were six big men in a long, big lifeboat type boat with a lot of cages on board. They slept with their guns under the *Seagull* cabin and did not speak to us 'gringos'.

Kevin said they were police looking for drug smugglers. I wondered, but then I have a thing about drugs. They cause so much waste of life and talent. A modern plague. The 'police' left in the palest light of dawn.

The Blasket Case

Much of what I have written was first penned on blank spaces on *The Irish Jurist* of 1997, as well as on novels and toilet paper.

This legal publication has always been my holiday reading. The volume has 500 pages of condensed high-class law. It should keep me reading for my whole nine days holiday. It has me in a mood for considering the Irish Constitution, as I am preparing for the Blasket island case appeal that is to come on shortly in the Supreme Court. This was a case to have an Act, the whole Act, declared unconstitutional. The Act was to annex to the OPW (Office of Public Works) and the state the Great Blasket Island. We won in the High Court after fifty days of most interesting evidence, but the State appealed it.

It is rather unfortunate that the magnificently presented and strong judgements of Mr Justice Declan Budd have not been fully reported. Every page of the 189 are worth reading.

Then you might not be as fond of the Irish Constitution as I am. My fondness may be due to the fact that we share almost a common birthday. The Irish people gave birth to their constitution on the 29/12/1937. My mother gave birth to me two days later – that fact is surprisingly not mentioned in Irish Constitutional law books! Editors are choosy people.

Update: We won in the Supreme Court. We all took mighty satisfaction in beating the might of the State. I really will have to write a legal article about it.

Update: I still haven't got around it yet!

Posse Origins

So, I must now return to *The Irish Jurist*. I am reading a piece by the learned Niall Osborough on the law about cattle stealing in 16th century Ireland. It begins:

> Under the Irish detector method of following the tracks for a person who had been dispossessed of livestock or other chattels, he was entitled to follow the trail left by the thief and to resort to self-help, to recover what had been stolen.

Now, isn't that fascinating stuff? In fact, one can see where the idea of a posse following rustlers, so beloved of the old 'westerns', came from, as there was 'the duty of my neighbours to assist me, to ride with me'.

However, my favourite sentence in the twenty-page article is the one dealing with the custom of riding off following the cattle tracks. Taken from a manuscript called *The Laws of Ireland*, where it deals with the difficulty of tracking, it says:

> *The Laws says, one need have no fear, the Irish were, incredibly cunning in that they were able to find the track by 'the bruising of a grass in the summer time'.*

Now wasn't that something. I have seen skills like that still in Kerry.

Poachers & Snatching

I remember the fascination of seeing a skilled poacher 'tickle' a salmon with his bare hands, slot his fingers into the salmon's gills and hoist him onto the bank. It is a skill I suppose that is passing.

I suppose I have a soft spot for poachers – sorry, alleged poachers. This is because early in my career I had two poacher cases.

The first case I ever had in Listowel District Court was a fishery case – what was then, and I think still is, described as a 'snatching' case by those learned in poaching lore.

'Snatching' is an offence of considerable skill. It involves the fisherman (I never had a poaching case involving a woman) spotting a salmon in the water – a difficult task needing a trained sharp eye, although aided in modern times by Polaroid glasses.

There was a bit about me in the Kerryman newspaper, about my introduction into Causeway court and the nice things said about my academic career. A few Sundays later I was collecting for the Red Cross in the village of Duagh. A man sidled up with his shilling for the Red Cross and said: 'I read about you in the papers. You might be able to do something about the water bailiffs with all the letters after your name. I will be in town tomorrow and will call in. Where is your office?'

I said my office was opposite Tarrant's Garage and I would be in all day. Of course I would, as I had nowhere to go. I hadn't appeared in Listowel Court as yet, four months on.

He (Mr O'C) came with his summonses and we agreed to a ten-shilling fee (€63½ now). The summons claimed the offence was under a 1914 fishery by-law. Unfortunately the facts were all too straight forward and neither he nor I could not see any way out of them.

He wanted me to get him time to pay the fine, which was a fixed fine of £2 (plus £3.30 costs), under a 1914 by-law.

He didn't approve of the tactics of a particular bailiff (Mr M). Mr M's vocation in life, Mr O'C claimed, was to prevent poor people getting a salmon for the Friday dinner – you remember the Church's rule of no meat on a Friday?

There is a rule among legal people, that if you cannot fight the facts then you fight the law. Nowadays, cynics say that if you cannot fight the facts or the law, fight the human rights' issues. We were not into human rights much in 1962 though. I had nothing to do but look into the law.

Surprise, surprise, no one had a copy of the by-law of 1914. The court clerk hadn't it, the Fishery Board's solicitor hadn't it, and no other solicitor in town had it. I eventually got a copy from the National Library.

It made very interesting reading to me who had been trained by Mr Justice Crotty for a year and a half in West Cork. I was trained in how to read the law. 'Mr Pierse, what is the law in this matter?' was his question to me, and to other young solicitors. So, I did my homework on the offence. The by-law read that in the River Feale one was prohibited from snatching or attempting to snatch salmon or trout by means of a rod and line with hooks on the end of it (what they call a strokehaul).

Luck is great when it is good. I was lucky on the court day. The local District Justice Mr F was off sick. He was a man who, I learnt later, did not believe in 'technicalities'. He just wanted everyone to plead guilty so that he did not have any bother. There are still a lot of judges like that unfortunately. Luckily, Mr F was not the justice for the great day.

I was proceeding up William Street, sweaty palms and all, with a big almost empty briefcase. A car pulls up and a voice said: 'Will you hop in to show me where the courthouse is Robert.'

I got in to Mr Justice Kevin McCourt's car. I knew him from my West Cork years. He was a roving, temporary justice. He had filled in when Mr Justice Crotty was ill or away in Dunamanway.

I told him that it was my first day in Listowel Court. I knew him to be interested in the law and not afraid of the prosecution.

The court started. Fishery cases were reached. Mr M the bailiff – or water keeper as they were officially, if not locally, known – gave evidence in a string of cases to which I listened carefully; £2 + £3.30 costs were meted out every minute or two.

Then my case was called: *Fishery Board -v- Mr O'C.* I said I was appearing for Mr O'C. Mr M swears that on the day in question, by the river Feale, he saw Mr O'C attempting to snatch fish with a rod and line by dragging his line through the river with a jerking movement.

Mr Justice McCourt says, 'any questions, Mr Pierse'? 'No Justice,' I say. The prosecuting solicitor says, 'that's the case (i.e., no other evidence)'. I hop up and say I want to apply for a direction. A direction is an application to the effect that the prosecution haven't proved their case.

There was a shocked silence. 'On what basis?' asked the justice. I produce and read the by-law and hand the justice a copy. I pointed out that the witness had not said there was a hook on the line. I said maybe there was nothing on it, that Mr O'C was practising casting.

The Justice said: 'I agree there is no evidence of a necessary ingredient of the offence (i.e., a hook). Dismiss and £3.30 costs to Mr Pierse.'

Another bombshell from the bench. Mr Justice McCourt said to Mr O'Reilly, the prosecuting solicitor: 'Mr M didn't give evidence of a hook in all the previous cases, so I am dismissing those also now.'

This caused a sensation in the fishing community (or the alleged poachers therein). Many of the people involved in those earlier summonses had been paying in their fines and costs in advance of the case to Mr O'Reilly's clerk by instalments. They all got their money back, so I got a bit of a 'hooks and fishes' reputation for a short time. The result was a number of people in the alleged poacher category slipped a salmon, with hook marks I must admit, to my mother or myself.

Appeal

The day Mr O'Reilly, prosecuting solicitor, came with the notice of appeal to my small, one room office, was a day when a man who had got £3 back had slipped me two white trout earlier; at about 12. I slipped them into a drawer in my desk.

Mr O'Reilly arrived at my office at 1 pm on that July day. I took the notice of appeal and Mr O'Reilly remarked, 'Robert, this is a fishy business', with a knowing smile and a sniff.

So, I get ready for the circuit court. I briefed a class mate of mine in UCD, Richard Johnson BL, with what I think was his first brief, first Kerry one anyway.

For some reason the case did not come until after lunch. My mother afterwards recalled that neither of us could eat our salmon lunch with excited anxiety. Our judge was the late Barra O'Briain, a great and patient judge, but also a fisherman. He was known to be no friend of alleged poachers.

When Mr M got into the witness box in the circuit court, his memory had improved to the extent that he remembered seeing a strokehaul hook at the end of Mr O'C's line. Richard Johnson BL said, 'no questions'. William Binchy BL (Maeve's father), who was prosecuting for the Fishery Board, said there was no other evidence. 'We apply for a direction,' Richard replied. Shock again.

'Why may I ask are you applying for a direction?' the judge said calmly as was his way. 'There was no evidence that there were salmon or trout in the river Judge. The bylaw is confined to salmon or trout.' Again, the bylaw was produced and dissected. William Binchy BL huffed and puffed about a reasonable presumption of a man using a rod-line and hook was likely to be fishing. Richard replied that maybe it could have been for eels or mullet.

I remember Judge O'Briain humming and hawing a bit, but he then looked at the anxious faces of two young lawyers. He decided for us. He dismissed the appeal and gave us costs. I got £15, which with the £3.30 for the district court made up almost a quarter of my income that first year.

However, my name as a district court practitioner picked up after that. I got a few handshakes outside the court later from the alleged poaching community. They were strongly represented in the back seats of the court. They wanted to see how young Pierse would get on. There's great interest in the law in the Kingdom of Kerry, especially if one wins against AUTHORITY.

The Judge

The Judgment was in a way a reflection of the nature of the good judge we had. He listened to a new point and applied the law. As he so often said, it was not his business to make the law as he felt it should be. We got on well over the next few years.

I usually did my own district court appeals, especially if there were knotty legal problems. I had plenty of time to go into the law, dig up old cases. You could not do that before a lot of the circuit court judges, as they felt it was presumptuous of solicitors to attempt to be advocates and lawyers. Some do even still.

Solicitors now have a right of appearance in all courts. When I use the right in the High Court, I do so only before those judges who encourage it.

Judge Barra O'Briain did of course encourage my interest in the law, as had Justice Crotty. I still have law books both of them had written. Judge Barra O'Briain had written one on the Irish Free State Constitution, and Justice Crotty on the district court. I have Justice Crotty's autograph on my much used copy.

Judge O'Briain spent part of his judicial career as a seconded judge in the divided Island of Cyprus. When I attended his retirement dinner, my wife and I were put sitting next to him, and we both spoke in Irish to him. He had a great love for our language.

I did ask him that night why, in his view, did he usually seem to get it right. His reply was he had the wisdom of much experience. He said his job was mainly to listen. He listened to the 'asides' of speech and intonation, for what he called the straws in the wind. He said when one saw, or rather heard, the way the straws were going, you learnt the direction of the wind. The one thing I remember about him the most was his unparalleled patience. Who was it that wrote:

> Patience is more oft the attribute of Saints,
> The trial of their fortitude
> Making them each his own deliverer
> And victor over all that tyranny
> And fortune can inflict.

I think it was Milton in *Samson Agonistes*. I am sure you know better than me on the subject of poetry.

It is a pity that, nowadays, clearing lists and 'moving on' cases is more important to many judges and governments than full, fair hearings. We do need more good, practical, learned and fair judges – which many of them are, but they are overworked.

Sir Walter Raleigh, Robert Emmet & the 'Min'

We were talking again last night about these solemn individuals who I have mentioned before, the 'min with the caps'. They believe they know most things about most people and the nation's affairs. This is especially if it is at the end of a fair day or a mart day.

Talking about fair days, these old legal institutions are much in the wane, except for the great horse fairs like the Cahirmee fair in Buttevant. That is where the French army horse-buyers bought Napoleon's famous white stallion.

Mikey Shanahan, a local historian and water diviner from Kilcolgan, Tarbert, once took me to a field near Ballylongford where he maintained that Napoleon's horse was born.

Mikey was wearing his cap as it was a bleak February day, and so was I. In a nearby field the Cromwellian forces killed three monks who had fled with the sacred vessels from Lislaughtin Abbey. The soldiers said they got none of the valuable sacred vessels, but who believes that? Although the fact they apparently disembowelled the monks before killing them, to try and force them to say where the sacred treasure was hidden, may lend truth to the idea they came away without the gold. Possibly people still look for them with metal detectors.

Mikey also explained, graphically, how the troops searched through the unfortunate monk's entrails, just in case they had swallowed any jewels. That evening was tough on my stomach!

As it so happened, I was reading that part of the life of Sir Walter Raleigh dealing with his death sentence for alleged treason. He's the guy who put his cloak on the puddle for his Queen Elizabeth. The judgment (taken from *Hargraves State Trials 1.211*) was short and terrible, and reads:

> But since you have been found guilty of these horrible treasons, the Judgment of this court is, that you had from hence to the place whence you came, there to remain until the day of execution; And from thence you shall be drawn upon a hurdle through the open streets to the place of execution, there to be hanged and cut down alive; and your body shall be opened, your heart and bowels plucked out, and your privy members cut off, and thrown into the fire before your eyes, then your head to be stricken off

from your body, and your body shall be divided into four quarters, to be disposed of at the King's pleasure, and may God have mercy upon your soul.

Tough courts in 1603. If I remember my history, Sir Walter Raleigh brought the first potatoes to Youghal. He was in the garrison in Cork and in conflict with Barry, the local Irish lord. Raleigh rode to Dublin to inform the Lord Deputy of Barry's outrages and to have him proclaimed a traitor. The Lord Deputy duly complied and commissioned Raleigh to seize the person, lands, and castle of Barry.

Barry hearing of the news set fire to his own castle and wasted his own lands. He also set an ambush for Raleigh, but Raleigh escaped.

Raleigh did not escape the judgment of the court above however. Raleigh's wife, Bess, did work to get the execution stopped. It was fifteen years before the judgment carried out, and only then in less revolting fashion. She got leave to visit him in his last night. He had recovered his poise and comforted her in her distress. She had the disposition of his body. 'It is well Bess that thou mayest dispose of it dead, that hadst not always the disposing of it when it was alive,' Raleigh said to her.

She left his cell at midnight but attended his strange and dramatic beheading the following day. It had a speech, a dance and a nobleman presiding in his honour on the scaffold. How did his distressed wife endure it?

If you want to go into the saga, get the second volume, *Life of Sir Walter Raleigh KNT* by Arthur Cayley, printed first in London in 1806, which I have here with me (a reprint of course).

Sorry, I have totally lost my theme of the men with the caps, or have I? Raleigh is always pictured with a plumed cap in pictures, and his gallantry, spreading his cloak for the Queen and so forth, is legendary.

Did you know that the bold Robert Emmet, the darling of Erin, had the same sentence passed on him? A sentence passed by Lord Norbury, who was described by Daniel O'Connell, our famous Kerryman, as a, 'judicial bully, butcher and buffoon'. That said, Norbury was in tears after Emmet's speech from the dock.

The full sentence of hanging, drawing and quartering was not carried out on Robert Emmet. He was hanged in the old way, by strangulation caused by pushing him off a plank in public with the noose around his neck. What was then the modern way of the 'drop', breaking the prisoner's neck, was not requested by the prosecuting lawyers. He was beheaded, but not disembowelled.

His defence was to be headed by the famous John Philpot Curran. However, the state pressured Curran to withdraw because some romantic letters were found in Emmet's belongings. These letters were from Sarah Curran, John Philpot Curran's daughter. Emmet's defence then passed to Leonard McNally, also a well-known barrister and whose son was Emmet's solicitor.

McNally did not defend Emmet properly. He did not raise the legal points necessary to defend a charge of treason. It was discovered, after McNally's death, that he was actually a spy in the pay of Dublin Castle. Most people do not know the difficulties Emmet had, including having informers among his friends. Emmet's speech from the dock remains one of the great speeches in Irish legal history.

Life According to the Min with the Caps:

> May you be in heaven half an hour before the Devil knows you're dead.
> A kind word never broke a tooth.
> Money is a poor master, but a good servant.
> Never make a bid until you walked the land.
> The whole world could not make a racehorse out of a donkey.
> You cannot run away from trouble forever, as there is no place
> far enough away.
> It's not the mountain we conquer; it's ourselves.

Or, as the lawyer master to whom I was apprenticed used to say: 'Never assume the obvious is true.' Or, as Oscar Wilde famously said: 'The truth is never pure and rarely simple.' All lawyers know that!

Nature calls for some relief. Also, I must arise and go now. Scruffy is waiting for me. Still no sign of Harry the hare.

The Galapagos

Well I am back. I find my island colony of family and friends playing cards noisily. I am not a card player, so I retired to my law books and these scribblings.

I came across a female lawyer recently giving out – she wants to be equal to men! Poor thinking! My mother thought the idea curious; why would any woman like to be the same as a man?

Scruffy has no views on women. He is like the turtle 'Lonesome George' on the Galapagos Islands, who has been waiting for forty years for a mate. His subspecies on the island is possibly extinct due to people either killing them or taking them away as pets! So, if you have a female companion turtle for Lonesome George do donate, otherwise George, who has a life expectancy of 150 years, will continue to be alone. He wasn't born when Charles Darwin evolved this theory of evolution after a visit to the Galapagos Islands. Interesting and still controversial chap, Mr Darwin.

If you ever get a chance, go to the Galapagos. We did on one occasion. I could see how it was used to forward Darwin's theory of evolution. We had a local marine geologist. He was proud, protective and professional in his approach.

He took us to a small, rocky island on the first day which had hot water on one side and cold on the other. Our boat had young Americans mostly – in their 20s. We were well more than double their age, so we were the old fogies.

We were let off our sailing ship (32 passengers and 10 crew) to swim for an hour. We swam off and did our hour. The most interesting thing being the hot water coral and fish were completely different to those on the cold side.

When we got back to the boat, we found all the other tourists were back much earlier. They couldn't 'take' the cold water! They weren't used to the cold Atlantic of Kerry Head. We were not regarded as old fogies after that.

It was a most educational and entertaining ten days. When you leave the boat to get the plane back to Quito in Ecuador, you are simply left off onto a flat rock. You then climb a few steps to a bus stop. When we got to a bus stop it was occupied by a big, sleeping seal.

The animals, birds and fish are all human friendly. We swam among seals, turtles, sharks and rays, throughout our time on the island. They were all around you on the beach. There are some wonderful books on the Galapagos – but get one with a lot of pictures! There are also some wonderful documentaries by David Attenborough – what a wonderful man he is!

Update: Lonesome George died unmated in 2011.

No Sisters

Having grown up in a household of seven boys without the domination of a sister (or should I say 'guidance of a sister') I profess to little understanding of the very opposite sex.

No doubt my mother was a member of that rather difficult half of humanity, but mothers are mothers. Sons do not regard mothers as really women; they are just mothers and so are great. Indeed, they are so good one ought to have two or three of them – one only with a wooden spoon though!

It is hard to go into all that about women on this island. I notice my sons, who have the benefit of three sisters, do not seem to have the same difficulty in understanding woman as I have.

I remember the wisdom of our eldest, Risteárd, when failing to cope with his three-year-old sister, who was standing in front of him and preventing him from riding his new Santa-produced bike. She wanted the first ride. Her cheeks were puffed out red over her dark green coat. He gave in to her demands, and got off his bike. Then, he watched his bike thrown on the ground as she turned away. I remember his words of deep perception: 'When she could not get it she wanted it, when she could get it she did not want it.'

Tuberculosis

As a teenager, I found the mysterious half of the population increasingly interesting. What had been 'just girls', who would not play games like the lads, suddenly became 'girls'. How come they were of new interest?

Of course, I was interested, but that budding interest was nipped in the bud when I got tuberculosis as a young teenager, and was sent to a sanatorium for a year and a half.

My parents were terrified of TB. My maternal grandmother died of it. As I mentioned earlier, my father was the vet who killed TB cows.

The women in the sanatorium came in two types, nuns and nurses!

The nuns: they were in the control of category and were not really regarded as women. They were in fact marvellous women when I look back on it. They maintained discipline over a hundred frustrated men. Cute they were.

For instance, in the ward of seventeen men who had nothing to do all day except lie in beds, who did they put in charge of the radio and the Rosary? Me! Why? Well, it was because I was the youngest and no one could give out to 'the boy' from Kerry without being considered a bully. Good psychologists those nuns. There were three other Kerrymen in the ward also, and they gave me some protection.

The nurses: These again were divided into two types: staff nurses and probationers.

The staff nurses: They were half way between the nuns and their lesser beings mentioned next.

The staff nurses wore a blue top to their uniform. They always had a stern frown as they ordered you to turn sideways, pull down your pyjamas and expose your backside cheek for the often badly blunt needles, usually in the hands of frightened probationers.

The probationers, especially the new ones, always got a rough time, anonymous whistles included, as they walked through the ward. Their first day making the beds was a dreadful ordeal for them. Well, I suppose it was, the female mind, like I said, is a mystery to me. Their blushes were glowing red.

Then their learning to give injections was an ordeal for us. They didn't want to hurt us, but their hands would shake and the needle hurt. There was one nice Wicklow girl who was so bad, one day I caught her hand and shoved in the needle myself, saying, 'just get it over'. This big injection of streptomycin always gave one a sore, lower red cheek!

I was 'mad' about a different nurse every week, and always the probationers, as they were really innocent young women. After six months they put on the blue tops and acquired that tough, hardened stare! Alas! Well most of them did.

I am also very grateful to the late Noel Browne, then Minister for Health, for keeping me alive. I always resented how the bishops treated him.

There ought to be a Law

I took consolation in PG Wodehouse. I was introduced to him by a member of St Vincent de Paul, while in 'the san'. Jeeves and Bertie Wooster became pals between study.

Great guys, those Sunday morning St Vincent de Paul men. One of them got me the book-list for the matric exam two years down the line – he was a teacher with a brother in the Department of Education.

I took up study, which actually was wonderful in motivating me out of the hopelessness of being a 'consumptive', especially when the good man next to me took a month to die – he drowned in his own sputum. TB was a tough, killer illness.

I would giggle over a chapter of PG Wodehouse before lights out at 9:30 pm – I still do, only in different circumstances thankfully. I began to regard myself as a Bertie Wooster, without a Jeeves! Can one not learn a lot about women from Bertie?

My favourite piece was when he was blackmailed by a female pal, Stiffy Byngs. Bertie was trying to match his old pal Gussie Fink-Nottle with the high-minded Madeline. Things were not going well as Gussie was not sticking to the spinach diet prescribed by Madeline. Madeline had declared that if Gussie did not stay on the diet, she would marry Bertie Wooster. This was a fate worse than death in Bertie's mind.

Stiffy Byngs wanted Bertie to steal an object of art. Bertie was more than a little reluctant to become a burglar. However, Stiffy threatened to reveal to Madeline (woman to woman help, of course) that Gussie was slipping down to the castle kitchen at night, shovelling steak and kidney pie into himself.

Bertie grasped the true result of such female to female assistance – Madeline leading him to the altar, a fate worse than death for Bertie. His view:

> Blackmail, of course, but the gentler sex love blackmail. Not once but on several occasions has my aunt Dahlia bent me to her will by threatening, if I did not play ball she would bar me from the table, thus dashing (her French chef's) Anatole's lunches and desserts from my lips.
>
> Show me a delicately nurtured female and I will show you

a ruthless Napoleon of crime prepared without turning a hair to put the screws on some unfortunate male whose services she happened to be in need of.

There ought to be a law.

O'Toole

Well as I am writing about under the bed and women, I heard a story about 'O'Toole'.

He goes into his local bar and says to Mike, the bartender, 'pour me a stiff one, just had another fight with the little woman'.

'How did this one go?' Mike asks.

O'Toole replied: 'When it was over, she came to me on her hands and knees.'

'Really,' says Mike, 'that is a change, what did she say?'

'She said, "O'Toole, come out from under the bed you coward", on her hands and knees, looking for me with fire in those pretty eyes.'

Now, am I a lucky man not to know such females? Well, only a few. Or well, maybe not so many!

I have been known to say, 'thank you God for giving me seven sons and only three daughters'. I know my sons say my daughters make a complete fool out of me. They practise their female wiles on me.

But then as Bryan MacMahon said, 'children sharpen their claws on their parents'. I think my lovely, 'innocent' female progeny have sharp pointed claws.

In saying that, I love the song (which I think is from the wonderful film *Gigi*):

> Thank heavens for little girls,
> Without them, what would little boys do?

The Spanish Computer

I go to Spain now and again. I love the Spanish people. There is a Spanish of sorts spoken here in Belize. It was also in the Galapagos. Well, here is a story I heard in Spain.

A Spanish teacher was explaining to her class that in Spanish, unlike English, nouns are designated as either masculine or feminine.

'House' for instance, is feminine: '*la casa*.'

'Pencil' however, is masculine: '*el lapiz*.'

A German student asked, 'what gender is computer'?

Instead of giving the answer, the teacher split the class into two groups, male and female, and asked them to decide for themselves whether 'computer' should be a masculine or a feminine noun. Each group was asked to give four reasons for its recommendation.

The men's group decided that 'computer' should definitely be of the feminine gender (*la ordenador*) because:

i.   No one but their creator understands their internal logic.

ii.   The native language they use to communicate with other computers is incomprehensible to everyone else.

iii. Even the smallest mistakes are stored in long-term memory for possible later retrieval; and

iv.   As soon as you make a commitment to one, you find yourself spending half your pay-check on accessories for it.

This gets better!

The women's group, however, concluded that computers should be masculine (*el ordenador*), because:

v.   In order to do anything with them, you have to turn them on.

vi.   They have a lot of data but still can't think for themselves.

vii. They are supposed to help you solve problems, but half the time they are the problem; and

viii. As soon as you commit to one, you realise that if you had waited a little longer you could have gotten a better model.

The women won!

They always do one way or the other. Odd, in the old days they rarely used to admit it. They let the 'man' believe he was the boss. The men knew they weren't, but liked to believe it. Peace reigned. Changed now, don't you think?

The immortal John B put it well, when he said: 'The women are the bosses when the trousers are over the end of the bed.'

I got into trouble last night because of another John B story I told in the *Seagull* cabin. When we got back to the *Laughing Bird*, Olive told me I should have higher values in my story. Indeed, I will be in trouble again for putting it on paper, so if you are of a higher value discernment stop and do not read the next story.

I think it was the night of the first wren boys' competition in Listowel, where 'wren boys' dress in garish, pagan-type costumes, and sing and dance on stage. This is a big event on the Friday night of our autumn festival in Listowel, 'The Races'. The first wren boy event was sponsored by Guinness. So, well it may, as an ocean of Guinness is consumed that week in town.

Lord Iveagh and his wife were on the platform with the MC, who was John B. I think John B was a bit nervous as MC. The wren boy groups were slowly coming down to the platform to perform and be judged. John B was slipping into the Listowel Arms for 'quick ones'. His MC stories were getting 'stronger'.

Suddenly he says: 'Did ye ever hear about the man from Bally who got married and was to get a fortune of £1,000?' We all shouted, 'NO JOHN B'. 'WELL,' he said, 'he only got £500 on the day of the wedding, the other £500 was to be paid in three months, when the cattle were sold in the autumn.'

A year and a half later his father in-law said to him: 'Where's my grand-child? I should have one by now.'

The son in-law said: 'Well I am not going to unbutton my fly until I get the other half of the fortune from you.'

The crowd roared, but the shock that registered on the faces of the Dublin glitterati had to be seen to be believed.

The 'min with the caps' had their own way of getting their own way.

Talking about John B and the men with the caps. These cherished citizens of Listowel would meet for their daily review of the situation at McKenna's corner, opposite John B's pub. They would stand in William Street if the wind (and rain) was coming from the south west. They would stand in Market Street if the wind was otherwise. Market Street got more sun as it faced south. They had their cap on all weather, to protect their innocent heads from rain or sun.

Robinson Crusoe & Isolation

Now I have definitely the writer's cramp and it's getting dark. No switch to turn on the light. I must go off and be sociable anyway. I am not an Alexander Selkirk, the model for Robinson Crusoe. He had been ship-wrecked and found much later, alone on the island.

Did you know that Daniel Defoe's book was one of the first bestselling novels? Another bit of useless information we might discuss tonight is, why Selkirk turned out to be a bully? Why Defoe could write a book about the unusual adventures of a man he never met? I think about this piece of school poetry about Alexander:

> I am monarch of all survey
> My right there is none to dispute,
> From the centre all round to the sea
> I am Lord of the fowl and the brute.

I often wondered about people in solitary confinement. What are their thoughts? I have read that it is an extremely cruel punishment, as it is disorientating.

Here on our island, while isolated from the teeming millions, indeed billions, of humanity, I have a little sense of disorientation. In a way my ability to be able to write my random thoughts is a therapy – but then my late wise mother always said I was bookish. A few more lines about Alexander Selkirk, from Alexander Cowper's *The Solitude of Alexander Selkirk*, came to mind here in the sand:

> Oh solitude where are the charms
> That sages have seen in thy face
> Better dwell in the midst of alarms
> Than reign in this horrible place.

Isn't there a strong contrast in those last two lines? I was on the Robinson Crusoe island of Tobago in fact, but could not describe it as a horrible place. It was a sort of an adventure three of us, my father, my brother in law Fr Gearóid O'Donoghue and I undertook many years ago.

That beautiful island had belonged to the British, and they did try and develop its roads. Then a group, I think it was the Black Panther Movement, sought to get the Brits out. They succeeded and the economy of the place collapsed. Roads ended in the middle of fields and led to nowhere. Food was in short supply and people lived off what nature provided – which was mainly fish.

Interestingly, as there was little or no electricity there, and no fridges. When the fishermen came in with a boat load of fish, they took away personally what they wanted for the day. Everyone else came along and just took what they wanted for the day – no payment. In fact, the women seemed to spend most of the day swimming, or rather standing in about four feet of water on the beach keeping cool and gossiping.

I remember their beautiful and colourful headdresses, bobbing around the sea until the daily, awesome sunset. I did not know where the men were.

To get on or off Tobago island, there was only one small plane. We ran into trouble when we went back to confirm our return flight. 'There has been a mistake, your booking is not registered, the flight has been cancelled,' and so on. We go back to a Scotsman who lived on the island, and he said: 'Give them $10 each and you will get your confirmation.'

We went back. We refused to pay a bribe. We stayed at the counter for about an hour and a half, and they got so fed up they gave us our confirmation without the bribe. Principles you know!

I remember an Irish diplomat telling me about his experience on a trade mission, where a bribe secured a big deal in a north African country. This Irish delegation arrived, bringing samples of their wares. They met ministers and officials. The goods were considered excellent but there was a lot of haggling about price. The minister left, and his son kept the negotiations going for hours, but no deal.

The Irishmen were back the following day. They dropped their price, but still no deal. On the second night one from the Irish group went on a binge with an Englishman. In the course of the night he learnt the solution. Simple – add 10% to the price, then give it back to the appropriate intermediaries as 'expenses' unrecorded and tax free. A dig out to dig out sales. It worked and they got a higher price too, even with the 10% added for expenses.

Life goes on. Now hello to money! As the song said, 'money talks, it don't sing and dance, but it sure talks'.

Lesson: 'Expenses' are a spoke of the great wheel of commerce. Now called 'top ups'?

The Book of Kells

I suppose it was my parents who gave me a love of books, particularly my mother. She read books like *The Wind in the Willows* and *Six O'clock Saints* to us as children. Later, we became fans of Agatha Christie and Georgette Heyer, which my mother bought.

Sometimes, when one of her authors was not up to scratch, she would slam the book shut and say, 'pot-boiler'.

Listowel has its famous entertaining and educational Writers' Week. It is the first weekend, with a bit before added on, of June each year. Do come and enjoy. You will be the better for it.

Now, to turn to a national treasure.

My brother John got me a Swiss-made copy of the *Book of Kells* some years ago. It and the 1399 others I believe were copied from the original in precise detail. The bookworm holes are all there, as are the edges you can see cut off in the original. The cut-offs in the original were apparently done by a book binder, so the manuscript would fit into the cover he made. Stupid man. The Swiss copies were made on special paper to hold the colours. The copies are truly magnificent.

The original *Book of Kells* is in Trinity College Dublin. It is probably the greatest book of illuminated gospels in the world. Indeed, it has been described as the most beautiful book in the world.

It comprises the four gospels in Latin. It is the work of three (at least) monks who, assisted by scribes, created it in the monastery in Iona, in the early 9th century, around the time of the Viking raiders. These raiders caused it to be moved to Kells in Ireland.

What fascinates me the most is its most microscopic details. There are Byzantine and other influences, as well as some smashing Celtic designs. What attracted the raiders was its cover, a rich gold & silver binding with embedded jewels. It appears that the thieves, having taken the jewels, gold and silver, threw the book into a ditch; hence some of the book is damaged by water.

Part of it is on display in Trinity always, and normally queues are waiting to see it.

The Book of Durrow

I have a weakness for books as I said. I have a copy of the *Book of Durrow* which is also an early medieval manuscript. It was written in Durrow, Co. Offaly.

The Book of Durrow was written in Latin, in a Christian monastery in Offaly in the mid-7th century. While it is older, it is not as glorious as the *Book of Kells*. However, a few of its best pages have been reproduced in colour.

While written in Latin, an Irish inscription was added much later:

The prayer and Blessing of Colmcille for Flann,
son of Maolshnaill, King of Ireland, who had this shrine made.

The shrine was probably the jewelled, silver reliquary in which the book was stored, when given by the protestant Bishop of Meath, Henry Jones, to Trinity in about 1661. This reliquary was stolen, probably during the military occupation of Trinity College in 1681.

The Book of Durrow is the first masterpiece of Irish Christian art. It is also housed in Trinity College.

Colmcille was of course a character – a lot of these 'saints' were.

As for the *Book of Kells*, if you haven't gone to see it in Trinity College you should be ashamed of yourself.

Now, I say goodnight to my absent audience in this non-solid, shifting and sandy island, amid the alarms of a continuing tropical storm. The lightning will guide me to *Laughing Bird*. I will not be able to see falling coco nuts though – I will duck and weave. Scruffy awaits impatiently. The length of this storm is most unusual.

DAY FIVE: SOLEMN THOUGHTS

Poetry in Belize – 5:30 am

Waking up here this morning has not been like waking up in my own Kingdom of Kerry. At home in Ireland for most of the year there is the sound of birds twittering in soft rain. Here, this very early am, it was the crashing sounds of sand being beaten by waves, a rattling, swaying cabin, swishing trees, and everywhere the constant howls of wind. Everywhere disruptive noise – and I am a man who likes peace.

It's going to be a long day of storm I believe. Heavy clouds hang everywhere in the wild wind.

I suppose it is not as bad as Alexander Selkirk – you know the real Robinson Crusoe I was writing about last night.

As you probably guessed, I like the condensed wisdom of poetry, 'the sweet music of speech'. You are probably wondering why?

Now, this isn't a gripe, or a claim of childhood abuse, something so prevalent nowadays. However, I did experience what would now be termed abuse at the hands of a priest teacher, a Father O'Connor, who is no longer with us. I don't want to say much about him, as it can do no good. He beat us unmercifully in the belief it would get us better results in our exams.

However, I owe my love and knowledge of poetry to a man who shared his surname, but nothing else, the late Timmy O'Connor, or 'Timmy', as he was known to us in the infamous class A.

He was a portly, calm man whose class succeeded the stormy class of his unrelated namesake. He would present himself to soothe our shocked senses and battered bodies. He would address us as 'gentlemen'.

The late Fr O'Connor was the only person I could not bring myself to pray for when I heard he was dead. I suppose I was wrong, but there it is. He shattered so many young lives with his uncontrollable and uncontrolled temper. His Greek class was a terrifying experience. I remember some of my classmates vomiting before it because of its terror.

Perhaps there is a wee bit of its terror here now – is my pregnant daughter-in-law going to be OK? I am an old-fashioned man when it comes to protecting pregnant women. Life is so precious and wonderful; I cannot stand that daft crowd who talk about the 'right' of pro-choice. Fat lot of good it is to talk about rights of a child when you are killing the child, so that he/she gets no rights. Downright unnatural.

I wonder again. I am a bit cross with these negative thoughts. Come on be positive! I hop out for a few minutes into that unseen, but much felt and heard, wild west wind. Scruffy only opened one eye. He did not join me in my three-minute walk around the island in the wind.

Back again – I actually hopped twenty times on each leg. Great exercise. I have to do these exercises as my feet are flat. Last year my giddy (per my mother) brother in law, Fr Gearóid, and three of our sons went missing in Donegal bay sailing down from Scotland. I spent an anxious time on cliffs and telephones. I promised to do Lough Derg. I did. It is very tough. My arches fell on those cruel stones.

Michael Collins' Blackthorn Stick

Back to work on this piece of toilet paper – I have sneaked a roll and a half from the toilet. What would Timmy O'Connor think of me now? Timmy would come in in his neat suit and waistcoat – he taught us that you always leave the bottom button of the waistcoat open. In Timmy's case it was necessary because of the protruding tummy. He dined not unseemly, but too well.

However, Mr McSharry in Dublin confirmed this is correct for a waistcoat, to have the bottom buttons open. Kennedy and McSharry's shop has dressed my grandfather Seán Collins, as well as his more famous brother Michael. I have a poor copy of a bill paid by Michael Collins about six months before his assassination.

I must look up what was happening on 10/12/1921, as I think the Treaty was signed about that time. Olive says it was the 6th of December. I know the divisive Dáil debates began on the 14th December 1921, and the main issue was the oath of allegiance, which caused many to walk out. My mother told me he came home to Woodfield that Christmas, but was worn out. The purchases would have been during those days of huge tension and public debate.

Collins found the London treaty trip difficult and Frank O'Connor commented on that in his book:

> *Collins did not like the London trip. It involved a certain amount of social contacts and four years of secret life had been a bad preparation for that. He had always been shy and rather self-conscious, hating formalities of any sort; most at ease when he was with simple people. His companions noticed that he tried to dodge functions and when it was necessary for him to attend any he was ill at ease.* (Frank O'Connor, *The Life of Michael Collins*, 1937, pg. 221.)

My mother says the Collins men dressed well, but Michael dressed shabbily (sometimes) in order to fool the British. He would tell my mother that he dressed like a civil servant usually, because the Tans respected 'British' civil servants. That was also the reason he used a bicycle.

The thing that surprised me most about that bill was that number on the phone, 1291. I remember in the 1940s my father's number in Listowel was 27. We used to crank it up to talk to the operator, who would eventually put you through to Dublin or even to the US of A in times of crisis.

Kennedy & McSharry, now in Nassau St, also have 'dressed' my grandfather, myself and my sons – that is tradition for you. That is until 2013, when their business closed down.

But you youngsters are not for tailors mostly. You are too much under the thumb of the Americans, using those awful blue jeans. Women are better dressers usually, but again those awful blue jeans make people look poor, and all to conform to a misguided sense of utility; or 'let's be as bad as the men'! Is there anything as alluring as a pretty, well-dressed woman?

I like going to weddings to see the style, particularly the ladies' hats. When I make up my mind on which lady has the nicest hat, I tell her so, and she loves it. It's a bit of glamour. Indeed, I noticed over the years that if I told a lady client she had a nice hat, the next time she visited she would have a different one to be suitably admired.

I had a number of widow or single lady clients who liked to tweak their wills every few years. On one occasion, I had a widow client who had a lovely Paul Henry print that she wanted to leave specifically to one of her two daughters.

'But Mr Pierse, what will I leave to Mary my other daughter?' she said. I said go up to the National Gallery shop and buy another equally good Irish print. She did and we re-did the will some months later.

When I was a young solicitor, I was doing a bit of business for a man called William Moore, RIP. He had retired home (and home was Pound Lane, Listowel) from the USA after a lifetime of work there.

When he discovered that I was a grandnephew of Michael Collins, the great man as he called him, we became friends. On a later visit to the office he presented me with a smashing, blackthorn walking stick. He told me the story of how he got the stick.

He had been in New York for about ten years, and had been involved in Irish republican societies. He was upset by the apparent disaster of 1916, but was heartened by the War of Independence and the Treaty. He came back on a long holiday in 1919 and, while in Dublin, heard that Michael Collins, then Minister for Finance in First Dáil, was selling their new bonds.

So, William went to Pádraig Pearse's old school, St Enda's, where the launch of the bonds was taking place. William was one of the first up, and bought $500 worth. Michael said: 'These dollars are much needed, and since you are the first man up, here is my West Cork blackthorn stick.'

William had told me there was such a sense of history at St Enda's. The fact his hero Mick Collins was up there, sitting by the wooden block on which Robert Emmet was beheaded.

William gave the stick to me, as he had no children. Unfortunately, one day I was out walking, and there was a fire on the farm and it was getting out of control. I used the stick to beat it down, but the bottom of the stick caught fire. It is a few inches shorter now. I got it fully restored and it glistens when in the light.

Now, how did I wander into Michael Collins' stories? I must talk about him tonight in the *Seagull* cabin.

I go back to those Timmy O'Connor days in St Michael's College. I remember after one stormy and battering session with 'The Priest', Timmy O'Connor saw us, saw what had been done to us, and said wisely, in his calm melodious voice: 'Gentlemen, I came upon this sonnet about the sea last night.' He then recited William Wordsworth's fourteen lines:

> The World is too much with us, late and soon,
> Getting and spending, we lay waste our powers
> Little we see in nature that is ours:
> We have given our hearts away, a sordid boon!
> The sea that bares her bosom to the moon;
> The winds that will be howling at all hours,
> And are up-gathered now like sleeping flowers

For this, for everything, we are out of tune,
It moves us not – great God! I'd rather be
A Pagan suckled in a creed outworn;
So might I, on this pleasant lea,
Have glimpses that would make me less forlorn;
Have sight of Proteus rising from the Sea;
Or hear old Triton blow his wreathed horn.

You will remember Proteus as the prophetic god of the sea. He had the ability to change himself into whatever form he desired. In the *Odyssey* he could mutate with the flocks of the sea creatures belonging to Poseidon. Triton was also a sea god and was the son of Poseidon.

Wordsworth wrote the sonnet as a criticism of the industrial revolution's focus on material progress, at the expense of the natural world.

Isn't there much in that poem that applies now? There is obviously going to be another boom period. I remember the Jack Lynch/Martin O'Donoghue one, when a lot of money was wasted on unnecessary items and little put into real economic development. The bubble will burst. The world is too much with us getting and spending. Maybe we are spending too much again in Ireland.

Update 2019: How right I was? But it may happen again in our 'democracy'!

The first four lines of the sonnet contain a lot of wisdom I think – contemplate them! Contemplate, what is wisdom? Read Socrates *a la* Plato, and the most rational of all Plato's pupils, Aristotle. How I love Aristotle!

Heavens I've gone classical, but I suppose the line, 'the winds that will be howling at all hours' got to me. I did study Greek in St Michael's – through Irish with English textbooks to get extra marks for 'The Priest'. It is no wonder I am mixed up.

Scruffy, my canine friend, is back outside the door. He has decided I need exercise. Then we will have breakfast. He knows I sit near the open door in the *Seagull* cabin. He knows if he is outside that door he gets an extra few bits. He knows lawyers are really soft-hearted!

Morning Verse

What fond and wayward thoughts will slide into a lover's mind

So, the Wonderful William Wordsworth (WWW) wrote (I hope).

Here it is difficult to be a lover in the howls of the wild wind and the bellowing of the breaking waves. It is easy to slide into wayward thoughts.

One of these is the music that exists. There is sound and rhythm there, a wild, uncontrolled music. Even the vibration of the boards over me add to the sense of a band of musicians gone wild. I am not used to this wild music in this small patch of strand we huddle on. I am used to it in the form of waves beating against the cliffs off Ireland's coast, the rhythm of their sequential approach, their aimless crashing against the rebutting rock.

On poetry, my favourite sonnet is the one I set out elsewhere – *Evening on Calais Beach*. Indeed, I prefer sonnets to any other form of poetry. Their perceptiveness, order and brevity appeal to me.

One of the many reasons I while away the storm-strewn hours by scribbling, is, as I have already said, my son Gearóid (No. five of ten) has been urging me to put some non-legal thoughts and stories on paper. He may read this and if he does, I am sure he will not know who these Greek guys were – or most of them. Interesting guy Gearóid. He has nine interesting siblings, who are also accumulating many interesting in-laws. Young people are great.

Shakespeare, the Bard of Avon, lived in an interesting old house which I visited many years ago – that is if you believe that version as to who he was. You should follow him up as he was a wise, philosophical guy and one heck of a poet and playwright.

One of his characters said about law: 'The sharp quillets of the law'. You know those legal distinctions that annoy the populace?

Bigamy

There was a conversation between a solicitor and his client outside the court after a long and difficult case. The solicitor had been very impressed by the calm way his client had answered in a severe and long cross-exami-nation. The solicitor queried:

'That cross-examination did not seem to worry you at all. Have you a lot of experience?'

The client replied cynically, 'three wives and three mothers-in-law'.

Then, there's the rhyme about three wives:

> There was a man who had three wives at one time,
> When asked why the third?
> He said 'one is absurd,
> And bigamy, sir, is a crime'!

I had better get off that subject. I seem to have forgotten the wisdom of 'the min with the caps'. They say stay in with the women!

Daniel O'Connell

Then there is the story about that great Kerry lawyer and parliamentarian, Daniel O'Connell. He was acting for a plaintiff who was disputing a will. He claimed the man who had 'made' the will had died before signing it. This was put to one of the witnesses to the will by Daniel O'Connell (D O'C) – the witness was a man with a cap no doubt.

> D O'C: 'The man was dead before the will was signed?'
> Witness: 'No counsellor, there was a lot of life in him.'
> D O'C: 'I see. What was the life in him?'
> Witness: 'We put three live flies into his mouth, shut it and signed the will, so he had a lot of life in him.'

Guess who won?

Adam and Eve

Where was I? I had gone a bit classical in my poetry. I like the psychology of classical stories. Take the story of creation in the Bible. All done in six days, then a rest day. Unlike the big-bang theories so fashionable nowadays, it was a simple story for a simple people.

It is the bit in the story about human nature, about Adam and Eve, that I find so wise. The urgings of evil (named the Devil); looking for the other guy's apple, even when you have enough of your own; greed, envy and jealously were then, and still are now, basic human characteristics; then you have the urger, temptress or 'adviser', followed by the blame game – man to woman, woman to snake.

You see a mighty amount of all these in the practice of law. Good psychologists those bearded boys, writing that Bible. They had to explain to their simple people the mysterious sources of unhappiness and life's difficulties.

I brought all this up in the *Seagull* cabin last night, and caused a bit of controversy. The reaction: the story is for the birds, and the Bible is for the birds. None of us are humble enough to accept that there must be a Creator, who is a mystery to us, beyond our ability to even conceive. A self-creating Creator from nothing. No one could understand the relevance of the Adam and Eve story for today's world.

Kevin asks, does it matter? Are the theories of religion and science arrogant attempts to explain the unexplainable?

I of course accept evolution, but there must also be a cause of matter, a cause of the evolutionary power and design which has produced such variety.

A Being whose plan and design we cannot understand. The First Mover, the Energy, the Designer, or St Thomas Aquinas's Uncaused Cause.

Of course, the younger members of our caye team say science will explain all in time. I wonder.

Let me off for a stroll to see the minute mystery of this little bit of the unexplainable, creator's work – something that was created by a self-Creator.

It is of course a mystery, but I think of the God-Creator as a circle with no apparent beginning or end.

I find Einstein a humbling scientist in so far as I can understand him – which is unusual for that subspecies of humanity. But as Churchill said of, I think Disraeli? (No, apparently it was Clement Atlee.) When Atlee was described as a humble man, Churchill said, 'he has much to be humble about' – I have too.

Einstein wrote:

> What I see in nature is a magnificent structure that we can comprehend only very imperfectly, and that must fill a thinking person with a feeling of humility. This is a genuinely religious feeling that has nothing to do with mysticism.

Interesting do you think, or do you not think so? I would like to have asked his view on what religion is. 'Religion,' like love, is an abused word.

I understand the Swiss are building a machine in a tunnel to try to find, or re-create, the ultimate particle or anti-particle. It is going to take about fifteen years to build.

However, no one is asking the most important question: is the machine going to show the Uncaused Cause of creation? I wish I could live another couple of hundred years. I might know something about something.

'*Ancora imparo*' as Michelangelo said, translated in Ballyheigue as 'I am always learning'. I actually keep a plaque outside my office door, with *ancora imparo* written on it.

2018: What has the machine achieved? I am not sure, but it seems to have proved someone's theory was correct.

To lighten my mood, I should be thinking of more poetry. I am not really in that mood. I turn to its near verbal and phonetic neighbour, music.

Music

It has not really been a beauteous evening here, but thinking of that poem has helped my mood. I have recited it to those in the *Seagull* cabin. Here it is hard, '*muy mal*' as the Spanish say. Here there is wind, rain, noise, but also good company. I relax and imagine what music I would like to have. I believe Tennyson would have a name for me, I am a lotus eater. Tennyson wrote:

> There is sweet music here that softer falls
> Than petals from blown roses on the grass ...
>
> Music that gentler on the spirit lies,
> Than tired eyelids upon tired eyes ...
>
> Death is the end of life; ah, why
> Should life all labour be?

Certainly, my eyelids are tired and I would like God to hear the cry of the lotus eaters in relation to us: 'Why should life all labour be?'

However, let's get back to the main point:

> The man that hath not music in his soul; Nor is not moved with concord of sweet sounds, Is fit for treasons, stratagems, and spoils.

If I were on my local radio, Radio Kerry, as a guest of the imitable Ted Carroll, what music would I play? I like *The Beautiful Blue Danube*. That is the proper name of the Strauss waltz. Then I suppose I would go to Irish local, in particular the many marvellous pieces in Shaun Davey's CD *The Brendan Voyage*. Having crossed the Atlantic from the USA to Ireland, I am a total disciple of St Brendan.

I know it is hard to convince the Yanks that our Kerry saint could, and I think certainly did, sail in his leather currach from the West Kerry shores to their mighty shores. However, I recommend that they read Tim Severin's book *The Brendan Voyage*, on which Mr Davey bases his very appropriate music. What an adventurer Tim Severin is – read all his book for real life adventure.

I recommend you also go and see the boat he used crossing the Atlantic at Craggaunowen Visitors Centre near Bunratty, in County Clare. I am familiar with the wonders of a currach, as I have used them all my life. I fished lobster pots from them.

By the way, if you are down in the Tralee area, go out to Fenit. Go see the bold and daring statue of St Brendan at the end of the pier. Sculpted by Tighe O'Donoghue. Many of the sketches in this book, including

Scruffy & Harry, are done by Tighe O'Donoghue – thanks! Even drive 'The Brendan Way', the area around Fenit and Ardfert. What history!

I snoozed off there, thinking of music, but an almighty shake of this cabin makes me alert again.

Would I play Handel's *Water Music* on the radio? Probably not, it is too sweet, I much prefer his *Messiah*. *Water Music* was first produced on the Thames, the Messiah in Dublin. I am being childishly territorial in my taste I suppose.

I would certainly include Tchaikovsky's *Swan Lake*, and for contrast, Elgar's *Pomp and Circumstances*. The absence of pomp here in our circumstance made me think of Elgar. That poor man was underrated in England because he was a Catholic.

Most of all my dear friends, Beethoven's pastoral symphony would need to get an airing – what peace? Probably the *Shepherd's Hymn*! I would also include that great master's *Moonlight Sonata*, as there was such a beautiful moon here on the night before this storm. However, nature is tempestuous here in Belize, and what I would not give to play is something like *Aladdin's Dream and Dance of the Morning Mist* by Nielson.

I would have to include my favourite piece of classical music, *Meditation* by Massenet, probably played by the controversial Nigel Kennedy. I'd also get in something from *The Merry Widow*, *The Student Prince*, and '*Thank Heavens for Little Girls*' from *Gigi*. Those costumes in the film *Gigi*, wonderful. I think someone should compose a song: 'Thank Heavens for wives, without them what would we men do?'!

I also love James Galway; *Lady in Red*; James Last playing *The Rose of Tralee*; Seán O'Riada's music; *Danny Boy*; and *The Coolin* played by Geraldine O'Grady. I could go on and on.

Don't tell my children of my selection. The would say, 'you are for the birds', 'fuddy daddy' and so on. Although the older ones are accepting these type of CDs. I gave Risteárd Mendelssohn's *Fingal's Cave* recently. He had a free night in London and went to a symphony concert which included Mendelssohn's Scottish symphony. He loved it. Now that's progress! Of course, he sailed Scottish waters with Fr Gearóid, his uncle.

What do you think? Write down your 3 favourite tunes.

1. ______________________________________
2. ______________________________________
3. ______________________________________

Then read my line from Shakespeare's *Merchant of Venice* above. Interesting guy Shakespeare. As was Milton. I like Milton's sonnet about his blindness, especially the last line: '*They also serve who only stand and wait.*'

Think about that. As I get older, I can see marvellous wisdom in that line. I did not really grasp it when Timmy O'Connor, our teacher, read it to us back in the 1950s. But does a stressed mind which had endured an hour of Greek, learnt in Irish but using English books, really have a grasping for wisdom? What a pity Fr O'Connor wasted so much of our education in seeking honour for 'his' school by high examination marks. We all paid a terrible price!!

All Human life

We reminisced about Listowel last night. It gives us a sense of security. The town that I have lived in for most of my life is rich and big in the drama of life. It may be small in number of people but, as one English newspaper puts it, 'all human life is there'.

This of course is particularly so to a lawyer, who has to listen to the confidential problems of so many friends and clients. One of the difficulties with being a lawyer in this country is the EU and Government are obsessed with confidentiality. It is now a bad word, but our privacy is being eroded. Ireland is full of inspectors who have too much power to interrogate, search and deprive citizens of their privacy.

National School

In school, I got on great with Mrs Crowley, the high-infants teacher, however Tom, my younger brother, did not.

Tom developed a trick of throwing himself on the ground and bawling when she came near him. One day, after one of these scenes, I, as older brother, was sent for, apparently to report Tom's behaviour to my mother.

There was Tom curled up on the floor bawling as if in agony. When he saw my feet, he looked up and gave me a big smirk and a wink. I burst out laughing. I got a smack in the ear and was sent off, for being as bad as 'him'.

Years later Mrs Crowley met my mother and told her about these incidents. She said my mother – God be good to her and I know he is – was the toughest woman in town. But my mother expressed considerable surprise at hearing what Mrs Crowley had to say.

Mrs Crowley said: 'In all the years when I sent notes home and sent complaints back to you about your children you never came up to talk to me about it.'

My poor mother had to say: 'I never got a single note or a single complaint from any of them.'

We were pretty loyal to each other as brothers. Of course, there was no such thing as a parent/teacher meeting at that time.

Mai Crowley's husband Amady had a big shop in town. Amady was the son of James Crowley, the first pro-treaty TD in North Kerry. He was a local veterinary surgeon. My grandfather John Pierse was also a local vet at that time.

In 1948 a new era began in our lives. Ration books began to disappear and exotic fruits began to appear. We were in school one day when, after lunch, Mai Crowley's son and his pal arrived with a banana and an orange. We crowded around to see these new fruits. We crowded so much that the two lads climbed up the stairs to show them off and to eat them in front of us. They had a tough job eating them. They did not know they had to peel them first!

My teacher in first class took a great liking to me. She was a Mrs Griffin. Other pupils regarded her as a difficult teacher. Because she took a liking to me, she asked my mother to keep me for a second year in her class. I had in fact started school when I was under four years of age, because I was a 'precocious child'.

For the second year, Mrs Griffin and myself ruled the class with a fairly small stick. When she left the room for any reason I was put in charge, which meant I was the 'teacher's pet', something that gave you both power and problems.

The following year our teacher was Mr Tadhg O'Flaherty, who had a very poor opinion (correctly) of the school. He used to sprinkle disinfectant in the morning, because he thought bugs were coming up from the septic tank under the school. He would also get the farmers' sons to bring in turf because the place was so cold.

Shortly after that, my parents had a row with the local canon, the Fine Gael parish priest, who prior to that had been a great friend of ours. At a meeting my father accused the canon of gross and ghastly inertia in failing to get a new school. It ended a family friendship, but a new school was built in Listowel some years later.

My father was one of the very few people who would stand up to the then powerful clergy. He did not see them as being on an untouchable pedestal. Oddly, I remember most of them respected his views very much.

He was the vet nearly all the parish priests in the locality turned to when needed. The parish priest normally had a bit of parish land, where he kept a cow and calf. Let's not forget, most of them were farmers' sons.

In third class I had the good luck of being with Bryan MacMahon. Indeed, I could write a whole chapter on Bryan MacMahon. He was of course later known as 'The Master', after his most famous book, a recording of which was also broadcast on RTE radio. One of my sons in Germany heard that broadcast, and I have since then been trying to get a copy of the tape. He only got bits of it and he wanted to hear the full programme, as it was the story as told by Bryan. I think listening to Bryan tell the story is far more satisfying than reading it.

Getting back to my school days with Bryan MacMahon; I have two really odd memories of him, outside of the fact that he was a very good and entertaining teacher. He was very much committed to Irish language and culture, and to instilling a love of our town in us. It is a legacy that has remained with me, because I still love Listowel, all its quirks, characters and peculiarities.

My two memories of Bryan, my teacher in 3rd class, were:

That he used to catch me by the side of my cheek as a punishment, hold me up in front of the class, and say: 'Now Master Pierse, why didn't you do your homework last night?' Not nice. You see, I liked going out around the country with my pal, my father. As I got older, I fell in love with books.

I also remember something he told me once. One day, a music inspector was coming to the class, and Bryan asked me not to sing, as I was, 'a crow and a bad one at that'. Not nice, but true. I haven't a note to sing even though I love music.

Moving to the other end of Bryan MacMahon's life. We buried him on the 16th of February 1998. The whole funeral, from my point of view, took from 10:30 in the morning until 4:30 in the evening. There were so many people I knew at it, so many interesting characters, much chat, and dare I say it, entertainment.

His sons, their wives and their children did him proud. An oration was given by Eamon Murphy, son of a great friend of his, Louis Murphy, and an extract from one of his books was read by Gabriel Fitzmaurice, a poet from Moyvane.

Because three of his sons were lawyers, and also because of personal friendship, Mr Justice Hugh O'Flaherty of the Supreme Court attended, as did the President's ADC.

I remember going to O'Carroll's funeral home for Bryan's removal, and being surprised to see a book of his at his feet that I did not have. I thought I had all his books at that stage. Indeed, I had autographed copies of many of them. He used to autograph droves of them for me, and I would send them off to my children who were spread all over the world. I did the same for John B Keane's books – different in content to Bryan's.

The book I didn't have was called *The Final Fling*. The following morning, before the funeral, I called to Danny Hannon's bookstore and asked Danny why I had never heard of this book. He told me the story behind the book. It had just been written and only came off the presses that Thursday.

Apparently, Bryan's sons took a copy of it to Bryan on that Thursday. Bryan saw it and was not too happy with the title, and, remarkably, he was even wondering what he would call his next book. Bryan died the following day, so he was good up to the very end.

At his funeral one of his sons told of how Bryan loved Listowel and Listowel loved him. As an example of the latter he told how the women of Church Street baked loaves of bread that would fit in the letter box opening, when Kitty, Bryan's wife, had died. Now that is how wonderful the women are in our town.

Thoughts on Lady Chatterley & Teachers

Some years before that, when Bryan was about 78 and I was about 50, I met Bryan in Church St, near his home. I had been reading one of Bryan's books. I think it was *The Sound of Hooves*. I had come across what I felt was a fairly 'hot' passage the night before.

At that time, I was personally involved in a local hubbub about the staging of *Lady Chatterley's Lover*, in a fairly explicit fashion I might add, in our former Protestant Church, now St John's Centre.

I said to Bryan: 'Bryan I was rather surprised last night when I read that story. I am surprised at a man of your age writing a *Lady Chatterley's Lover* type of story.' He looked me up and down and said: 'Robert, the difference between you and me is that I can only write about it, you can practise it.'

I forgot to ask him when does one stop practising sex! I do not know yet anyway.

St John's theatre, by the way, is run by the astute Joe Murphy, commonly known as 'Vicar Joe'. Great man and great venue.

I do know that my great grandfather sired his famous son Michael Collins at the age of 75. My father in law, Donal O'Donoghue, used to always say that you would be a full day dead before you would be finished with that sort of thing. You would certainly be three days dead before you stop looking. One should not be saying things like that. No doubt somebody will allege sexual harassment after reading these comments.

I was genuinely annoyed about that Lady Chatterley incident. I wanted to stop it being staged in what had been a church, even if deconsecrated. I had been involved, as an urban councillor, in the handover, and we had assured the donors that the building would be respected.

I thought a cultured town like Listowel should be above that kind of voyeurism. I got a lot of stick from people about it. One councillor took the view that, 'It's great to have a fine looking, half-naked woman in the stage'. What do you think? Is there a country culture that is more sensible than the city culture?

Another great teacher was Michael Keane, any knowledge of history and geography I have certainly comes from him. He used to make us place mountains on maps all over Ireland and Europe with Plasticine. History was always exciting, battles, blood and bullets, and he introduced us to the politics of power.

I met his son, Aidan, at Bryan MacMahon's funeral in 1998 and again I have to comment at how extraordinarily like their father sons become. That is when you get to know people at an age you first knew their father.

I remember Aidan as a youngster fell off a tree and broke his leg. The doctor put on a plaster and said, 'before you climb a tree again, grow a tail like a monkey'.

2018 Update: On the 24/5/2018, I had the privilege of listening to Una Keane playing her beautiful, relaxing music in St John's. Una is the granddaughter of Michael Keane and daughter of Aidan Keane.

We had a neighbour a teacher, Micheál O'Sullivan, who was a great Irishman and Irish speaker. He lived near us on Pound Lane. He was not a fan of 'The Priest'.

I then had a very good relationship with Denis ('Mocky') O'Shea. This was developed during my Intermediate Cert year (now Junior Cert). By some sort of coincidence, I got honours in the three subjects he was teaching me. After I got the results that evening, I saw him talking to another teacher while walking up the street. The other teacher turned around and said, 'Robert, how did you get on'? I replied, 'I passed your two subjects sir'. Mocky O'Shea then said, 'well, how did you get on in mine'? I said, 'I got honours in all three sir'.

I can remember the magnificent smile on his face as he turned to his colleague. From then on, I could do no wrong. After that he would say to me, 'laddie Pierse, will you open your blasted eyes,' when I was trying to phrase and analyse a bit of Latin.

Mocky used pray for me when I was in the sanatorium, and when I came out he organised my tutoring for the matric exam.

❧

The street I walked up after my exam results was the street John B Keane wrote that lovely poem about. The street he looked out on from his upstairs eagle's nest and watched every day. I used to think of John B as someone who wrote about North Kerry with the insight of belonging. As someone said about Shakespeare: 'Others abide our question, thou art free, we ask and ask, thou I smilest and art still.' So here is John B Keane's *The Street*:

I love the flags that pave the walk.
I love the mud between
The funny figures drawn in chalk.

I love to hear the sound
Of drays upon their round,
Of horses and their clock-like walk.
I love to watch the corner people gawk
And hear what underlies their idle talk.

I love to hear the music of the rain.
I love to hear the sound
of yellow waters flushing in the main.
I love the breaks between,
when little boys begin
to sail their paper galleons in the drain.
Grey clouds sail west and silver-tips remain.
The street, thank God, is bright and clean again.

Here, within a single little street,
Is everything that is,
Of pomp and blessed poverty made sweet.
And all that is of love of man and God above.
Of happiness and sorrow and conceit.
Of tragedy and death and bitter-sweet,
Of hope, despair, illusion and defeat.

A golden mellow peace forever clings
Along the little street.
There are so very many lasting things

Beyond the wall of strife.
In our beleaguered life.
There are so many lovely songs to sing
of God and His eternal love that rings
Of simple people and of simple things.

John B had been a reluctant attendee at St Michael's too. Like myself, he was no fan of 'the Priest'.

Also, with us was the late Paddy Rochford. I think that Paddy Rochford started in St Michael's the same day as I did and went on to become principal. Again, time softened him. I remember he was very tough at study when we started.

When my children were going to him he was considered to be 'not too bad', which means, in young people's language, he was probably a softie, and he was probably even softer by the time he retired.

We also had John Molyneaux, who was a Latin teacher. He had a wonderful grasp of grammar, which I am afraid I could never really pick up. John is a golfing madman now, but it takes all sorts doesn't it? Interesting too that two of my fellow pupils at St Michael's went on to become teachers there – Johnny Flaherty and Pat Gibbons, both of whom became writers. Paper got ink in Listowel from many pens.

I think we all were all keen to remain in Listowel. It was unfortunate that so many people who were keen to remain in Listowel had to go. After Christmas was a sad time in Listowel when I was a young lad, one would see the droves of people, young men particularly, heading for the railway station and the boat to England, with their small brown suitcases and Christmas gift scarves.

John B Keane wrote *Many Young Men of 20* about the massive immigration from the area. I think the precipitating event was when half the Ballyduff team emigrated together. John B spent much of his early life in England. A great man John B, who had great time for the 'min with the caps': 'I love to watch the corner people gawk, and hear what underlies their idle talk.'

2019: There is a new Irish stamp showing the brown suitcase.

TB Schooldays

In St Michael's College I had the misfortune of picking up TB, or 'consumption' as it was known at that time.

It was a terrible affliction, it meant all sorts of health regulations, and we were almost quarantined off as a family. My father always refused to believe I had it, even when I was in the sanatorium. I will deal with that someplace else.

To the credit of St Michael's College, it helped. When I came back from the sanatorium, I was only allowed up out of bed for two hours a day. I had been studying while in hospital for the matric exam.

I came home just before Christmas after my second year in the sanatorium. All the teachers of St Michael's College voluntarily, and free of charge, tutored me for an hour each night to try and get me through that exam. And they succeeded! These are the things that make Listowel town such a great town to live in.

I love that song, *The Town I Loved So Well*. I feel it was written about Listowel – thank you Phil Coulter.

The Tide & the Corkman

There is not much of a tide here on this small island caye off Belize. Maybe it is the storm that is making the sea and the sandy shore look the same all day.

That reminds me of a story of an innocent Corkman, Tom, who came to Ballybunion to get some seawater to take home for his mother's 'pains'. Seawater with some seaweed in it was a well-known cure, or so it was said.

He came from the North Cork county bounds in his horse and car – it was before my time; or maybe it wasn't!

Horse and cars, donkey's cars, and horse and traps were the main means of moving around in my young world.

Anyway, the Corkman arrived at the top of the cliff in the men's strand. No woman was allowed on it then, as they had the ladies strand at the other side of the castle green.

The Corkman had a large churn, as he had been instructed to bring home about 20 gallons of seawater. The tide was in, right up to the bottom off the cliff.

There was a not so innocent Kerryman standing nearby, a county council worker, a man of obvious importance, or so our Corkman thought.

He said to this official looking person, who was leaning thoughtfully on his shovel: 'Are you in charge here?' 'I am,' said your man guessing he might gain something.

The Corkman then explained the purpose of his visit, the 20 gallons of seawater for his mother's pains. Our council man says, 'I will have to go down for it for you'. 'And sir,' said the Corkman, 'what will that cost me'?

The Kerryman's reply was, '1 penny a gallon – one shilling and eight pennies in all'.

Tom paid up. He took his churn of 20 gallons of Atlantic sea home. His mother was greatly improved by the seawater, so much so that she had it all drank by the end of the winter, or rubbed herself down with it, in the privacy of the room at the back with the fire that she slept in because of the heat. Heat was good for the 'pains' too.

In houses back then, the back of the fire room was always kept for the old pair, somewhere for them after the farm was transferred.

That April, she sent the son back to Ballybunion for a new supply. The council worker was still at the top of the cliff leaning on the shovel, but Great God the tide was out.

Tom, the Corkman was frightened. He said, 'my dear friend, you are running out of water'. The council man looked at the churn, remembered Tom, and said, 'well, there is great demand from people with pains'.

'So, can I get any?' asked the Corkman. 'You can,' says the Kerryman, 'but the price is now 2 pence a gallon!' This was a whole three shillings and four pence. That was the price of banbhs (piglets) in Kanturk that year.

However, the son was a good son and paid up. Unfortunately, his sow had no banbhs the following year, so he never came back to Ballybunion the following year or since that we heard of.

The following year, Tom, the Corkman, had to travel all the way to Lisdoonvarna to get a wife. You see his father was dead and the mother's pains were so bad she could no longer milk the cows, nor could she stand on the wynnds of hay. In that part of Cork, they made these big wynnds of hay that some lively person had to stand on to build them up. They can be ten feet tall.

So, three days in Lisdoonvarna became necessary. His aunt went with him, his mother's younger sister, to make sure he did not get fooled by a *bean Domhnach* (Sunday woman).

You see the shawl was going out of fashion with these young women. Since they got the vote a lot of young women were forgetting their station, the aunt said. Not dressing properly and fooling the men.

So off went Tom and the aunt. The aunt got the best matchmaker and spent an hour plying him with expensive whiskey. She explained the case well and within three days of tough bargaining over the fortune the match was made.

The girl was a fine, strong, weighty, and well-developed young woman. Her fortune was only £150, but she could cook and sew. She had years of helping her father on the farm as her younger brother had gone to join the Gardaí. They were a very respectable family from the Tipperary/Cork border.

The 'bindings' were made in Charleville. The mother kept the room at the back of the fire in the 'bindings', and would be given a pound of butter a week and 3 potatoes per day along with other food and necessities, as the pension wasn't great.

The 'fortune' was paid. A fortune was important, as it meant the wife could say she paid for her 'stand on the floor'.

The following year the young woman was expecting during haymaking in July. They were all in a pucker, but as luck would have it didn't her garda brother get holidays. He came down by train and solved the problem. Tom thought it was very strange for someone not to have work for two weeks.

Then, even more strangely, Mick the guard said to Tom he only worked five and a half days in the week. 'No wonder the country was in the state it was in,' Tom said. You could not run a farm like that, thought Tom.

2018: You still can't!

You know it's a good job wives never formed a trade union. 'Feed them well and they'll work away,' Tom would often say!

That silly story had the kids roaring with laughter last night. Good medicine in a storm.

Helena's Shoes

The sea was something my daughter's mother-in-law, Helene Kolb, saw for the first time when she came from Germany in 1990 to the marriage in Listowel of her son, Jürgen, to our daughter Máire.

One day we went with her for a stroll along the golden sands of Ballybunion. Olive and I saw the wave coming in and moved up a bit from it. Helena did not and the wave went up over her shoes. She was dumbfounded. She baffled us when she told us she had never seen a wave or the sea until then.

She loved Ireland. Loved things like wild furze, blackberry bushes and birds. These treasures are gone from Germany due to the over use of land, fertilizers, acid rain and the likes.

We should watch our environment more. It really is important. It is suffering from abuse on a daily basis worldwide. It annoys me the way politicians, local ones mostly, pull 'Section 4 strokes' under the planning law for pink bungalow monstrosities along the coast.

Anything for a few votes! Democracy is probably the weakest form of government, but it does not get the care it should from us, the *demos*. Ordinary citizens should be extraordinarily careful about the law and lawmakers.

Of course, one should add what Churchill said: 'Democracy is the poorest form of government until you compare it to everything else.'

Helene had grown up, grew into young womanhood and got married, at the end of the Second World War.

Her late Husband was a prisoner of war (POW) by the French. He always hated the French – we learnt from him that cruelty towards POWs wasn't one sided.

I always remember one little story she told me about the Marshall aid. She had a leak in her roof but no slate could be got. She got a tin of beans at an American food centre. When the feast of eating it was finished, she got a stone, carefully hammered the tin flat and put it in the hole in the roof. It worked; the Marshall Plan was working!

The mention of Churchill reminded me of a little story. His cranky friend, George Bernard Shaw, sent Churchill two tickets to the opening night of one of his plays, adding, 'bring a friend, if you have one'! Churchill replied: 'Can't go to your first night. Will go to your second night, if there is one.'

A Funeral

I remember the very impressive funeral of Jorg, Helena's husband – the man who had been a POW. Olive could not go for some reason. Funerals are always important to country people, be it Ireland, Germany, or China.

I flew to Zurich, where Máire met me and on we went over the (almost invisible) border to Germany, to Kisslegg to be precise.

I was tired but Jürgen, my son-in-law, found a nice sunny spot at the side of the cow stall for me. He gave me a big jug of hot soup. I did not realise until much later why it tasted so good, and why it bucked me up so much.

Jürgen, now a chef of international repute, had put a good glass of whiskey into the soup. It had a big effect on a pioneer!

The funeral the following day was like the old Irish funerals. The farmers dressed in their best, with respectful black coats and hats, and their hands hard from toil.

They reminded me of those decent, respectful farmers at my father's funeral (RIP).

We walked behind the coffin from the Kisslegg church, after a long mass that took over an hour. The coffin was placed upright in the family grave in the neat and flowerful graveyard.

I was introduced to many mourners by Helena. I think it did much for Máire in the village, that her Catholic father had come to bury her Catholic father in-law.

I sent Máire a bit of a dowry as they were doing up their restaurant. This had a big effect. The bank managers of both banks came out to dinner the following Saturday. Kisslegg had its grapevine too. Money talks, it don't sing and dance but it sure talks.

I could never understand how Germany recovered so quickly. It seems there are a number of reasons: The women who cleared the rubble; the government structures which tried to instil a revival spirit; the allies by-passed villages and small towns in their attempt to get to Berlin before the

Russians, which saved the towns from destruction; the Marshall Plan; and the foreign currency the American troops introduced. They built factories first – then houses.

Most of all, it was the will of the people not to accept defeat.

I will admit, the great thing about the common market is there has been no major European war since it was introduced.

One woman there told me about her experiences in Dresden as an eight year-old, when the war was on. Her father had been conscripted and wounded on the western front. He was given three months leave, but this was cut short and he was sent to the Russian front.

The allies were bombing Germany regularly, but they went to a cellar when the sirens started. They had a packed suitcase permanently inside the backdoor. Then came the night when the allies bombed Dresden, killing over 100,000 civilians.

This eight year-old girl and her mother realised that, one by one, the streets were being flattened. What was happening was 'pattern' bombings. The bombing radiated out from the church spire, which the bombers left standing as a landmark.

So, mother and child grabbed the suitcase and ran through the bombs to a field where they found a crater. Her mother made her lie down, then put herself on top of the child, put clothes over both of them, then put a suitcase half-filled with earth on top of the clothes.

They survived, but no other neighbour on that street survived. Their house collapsed into their cellar on a direct hit. War is an evil thing, said Padraig Pearse. He was right.

2019: I wonder are they undertones of this historical animosity in the Brexit mess? When I was in Germany, I remember one man saying: 'They carpet-bombed us; the old, the women and the children.' He was so bitter about the British. I wonder will the EU last with all this historical animosity?

One UK voter has said to me: 'The Germans have it in for us, and the French and the rest of them have forgotten what we did for them.' I wonder.

Sleep

Well now, Olive says 10 minutes to tea time. I am hungry. So, I had better finish off this portion of script. I expect that there will be a lot of chat and cheer over the meal. The wind definitely seems less.

I have been writing at the cabin table. Kevin has been fishing with the lads. He is throwing a bucket of water over the 'gutting table' where they have been busy. He always throws the offal into the sea – for tomorrow's fish!

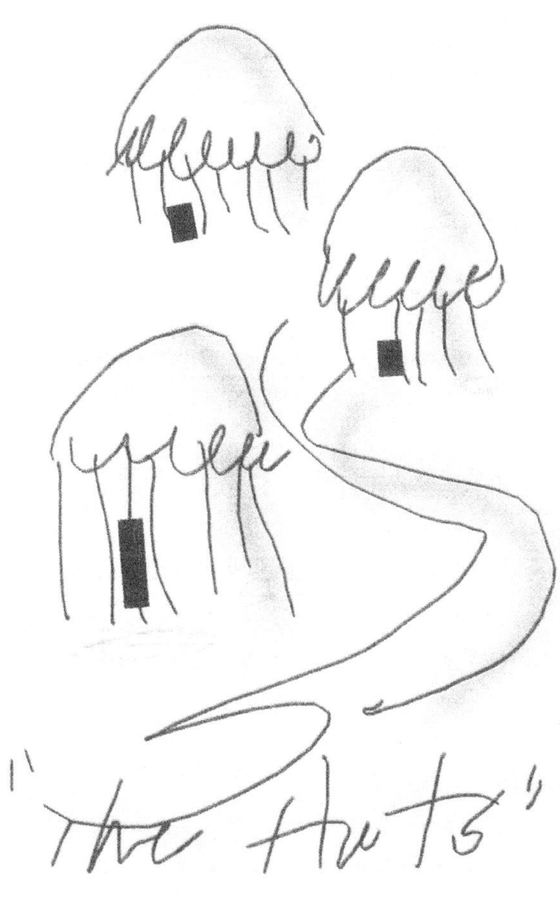

We'll then try to 'wrap up the ravelled sleeve of care' and get sleep, the innocent sleep, the death of each day's night.

Oh heavens, I am back in gloom in this disappearing island. Think positively Robert, still a good bit left. I think the storm is abating.

What foolish and wayward thoughts slide into a lawyer's mind!

Apologies to WWW (Wonderful William Wordsworth). Is WWW going to be an internet code? Not that I am much good at that as Olive is my cyber chick. She is a www. too – a 'wonderful wife and woman'!

She who must be obeyed calls me now. So, it's shoes on, jacket on, bend low, hold hands (I like that bit) and head into the wind! Off to the *Seagull* cabin. I will tell you tomorrow our night's chat.

DAY SIX: STILL STRANDED!

Well now, what have I to report on Day Six? Bad morning again, but not as bad as yesterday morning. It is rough out there. Kevin says it is very unusual for these tropical storms to go on this long. However, we are in the hands of the Man Above and He does not wear a cap that I know of.

Of course, when I mentioned that Man Above last night it raised all sorts of issues. I am old fashioned about the Creator. I simply accept that something (the beginning, the galaxy, the quark; call it what you want) is there and eternal.

I wonder where Harry the hare is and how he is surviving? Let's go back.

In the Beginning!
Adam was hanging around the Garden of Eden feeling very lonely, so God asked him: 'What's wrong with you?'

Adam said he did not have anyone to talk to. God replied that he would make Adam a companion and it would be a woman.

God said: 'This pretty lady will gather food for you, she will cook for you, and when you discover clothing, she will wash it for you. She will always agree with every decision you make, and she will not nag you. She will always be the first to admit she was wrong when you've had a disagreement. She will love you and always praise you!'

Adam was impressed and asked God: 'But what will a woman like this cost?' 'An arm and a leg,' God replied.

Then Adam asked: 'What can I get for a rib?'

Of course, the rest is history ......

Maybe I should not write that sort of comment. It didn't go down well with these new-fangled women. The revolution in the role of women in society is actually very welcome (in most aspects). Great stuff most of it. Like the independence and wisdom of my wife, 3 daughters and new *iníon céile*.

I wonder will any women read this anyway? It is not a romantic novel. I myself see the romance of nature here – the swaying trees, the dancing waves!

The modern world has a romance with science. The 21st century is going to be very interesting. Pity I will not be around for much of it.

I believe there has been more change in this 20th century than in the whole of history before that. Think about that. The changes in thought and society brought by the humanist movement are reflected in consumer-ism, the decline in respect for authority.

Think about the wonderful world we live in at the end of that century. Enjoy it and mind it.

I do not know how, but the kids moved me away from religion and philosophy to romance. I began telling them about how Olive and I met all those years ago (July 1958). I will tell you the version I gave. Olive gave her own version – but I want her to write her own book. Now, would that not be very interesting? I told her just now what I am writing about. Again, she says no one is going to be interested.

Romance

It was in Dunquin, in the guesthouse of the 'Princess', Daughter of the King of the Blaskets, that I met a wonderful girl. She has been my wife, or rather I her husband, for the best part of 40 years.

I still remember my first sight of her. Her nice leg first of course, coming out of the back of a black Volkswagen Beetle car.

I was smitten very quickly and fortunately so was she. It was really when I was working with her trying to save the life of her dog, who had been poisoned (she was a medical student at the time) that we gave each other 'The Look' into each other's eyes. That made my heart go really humpty bump – still does you know!

I had been sent by my mother to the Gaeltacht with my brother, Tom, to see that he learned Irish for some exam. I was the minder.

I took my fishing rod, but it was I who was hooked by my Phantom of Delight from the first moment she 'gleamed upon my sight'.

We were together there only five days, but that was sufficient. We actually promised each other we would marry on our fourth day, but agreed only after we were both qualified. Provided we didn't change our mind of course. What a wonderful event it was, and it continues.

We were separating the following day. She was off to east Kerry and UCC. I stayed to fish and dream, as well as looking after my brother, Tom.

Do know that poem *She Was a Phantom of Delight*? If not, you should you know because fellows, even young fellows, use it as a romantic guide. In case you cannot put your hands on it here it goes – I think I can remember only the first verse, which may be just as well:

> She was a Phantom of Delight
> When first she gleamed upon my sight;
> A lovely apparition, sent
> To be a moment's ornament;
> Her eyes as stars of Twilight fair;
> Like Twilight, too, her dusky hair;
> But all things else about her drawn
> From May-time and the cheerful Dawn;
> A dancing Shape, an Image gay,
> To haunt, to startle, and way-lay.

That is how I saw Olive in 1958 in Dunquin, West Kerry.

Hold on! 2018: I recently remembered where I left my book of William Wordsworth poems in my study, and I read the poem again. The last stanza caught my attention; I felt it represented my view of Olive 40 years on.

I have since read it to my beloved, 60 years later:

> And now I see with eye serene
> The very pulse of the machine;
> A Being breathing thoughtful breath,
> A Traveller between life and death;
> The reason firm, the temperate will,

Endurance, foresight, strength and skill;
A perfect Woman, nobly planned,
To warm, to comfort, and command;
And yet a Spirit still, and bright
With something of angelic light.

Yes indeed! I am touched with the magic hand of true marriage. Young people urgently need to understand that marriage is a truly wonderful institution. A huge commitment produces huge lifelong dividends.

I hope I am not the last of the romantics. Olive and I still love the romance.

2018: Romance still going strong!

Olive's Father

Olive's father (Dad) and I got on very well. He was a teacher, had an LLB law degree and was a former Fianna Fail TD. We had great chats. While in Dunquin, we disposed of a dead dog's body together. He was such a good man.

Olive told a story from when we first met, about going home in the car with her parents.

Olive's mother (Mom), said: 'They were nice boys, but I don't think we will see them again.'

Olive's Dad however looked in the mirror and said in Irish, *beidh muid ag scríobh*, (we will be writing). He knew I was smitten.

Mom thought we were 'nice boys' for a particular reason. My mother had ordered myself and Tom to say the Rosary every night, and Mom was impressed by this: you never know what the Rosary can do for you.

The Binchys & my Favourite Book

We discussed last night what book we would bring to the island if we were marooned on it. Some people opted for a big compendium book by Maeve Binchy or some such writer.

I was in UCD with Maeve Binchy. A lot of the courses in those years were cross faculty. Maeve was studying arts and many of the courses in the arts faculty were attended by us law students – philosophy, psychology, history, Irish and many more.

It is different now. There is more concentration on the practice of law and less on the theory, or more on procedure and less on the basis of law and human motivation.

Maeve was a great talker – still is, judging by what I see on TV.

I was invited to her parent's home several times – what a generous household! I remember there used to be a big platter of sausages, rashers and black puddings in the centre of the table. As a student, it was marvellous.

I met William Binchy BL Sr and junior there. Some years later I began briefing William Sr. He was a great counsel. He was very interested in the law as theory as well as practise.

Later still I came to admire William Jr, that great champion of the right to life – what a man! I even went along to Trinity now and then to give a lecture at his legal seminars. I really do admire William – he is a great writer of law books and law articles, all of which I read avidly.

I would never admit it publicly, but Maeve's stuff is not for me.

Update: Maeve Binchy passed away in August 2012, RIP.

I share William Binchy Jr's disbelief at the recent amendment to the constitution. That the people of Ireland deliberately voted to give the country's politicians the power to legislate for the killing of unborn children shocks me.

I think is the start of a new civil war. Doctors being paid to assist in killing – shameful! We go back to that poet-politician, WB Yeats:

> The ceremony of innocence is drowned,
> The best lack all conviction
> While the worst, are full of passionate intensity.

Well, what book would I like to have brought? I plumbed for the *Good News Bible*. You know the edition that has those nifty drawings in it? Came out about 20 years ago? It's the Catholic version. However, I remember when trying to get an older text, a more authentic translation, I was given a Protestant edition. I always found the books by Protestant writers to be clearer on the nature and purpose of the 'good news'.

I believe, even if I was marooned here for a month or even three, I would not have got to the end of its subtle meaning and depth of thought, or understood the principles that the Bible contains.

Take the opening scene – about Creation. A story of huge depth. A mystery we have not solved yet. What is the nature of a Creator of a world such as ours, of a universe such as ours? Is he a he or a she, a HE or a SHE – obviously no!

Is the Creator a designer, who made Adam and Eve directly from energy and material, and out of 'nothing'?

Take the Adam and Eve story – obviously an attempt at explaining the mystery of Creation. Even when it comes to evolution, we still ask who comes from where? Who? What? When? Where?

Adam was like the person who wants a pint after the pub is shut, even though he knows it is illegal. Or the person who covets gold or wants to race a car at high risk.

Adam had everything except an apple. He is jealous; his pride is offended. He did not need the apple, but he was prepared to take God on and try to 'best' him. How often do I see that in compensation cases, in disputes about land, boundaries, and right of way? Or, worse still in family disputes. Then the blame game follows, just as it does today. No one takes responsibility. Adam blames God and Eve; Eve blames the snake.

'The woman (Eve) you (God) put here with me gave me the fruit, and I ate it,' says Adam.

Then Eve says, 'the Snake tricked me into it'. As God had created the snake the blame game had gone full-circle, back to God.

Looking for the other guy's apple is going strong still. Most law cases have an element of it. The blame game is stronger than ever, especially in politics.

Wisdom

In the *Old Testament*, the *Book of Wisdom* is one I like. Wisdom would be a huge prize if one had it. It would explain all and give meaning to all the apparent foolishness of life. But what is it?

Unfortunately, I do not agree with Solomon who says: 'Wisdom shines bright and never grows dim: Those who love her and look for her can easily find her.'

I suppose it is I who am dim. I have looked for her but I haven't found her, except for finding a wise wife. Maybe that is all I will ever find and maybe that is it. Now there are pointers I learned from my search. If you are searching, here are the tips:

> Get up early in the morning to find her
> Wisdom begins when you sincerely want to learn
> To love her is to keep her laws
> To keep her laws is to be certain of immortality

The Book of Wisdom also says:

> To fasten your attention on Wisdom is to gain perfect
>   understanding
> If you look for her, you will find peace of mind
> She is kind and will be with you in your every thought

I know I have not found her, have you? Let's keep searching. Wisdom is a great prize. It's all about having full knowledge of truth and action.

I was going to go on about my favourite part of the *New Testament*, about St Paul. It is too late? Maybe your concentration is flagging too?

In Ireland religion has become a forgotten word. People do not read St Paul anymore – what a pity.

Unfortunately, because some of the Christian messengers do not practise what they preach, the message is being set aside. *A la carte* Christianity is the practice of the day. Now they take just the nice bits, the ones they like. People say that religion has destroyed itself in Ireland. I hope not.

I am hopeful it will continue, and it could even last another 2,000 years – provided man has not destroyed the world.

Well you know Jesus's preachers, the 12 apostles, contained Judas, the traitor and weaklings like St Peter who was supposed to be his rock. So, if

HE could not find perfect apostles, why should we be shooting down the message because of the conduct of the messengers?

Religion is a pathway towards values in life. Its teachings are often unpalatable, but that does not mean they are wrong. It does not mean Jesus' message of 'love one another' is wrong. Maybe its wisdom helps peaceful understanding, peace of mind and it should be with us in our every thought!

As I wrote previously, I like Chesterton's remark: The great failure of Christianity is that it was never practised! I am going to be accused of being preachy, so I will move on.

I will go out of this shaking cabin and scout around, not that there is much to scout around on. However, it might be coming up to breakfast time in the *Seagull*, our social centre.

Olive also wants to say the Morning Offering and its appendages to thank God for letting us survive so far. It is amazing that the island didn't disappear, or that the cabin didn't get damaged too much in this storm. Just one of the steps washed away.

I wonder what is the religion of Belize? If it is basically Spanish, it is Catholic. But it was British Honduras, so maybe it isn't. All of the few people I have met here have been easy going and friendly, and don't seem to bother much about religion.

The 'Min' with the Caps; Just a Few More Thoughts!
You might have predicted that those views on women (that they are the dominant sex) that I rashly spoke out last night went down like a lead balloon. A romantic son rushed to their unneeded rescue. I am contrite.

I now want to pen another few words about that rare breed: the 'men (pronounced 'min') with the caps'.

They specialise in giving directions. They are prepared to sit on the fence in some remote area awaiting the arrival of the lost city slicker in his big car.

Window goes down: 'How can I get to Cork, sir, from here?' The voice from the leather seat says.

Now the man is pleased at being called 'sir' – very unrepublican – but there you are! The man climbs down, raises his cap to give air to his brain through his hair and then scratches his head to give more air (O2) to the brain. He pronounces, from the depths of his profundity:

Well I would not start for Cork from here. It is a bad place to start from, but I suppose you can't start from anywhere else today; but bear it in mind in the future. Now, boyeen, go south to Lerrig Cross. When you come there, don't turn right, don't go straight ahead but take to the left – that is the road to Tralee. There is a shop there with petrol pumps but they tell me that the juice is dear there so don't stop. Anyway, there is a contrary dog there. Go on then about 2 miles to the Quarry Cross. You can't see the quarry unless you look over the ditch. Instead of looking over the ditch, bless yourself and turn right. Go on then until you have to turn and go left. Go on again until you have to turn and go left. Now let me see ... about a mile on you will have to turn. Now you could go right there and reach the main road; or maybe you should go left and take a shortcut. The shortcut is a bad road to meet a tractor on. Well now it's up to yourself. Now it's time to be off. But before you go do you think Kerry will beat Cork again this year in the Munster Final? Or is your mother from Cork, because if she is she will always expect the Cork fellows to win. Women are like that. Good luck now – you will need it!

The min with the caps quickly advise you about your life as they consider themselves specialists. They might say:

- Love of life brings a life of love.
- Hatred is a wasted emotion. It's like talking a slow poison and then waiting for the other person to die.
- The pint after hours in the sweetest, especially if that sergeant is on patrol disturbing the peace of the working (sometimes) classes.
- Two words you should never use are always and never.
- Time waits for no man or woman.
- Short debts make long friends.
- May you be dead two days before the devil knows it.

We also had a competition for best *seanfhocail* last night:

> *Ní hé lá na gaoithe lá no scolbh*
> (A windy day is not the day for thatching)

> *Aithníonn ciaróg ciaróg eile*
> (One earwig knows another earwig)

> *Ar scáth a chéile a mhaireann na daoine*
> (People live in each other's shadows)

> *Níl aon tinteán mar do thinteán féin*
> (There is no fireplace like your own fireplace)

> *Ní haon ualach do bhrat*
> (Your cloak is no burden)

We used up the last bit of cereal this breakfast. We were very hungry. I wonder what we'll have tomorrow?

I notice the bread is being toasted which is not a great sign of freshness – we are cutting the odd bit off for Scruffy. I am told the green on it is penicillin. Scruffy believes that too!

Anyway, I wonder what Harry the hare is eating? Still no sign of Harry. I predict tomorrow will suddenly be better.

South America

I was in South America once – one of those trips we made every four years with the International Bar Association.

We were in Brazil first. What I remember most about Brazil was its poverty. There were warnings of pickpockets and bag-snatchers everywhere. But there was also its beauty.

We saw a beautiful cathedral in Rio de Janeiro, but every single window was broken; smashed in protest against this island of apparent wealth in the midst of dreadful poverty. And there is the famous statue of Christ the Redeemer, with his arms open to the world.

I went for a swim on the famous Copacabana beach. Olive didn't go in, she sat on a rock watching me. When I came out, I shouted at her: 'Don't move there is a big rat underneath you.' I went and cleared the rat.

We went on to Brasilia, the official capital. A truly beautiful city. I think the one architect designed it. Oscar Niemeyer was his name. Each ministry has its own façade appropriate to its purpose. The Department of Agriculture had a plough; Justice had the blind lady holding a scales. It also had stunning churches, designed, apparently, by a professed atheist.

It was a stunning city!

Actually, South America has stunning scenery. I was sorry we did not get around more. We got to see the magnificent Iguazu Falls. I flew over them in a helicopter.

There is a 007 film with a lot of stunning scenery. Actually, a lot of these films are made at wonderful locations.

I was in Chile as well, but my recollections are few. It was hot, noisy and poor. One paid a few cents to read the paper or a comic. These were chained to a wooden board under the watchful eye of a man with a stick.

We went on to Peru and saw the amazing Machu Picchu. I will never forget the young boy, of about seven or eight years of age, coming up to be at the bottom of Machu Picchu, saying, 'you speaky American, you have dollar'. The dollar was king everywhere I went.

One could write a book about South America – go there!

Morality and Words

Why do I come back to this? Well we discussed aspects last night. You are getting fed up with me? Skip the next few pages, I will not be offended.

I find the morality of the Catholic Church and other Christian churches generally very acceptable. This is because it seems to me to be based on reasonableness, love and nature. I think it is the distilled wisdom of the Jewish tradition on one hand, and the rationality of Aristotle and Thomas Aquinas on the other. I don't expect you to believe that and know

I am neither a philosopher nor a theologian. It is my private view and it sustains me.

I am not keen on ritualism, those bearded statues of God. My Creator, my God; He is the uncaused cause, the first mover and shaker. He is the designer, and the evolutionary planner.

I think that we simply cannot understand God in the context of a cause – at least I do not bother my very finite brain with trying to understand the riddle of concepts. What is 'good' or 'evil'?

As a lawyer much of my life is spent considering the meaning of words. Courts spend much time interpreting the meaning of words.

Take 'careless' as an example. Cases abound about carelessness – careless driving, carelessness at work and so on. Lawyers call it negligence. We nit-pick the circumstance of an 'accident' – an unfortunate word as most incidents we call accidents aren't accidents at all but careless events.

As I wrote yesterday, the main law about carelessness is based on the parable of the Good Samaritan. We have a duty to be caring, which comes from our human nature.

The Pope

I have been baffled recently by our Pope, John Paul II. I am one of his admirers, as anyone in the last quarter or third of his life should be. His courage and intellect are inspirational.

My view of the Pope is that when it comes to his public appearances all over the world, he is so, so modern, yet his doctrine is so traditional.

I found the key to understanding Pope John Paul II and his teaching in a book I was reading recently by Fr Hughes, given to me by my priest brother-in-law, Fr Gearóid of Fenit. Find the exact quote below.

The point is the Gospels are not presented as words of reason but are a record of what Jesus said and did with Divine Authority. You therefore have to accept them in faith rather than with reason, they are God's rules for stated roles of life; such as love your neighbour as yourself, do good to those that hate you, bless those who curse you and many more.

All of these are difficult, but I think they are based on reason also. If we did all of these things then there would be no more trouble between neighbours, between sections of communities, between states, and between ideologies.

Read the words below; isn't that the Polish Pope for you? As it happens, I was in Krakow the night the Pope died. Very moving.

I do not think Father Hughes was fair to my friend St Paul in this quote. Paul's theology is usually very reasoned and reasonable. Philip Hughes:

> The new doctrine, the New Testament, is not offered to the world as a reasoned philosophy. Its teachers do not seek to convince by any argumentation from principles, by any system of proof and dedication. It is presented as an indivisible body of truth to be received whole from the teacher, as he himself received it, and to be so received, not on any personal judgement of the reasonableness of its detail, but on the authority of the teacher. Nothing is more characteristic of St Paul's methods, no note so frequently sounded as this. It is to be, all through the centuries, the one answer of the church to innovators, its one practical test of truth.
>
> (*History of the Church*, Philip Hughes)

Update 2019: Jeremy Murphy, my editor, is also editing the late Fr Gearóid O'Donnchadha's final book; *Why? The Quest for Meaning in the Third Millennium: A Journey Through Science, Philosophy & Spirituality*. Why not have a read of it when it comes out. Fascinating man, Gearóid.

Fish & Paper

Kevin, Seán and Paul have just shouted into the cabin to come out as the fish are throwing themselves up on the beach, frightened of the sharks. No love your neighbour there. I go.

I see Scruffy awaiting. I wonder how Harry the hare is doing? Odd animal to bring on this small island. Odder still to see him playing with Scruffy on a Saturday. I must stretch my legs.

Well I am back. I had of course to visit the toilet. Not the most salubrious of places. It's up near the caretaker's hut, which is the highest point on the island. There is no such thing as a toilet, just the waiting sea with a current to remove any business.

Now I am a regular visitor, as that is where I get my supply of paper. My notepad is full. My *Irish Jurist* is full. The toilet paper seems to reappear mysteriously overnight, usually with 2 spare rolls of rather abrasive paper. I have not been numbering the sheets, so this is going to be hard to make sense of, if I ever want it to!

Love

I developed a 'feeling' for St Paul when I was a reader at Mass in Listowel. I never knew why I was dropped from that job. I think someone probably felt it was not inappropriate for a lawyer to read the words of Jesus.

I began to appreciate St Paul because of the beautiful way he reasoned matters in his letters. The one I particularly like is his first letter to the Corinthians. Corinth had a multi-party view of religions, and so had a statue to the unknown God in case they missed some God, or just in case one cannot really know God.

Paul's view of love in verse 13 of this first letter to his converts in Corinth is so lovely that I have to include it. You often hear it at weddings. I like weddings – such hope and trust. Paul of Tarsus wrote:

> If I speak in the tongues of men and of angels, but have not love, I am a noisy gong or a clanging cymbal. And if I have prophetic powers, and understand all mysteries and all knowledge, and if I have all faith, so as to remove mountains, but have not love, I am nothing. If I give away all I have, and if I deliver my body to be burned, but have not love, I gain nothing.
>
> Love is patient and kind; love is not jealous or boastful; it is not arrogant or rude. Love does not insist of its own way; it is not irritable or resentful; it does not rejoice at wrong, but rejoices in the right. Love bears all things, believes all things, hopes all things, endures all things.
>
> Love never ends; as for prophecies, they will pass away; as for tongues, they will cease; as for knowledge, it will pass away. For our knowledge is imperfect and our prophecy is imperfect; but when the perfect comes, the imperfect will pass away. When I was a child, I spoke like a child, I thought like a child, I reasoned like a child; when I became a man, I gave up childish ways. For now we see in a mirror dimly, but then face to face. Now I know in part; then I shall understand fully, even as I have been fully understood. So faith, hope, love abide, these three; but the greatest of these is love.

Now isn't that well thought out? It appeals to reason as well as faith and emotion.

I have been particularly blessed by a life of love. I have and do love my wife, my children (all 10 of them), their spouses and now their progeny, my parents and siblings and so many more around me. So, I believe in St Paul's words.

I do not accept that such a man could be anti-woman, as he is often portrayed. The view that he is anti-women is based on an earlier remark in that first letter to the Corinthians: 'It is well for a man not to touch a woman.' He was of course replying to a letter from a very divided group of early Christians. If you read the later portion of his letter (the bit I quoted above) you will see a very different and loving St Paul.

Many of his letters end with greetings to women. In Galatians he writes about equality in a way that was startling for his time:

> There is neither Jew nor Greek, there is neither slave nor free,
> there is neither male nor female, for you are all one in Christ Jesus.

Oddly, I have never gone to Corinth in Greece – must do sometime. Greece is the cradle of much of our Western thought on philosophy, values, democracy and law. What a treasury of wisdom. I could write a whole book on our trip to Greece. The western world is still basking in the sunshine of ancient Greek culture, civilisation and philosophy.

When I was in Athens, they told me there was nothing in Corinth. I wonder does the historical enmity and jealousy between Athens and Corinth still exist?

I often wonder how the Greeks thought and talked so much about equality and yet tolerated and enforced slavery? Wasn't it Aristotle who said: 'You must treat equals as equals; and unequals as unequals.'

One story I recounted from Greece involves tax. None of us like tax, or some of the purposes for which it is used.

We were crossing from one island to the other by boat, and when we arrived we decided to visit a very hospitable restaurant.

Mama Mia discovered it was one of our birthdays, so a great night of Irish & Greek friendship was had. Such fun and food!

I remember talking to the owner. He had such a large family, and was very proud of the fact. He was very impressed by the size of mine, even though I explained to him that I was not the head of the family, Olive was. Olive, of course, assured him I was, and Olive is Olive.

I remember discussing taxes. He said he didn't like taxes so he didn't pay them. I asked him how he got away with that, and he explained to me that his son was the official tax collector, and he never asked his father for tax.

No wonder Greece is in such a financial mess!

The Irish Constitution expresses similar views on equality to the Greeks, but they are applied for the purpose of positive discrimination and not for the negative aspects of the concept.

See *Article 40.1* which reads:

> All citizens shall as human persons, be held equal before the law. This shall not be held to mean that the State shall on its enactments have due regard to differences of capacity physical and moral, and of social function.

Of course, the drafters of the USA Constitution also had noble sentiments of equality but tolerated slavery. Funny things words!

St Paul you know studied law. Maybe that is why I can identify with his writing. But of course law was, among the Jews at the time of Jesus and Paul, the law of God and the prophets. In a way it was a law of morality and religious practices which has survived in different forms in the nature of man's reasoning.

'Morality' remains much talked about and much abused. I suppose it is like 'law' and 'justice' – much talked about but still much abused. But then the situation is like Humpty Dumpty (or was it the Mad Hatter?), people want these words to mean what 'I', the great 'I', want them to mean. Politicians are great at that.

I came across an unusual reference to St Paul recently in a startlingly unlikely case. It was a 1976 case of what the UK Money Lenders Act, in all its complexities, called *Oratipa -v- Manso Investments*. In his judgement Walton J quoted and said:

> There is a great text in the Galatians:
> 'Once you trip on its entails
> Twenty-nine distinct Dominations,
> One is sure, if the others fail.'

I can think of no better description of the complexities of the Money Lenders Act.

Obviously Judge Walton was no fan of moneylenders, but then Jesus wasn't either. He seems to have lost his temper with them and lashed them! He would be sued for that now.

I said before if I had to choose one book for a desert island, it would be the Bible, once it includes the letters of St Paul, but of course they are in the Good News version, so I will stick to that.

Read them for their logic, strength and wisdom, even if they often take the form of simple stories for a simple audience. Odd how Jesus wrote nothing and Paul such a lot, although he never met Jesus – or did he on the road to Damascus? What a pity that part of the world is still in turmoil.

Update: We got to Greece again in 2009 – before the crash. How wonderful Athens was and many islands. I went to Socrates' prison, it is there as you come down from the Acropolis, and the nearby marketplace was where St Paul spoke.

I could write a whole book about that trip. Go there if you can. Read the wisdom of its philosophers, and learn about its culture, its language and its achievements. Why do civilisations decay – jealousy and greed?

Travels to Downpatrick

I have another, very different reason for remembering the words of St Paul. I was very active about 30 years ago in twinning my town, lovely Listowel, with that delightful town, Downpatrick. We, the urban councils, worked at twinning the towns through an organisation called Co-Operation North. We still are twinned towns!

I have many stories about that twinning, but one hears so much about things like it nowadays that we have become news-saturated and turned off.

This is especially because the media are bad-news specialists. They are mostly so dour and destructive, those people in these newsrooms. Bad news is their good news.

The first time I went to a twinning exchange in Downpatrick it was very stressful.

I was, as chairman of Listowel UDC, to spend the first day up there with Downpatrick's council's chairman, Cecil Maxwell. I learnt he was a verger in the cathedral (Church of Ireland), high up with the Unionists, a postmaster and so on. Olive and I, after much discussion, decided the only thing I could talk to him about was St Patrick, who is supposed to be buried there.

So, on our way to the magnificent cathedral in Cecil's car, we start discussing St Patrick.

We view the grave, but as we headed out of town Cecil told me, pointing at a small church, that this was the church of Sábháil (he pronounced it 'Saul').

'Oh,' I say, 'Saul; well St Paul is my favourite saint.' Cecil said he read St Paul there at the previous Sunday's service. So, we stopped and went in. It was a little gem of a church.

It was apparently given to St Patrick by a local Irish chieftain, after the chieftain converted to Christianity.

Cecil read his bit from the Ephesians, and I read my bit from Corinthians – the bit above about love.

We spend the rest of the day like two cows in a cock of hay discussing the North, the South, Irishness, religion, town and district councillors' jobs, as well as many more topics.

That night Cecil hosted a welcoming dinner for us. He told how he had enquired about this man Robert Pierse, who was coming up from Kerry. He found out he was a (mad) Catholic with 10 children, a stuffy solicitor and, worse of all, a grandnephew of Michael Collins. Cecil said that, before we came, he and his lovely wife, Myrtle, spend many hours trying to find a subject they could raise in conversation with me – without success!

Willie Wixted, our Listowel town clerk, interrupted him then to report on what he had told me about Cecil; as above. I remember all of our speeches thereafter dealt with the difficulties that preconceived ideas and positions cause.

Myrtle, Cecil, Olive and I have been firm friends ever since, visiting each other through thirty troublesome years.

2018: We were still friends right up to Cecil's death in 2017. I actually went up to see him some weeks before he died. We had a man to man talk about life and death. He was a man of deep faith and had no fear of death. He rests in peace.

Possibly the most satisfactory thing I did in local politics was to push the twining of Listowel and Downpatrick. The Listowel UDC were great, open-minded, and not afraid.

We were helped by Cecil Maxwell, as I mentioned above. He was a man of vision, peace and openness. Of course, he paid a price for that. These were very rough times, long before serious inter-government talks. I made many friends up there. They are brave people.

On our first trip up there (1980s) we had a fiery urban councillor with us, the late Michael O'Neill, in the car. We were held up at a checkpoint – spikes across the road, frightened young 'tommys' showing off their 'tommy guns' and flack-jackets. Some were hiding in the ditch.

I explained who we were and told them to contact the town-clerk, Seamus Byrne of Downpatrick. They seemed to be unable to work their large field phone – a backpack. We sat there waiting in their suspicion and confusion.

Michael O'Neill said: 'Robert drive on, this is our country. It's wrong for us to be surrounded and questioned by these guys.'

I said back, 'Michael it may be wrong, but I have 9 children and a wife at home, so I am going to wait'. We waited.

We got through eventually with a wave and an apology from the officer in charge.

In fairness, I think those youngsters were afraid of my Kerry car registration number. We had a great time thereafter when we got through.

The first 10 years going up was so difficult at times. Cecil and I would have to plan the visit carefully.

One time, things were so 'hot', I had to attend the council's meeting in the public gallery. At the break in the meeting, Cecil pretended to notice me and bring me down into the members' tea room.

I remember having a lively debate with a DUP man. I received a rebuke from a Sinn Fein man. The Sinn Fein councillor called me a traitor, as I recognised the Crown by attending.

My reply was: 'So why do you, as I understand you, draw the Queen's dole and do not refuse the Queen's £ note?' The Sinn Fein people were actually the most difficult to deal with. The DUP were tough but not very insulting – rabid in their views though.

The first time the Downpatrick delegation came down I got them to call to my private home first as Cecil told me they were apprehensive. I gave them a shot of whiskey. All went well for the visit.

On the Sunday, I went with them to Tarbert Church of Ireland for their service. The vicar was not available, so it was officiated by an old friend, Dr Tim Jackson from Tralee. He was County Medical Officer. When he went up to the pulpit and saw me, he said: 'I had better be careful in what I am reading today as Robert Pierse is here.' The passage he read was the one about the lawyer questioning Jesus. A number of my clients were at the service, so there was a titter.

When the service was over, I invited Tim back home to have coffee. During our coffee he told the Maxwells and Johnstons about being offered a top medical job in the public service in Munster.

Stanley Johnston, also from Downpatrick, said, 'Tim, do they know you are Church of Ireland'? Tim said they do but it makes no difference down here in Tralee. 'But isn't Tralee mad IRA?' Stanley said to him. Tim said no, it was not, and he was reluctant to leave the town. Stanley was shaken out of his misconception.

Stanley and the others really enjoyed their regular visits to Listowel. I remember we had about 200 on one visit. Signs on, Stanley and his family's attitude towards the south changed rapidly.

I developed the habit of going to the Church of Ireland services with Cecil and Myrtle. It helped, but Olive claimed I would be excommunicated when she saw me taking communion. Cecil always goes to mass with us on Sunday morning.

That was before Mary McAleese got reprimanded for taking Communion in the Church of Ireland.

I think people take the minor rules of their religion too seriously and often forget the principle message; to love one another.

The UUP and SDLP were always reasonable, welcoming and courteous. It was a pity the aggressive and unreasonable people won out.

Update 2019: Pray there will be no hard border from this Brexit mess. Odd the way the 'Irish question' still disrupts UK politics.

Scotland, Iona & Facing the Past

I remember being on the island North Uist, and being surprised to find it so Catholic and Gaelic. Apparently, the Sassenachs did not think it worthwhile risking their soldiers for the conquest of a remote piece of rock, however beautiful. These English Sassenach guys weren't into tourism or aesthetics.

Neither were the Protestants after Henry VIII. I suppose he did not want any red-haired Gaelic wife. Tough guy that fellow, but all of them in the power game were. The power game at that time was a lot less subtle than it is now.

If you ever get to Scotland then visit Glasgow's Burrell Museum. I spent a great day there once. Its use of light is superb. On the other side of Scotland is Edinburgh Castle, the Royal Mile of Edinburgh, fascinating places and so near us.

Of course, rural Scotland is much more severe about religions than we are. My brother in law, a priest, was driving early one Sunday morning in the Highlands, while dressed in civvies. It was drizzling. He saw a tall man dressed in black striding along the roadside.

Fr. Gearóid pulled up and said: 'Do you want a lift?' The gaunt figure with a determined chin asked: 'Go ye to Kirk?' Gearóid said 'no' in reply. The man said: 'Ye nay go to Kirk, I nay go with thee.'

Incidentally, on the islands you can read the Gaelic signs as they are worded so like the Irish language. However, I could not understand the Gaelic they spoke.

It was on the Royal Mile that I bought my copy of the *Magna Carta*. That really was the start of individual rights, of producing a defined charter of them. It limited the state's powers, the power of the King. We owe more to the English than we Irish are prepared to admit, especially in our legal system.

One other wholly non-legal observation about the one-mile long road known as the Royal Mile is if you go into the side streets you normally end in a courtyard. Usually, you will see a very small, almost hidden doorway. These mini doors were used by the mistress slipping in and out!

If you do go to Scotland, and you should, Iona is a place you should visit. It is scenery with an atmosphere of peace, history, religion and spirituality that is pleasing to the eye, the mind and soul.

Monks, bishops, chieftains and politicians are buried there. It has that air of sanctity that it is so hard to describe – like the Sea of Galilee.

My first time there was while sailing off the jagged west coast of Scotland. I remember an incident from that trip.

We were in a bay in North Uist – the u is very long and strong in 'Uist', almost a spit on your tongue. I was going back by ferry and plane to work in the Kingdom the following day, so I wanted to stand the lads a meal.

It is a purpose fathers still have; standing meals to hungry children. I have long since become expert in saying 'the bill please', 'the cheque please' (in Dollar Land), *'le addition síl vous pláit'*, *'de recknon bitte'*, *'la cuinta por favor'* and so on. In other places you can get the message across by miming, with a biro or your finger, the writing out a bill, which leads quickly to the appropriate document.

That reminds me of the remark a West Cork farmer client made to me about 40 years ago – in 1960, when I worked in Powell's solicitors' office in Dunmanway. I had transferred his farm to his son so that he would get the old age pension, that very important steady income which gave great status to small farms back then.

There I was making out the bill 7/- (35p) for the folio, 30/- Land Registry fees, 10/- stamp duty (marriage deed reduced rate) £10-0-0 for the professional fee and so on. The farmer was listening with increasing dismay to this legal litany so he decided to comment. He cleared the throat and said:

> Farmer: 'Young fella, it's a queer school they sent you to.
> Me: 'Why so?'
> Farmer: 'They only taught you addition!'

I am a fright for wandering you know. It's the worst trait of lawyers that one, the tendency to wander into other points to impress, or annoy, the court.

Where was I? Yes, in North Uist Scotland, an island outside Iona, standing a meal to 4 other hungry sailors. When I got to the hotel, I found a meal would cost £6 a head. I had only £20 of the Queen's money, whereas I needed £30. Anyway, my Kerry tenacity made me sidle in the back door to explain my difficulty to the proprietor-chef.

I know the Scots are fond of the Queen's picture on the £20 note, so I produced that picture at the commencement of our discourse. I kept showing her smiling visage as I bargained. I am happy to report that a good meal and a good night was had by all thereafter. Thanks to an alien £20 note, we quiet Celts celebrated with the Scottish Celts our common hospitality.

So, my second visit to Iona began well but ended badly.

We had Mass on the Abbot's Rock, and then we had another Mass in St Michael's Church. Odd the way Christianity has split us up, and it is totally unnecessary.

We had our party in the Red Cottage on the Isle of Mull. It was a very beautiful setting, and our host gave a fine meal.

Unexpectedly, at the end of the meal, Olive volunteered my services with the statement, 'Robert will say something'.

All I could say in such a setting – I could see the sun setting in the sea to the west of our window – was the sonnet:

> It is a beauteous evening, calm and free,
> The holy time is quiet as a Nun
> Breathless with adoration; the broad sun
> Is sinking down in its tranquillity;
> The gentleness of heaven broods o'er the Sea;
> Listen! the mighty Being is awake,
> And doth with his eternal motion make
> A sound like thunder—everlastingly.
> Dear child! dear Girl! that walkest with me here,
> If thou appear untouched by solemn thought,
> Thy nature is not therefore less divine:
> Thou liest in Abraham's bosom all the year;
> And worshipp'st at the Temple's inner shrine,
> God being with thee when we know it not.

Oddly, the whole restaurant was quiet as I recited Wordsworth's *Evening on Calais Beach*, so I might have got it right.

I swear all that is from memory, I remember it almost 50 years on. A memory of that one English class and that great teacher, Timmy O'Connor.

As it happens, it is a poem I say to myself as I walk the cliffs at home to *Poul na Gloca* (the hole in the rocks). It is a rock that has 4 holes, and each hole has a rock in it. It is where the leprechauns live.

Because of the wind, the sea gets in underneath these rocks in different ways. Whenever we hear this rock roar, from our house in Meenogahane, we know the weather will be good.

My Brother, Fr Gerard Pierse

Olive and I travelled back the next morning, through Mull and on to Oban via a ferry. Our son Micheál, who was studying in England, dropped us at Glasgow Airport.

Before our flight was called, there was an announcement over the system: 'Would Mr Robert Pierse, a passenger travelling to Ireland, go to the information desk.' Off I go. I was told to ring our son Riobárd immediately.

These messages over public systems fill me with immediate foreboding: Who? What?

I ring and Riobárd breaks the news that my younger brother, Fr Gerard Pierse, CSSR, has drowned in Australia.

I was stunned and shocked as he was a powerful swimmer. He has been in the Philippines for almost 40 years, as a Redemptorist.

He had gone to school to the Redemptorists in Limerick when he was 14. After school in Galway, he went to the Philippines islands as a student of the 'Reds,' as my mother called them, who were starting a seminary there.

I contemplated all this on that flight to Dublin, and then on the hop to Kerry. The shock remained, but no sadness really.

Gerard, known to all as Fr Gerry, always wanted to be a priest and was very fulfilled in his ministry. Now he is gone to the Redeemer he believed in and worked for all his life.

I didn't think it was a time to be sad, but it was a questioning time. We will never have the exact details. It seems he was taking a break, leaving his base in Cebu for a tour of retreats around the Pacific.

While in Australia, giving retreats, he went for a swim in the Gold

Coast, in a creek he was told was safe. He was snorkelling in an inlet, when the tide changed suddenly and swept him away.

However, an elderly lady recounted seeing him struggling. He attempted to stand but fell, attempted again and fell again. The tide went out and left his body on the rocks.

We believe, from the marks on the side of his head, that he was rendered unconscious. It was his mother's birthday and he died unknowingly.

Why did a loving mother arrange this? In life, she had prayed daily for him. All I can say is she had great faith, so all must be well in Heaven. She probably took Gerard to save him from something worse.

Update: In 2007, I visited the place he drowned in, and I could see how it all happened so easily.

He was told the place was safe to swim in, but what he wasn't told is it is only safe when the tide is in. The simplest mistakes are often the most disastrous.

His six brothers attended his funeral on the 26th July 1999, in the old cemetery in a poor area of Cebu.

It was a difficult decision not to bring his remains to his mother and father's grave. However, he had told my brother Frank, the last year before his death, that he would retire to Cebu at the end of his days.

Afterwards, we were glad we acceded to his colleagues' request and laid him to rest in that shabby graveyard. It was quite a sight, him lying embalmed in a glass-topped coffin.

The wonderful locals came in their hundreds, with their stories of acts of kindness and Christian love done by Gerry.

The hospitality of the Redemptorist community was matched only by the wonderful Presentation nuns. We stayed in their convent, and it was a far livelier place than I had expected.

Those priests and those two nuns, Sister Lourdes and Sr Evelyn Flanagan from Galway, do marvellous work.

Poverty always horrifies me, so seeing what our Irish clergy and nuns do in Cebu was shocking. Why do the media constantly criticise the clergy, always give us the bad news? Why do they always write about Judas? Why do they not write about all the good things the Church is doing? Pity the media are so blinkered by their narrow vision.

I suppose, due to early sibling rivalry, brothers never understand each other, especially when there were seven boys. Why had he given up all his talent to people he didn't know?

My mother longed for a girl, but to no avail. She herself had to wield, with considerable accuracy, a wooden spoon on her charges.

However, I got a feeling of the type of Christian Fr Gerry was in my two trips to him, one while he was alive and one for his burial.

When we, his brothers, came back from the funeral we were surprised at the number of people who wrote to us or rang us about him, people who had been to retreats given by him and read his books. It is 'funny' how we often take our siblings for granted.

The flight to the funeral was wrecking. I had the misfortune of staying overnight in a guesthouse near Heathrow. And, because I am so tall, my legs kept getting cramped during the 23-hour journey. I really do not remember much of that first 48 hours. I was exhausted.

The Wake & Funeral ... And the 'Badagio' Pay their Respects
Gerard had been drowned near Brisbane in Australia. I was not aware of it, but he gave a lot of these retreats around the Pacific Rim. He was big into meditation and the Eastern temperament. He was much influenced by the Dalai Lama and others.

He also wrote quite a number of books. I still use his Sundays book. I like his little stories that make the gospel or scripture reading for each Sunday relevant to everyday life.

Gerard's wake was interesting. His body was in a glass-top coffin – there must have been an inbuilt cooling system in it, as the outside heat was oppressive.

Now that I mention it, I think there was an incident when some women tried to remove the top to touch his hands and crucifix. There were a lot of genuinely upset people around.

In some ways, this was comforting to me. It reminded me of my parents' funeral, the sharing of grief.

It was good for me to know that he had done his best, as our parents had always counselled us to do. I think it is important to know that a person had had meaning in his life, for himself and others.

That second night, at about 2 o'clock, I went up to say a quiet prayer of goodbye. That afternoon, I had, along with my 5 brothers, went to Gerard's cell to get his belongings.

It was a humbling experience: his few belongings included his few books, two shoe boxes of items, a clerical suit (which he did not wear often), 4 T-shirts, (which he usually wore) and two pants. The only other possessions were an old community computer, on which he wrote his sermons, books and the letters and e-mails he sent to people all over the world.

In one of the shoe boxes were family letters, mostly from my mother. In the other box were small items, like a letter from Fr Anthony Gaughan, one from John B Keane, and some cuttings of my law cases. There were letters from Jimmy Canty, who was called the 'Lord Mayor of the Lodge Cross' near Meenogahane, and family photos, including a photo of my conferring class.

Yes, it was humbling and it showed me the value of another value system, what was really a religious and moral-law value system.

He and I often had discussions on subjects such as the nature of the 'good', what is a good person, what is a good political system, and was there only one good church or religion? With regard to the last question, he certainly did not agree that there was only one good church.

What is good? Right? Wrong? What do you think? Or, do you think about these things?

Going back to where I was, my hoped-for quiet prayer at Gerard's coffin; it did not happen.

When I arrived at the coffin, an unusual ceremony was taking place. A Filipino tribe had arrived *en masse* to conduct their own ceremonial 'wake' for Gerard. The Badagio tribe.

They sang and danced all night; it was their ceremony of departure for a 'man who was good,' they said.

The chief had passable English, and a story emerged.

While giving a retreat in their area, Gerard had apparently heard of their plight. He was told that all their boats had been sunk in a sudden, violent storm. Worse still, the only two outboard engines were gone. This was disaster for the tribe, as their whole livelihood and sustenance came from the sea.

The chief described to me how this tall, gringo white man arrived on his old motorbike, and talked to them. He told them to rebuild their boats. He gave them $50 for timber.

Then, the tall gringo went off. However, two weeks later he was back and he had an outboard engine. A further week later again, the tall gringo was back with another engine.

The tribe were back in business and they never forgot. They came to honour a good friend that night, and they were still there at dawn's coming.

I remember asking the chief one thing; were they good engines? Of course, I knew they were, as I remember Gerard had rung for funds!

The chief told me the engines were better than the old ones and were still going strong. He could never understand how a gringo padre knew so much about good outboard engines.

I explained to him that Gerard had learnt this from his father. Our father was one of the first men, along with Bernie Holyoake and Jack McKenna, to put a funnel into a currach for his outboard engines. The engines were a Johnson Seahorse from the USA and a Seagull from England. These were inserted into canvass boats.

The chief was also impressed by the fact Gerard never tried to convert them. This actually became the basis of their friendship. Gerard accepted their values and their spiritual outlook.

Update: The Pierse family are still helping out, and we are currently helping to build houses for the tribe and helping out education-wise, as a memorial to Gerard's love of people. Like most priests, Gerard believed education could set people free.

❦

During the funeral mass, I listened to many people explain Gerry to me. I also had the pleasure of saying thanks to the Redemptorists and the people of Cebu.

When the time came for me to say something, I again turned to a poem Gerard and I learnt about 45 years earlier.

You see, Gerry was always positive about all people. No one was hopeless and no situation was hopeless. His belief was a good God aided everyone in ways people just did not understand.

So, I quoted Longfellow's *A Psalm of Life*:

> Tell me not, in mournful numbers,
> Life is but an empty dream!
> For the soul is dead that slumbers,
> And things are not what they seem.
>
> Life is real! Life is earnest!
> And the grave is not its goal;
> Dust thou art, to dust returnest,
> Was not spoken to the soul.

In trying to analyse my brother's hope, love and faith, I had to give credit to our parents. I told the full church of my parent's advice to us. My father's advice to Gerard, when he left Ireland 38 years previous, was: 'Do your best every day. You can't do better than that. If you do that, don't worry no matter what the results are.'

This was the advice he got from his father and he passed it on to me. I passed it to my children, and now I pass it on to my grandchildren.

My mother's advice was: 'Remember, women outnumbered men three to one at the foot of the cross, and it is still that way.' This went down well with the ladies in that big, open church in Cebu. Three quarters of the heads in the church nodded in agreement with my mother, RIP.

I told them about us growing up together. I told them how, as a young man, I didn't like sleeping in the same room as Gerry, because he snored. I would only see his nose on a cold morning.

I told them of his joys, his sorrow and his hopes for the Philippines. In particular his thoughts on freedom, and the Filipino prison system. He had been a prison chaplain.

To express my brother's optimism about life and the people of life, I went back to the last two stanzas of Longfellow's, and recited them as we had learnt them together:

> In the world's broad field of battle,
> In the bivouac of Life,
> Be not like dumb driven cattle!
> Be a hero in the strife!
> ....
> Let us, then, be up and doing,
> With a heart for any fate;
> Still achieving, still pursuing
> Learn to labour and to wait.

I actually read those stanzas of Longfellow's again – a lot of philosophy in them! (One of my sons, who was present, told me the women loved them.)

I said all of this to a church packed with Gerard's parishioners: to the cardinal; two bishops; almost 80 priests; and local politicians.

I was very pointed in my remarks about the prison conditions. He was a prison chaplain, and I had visited one of 'his' prisons. I gather that the politicians did not like my pointed criticisms.

I spoke of and to his many friends and helpers, including Noreen Trota, who is now back in Listowel.

Come to think of it, what I remember most was the people's reaction along the street. Bowed heads, bowed knees at times, and blessing themselves.

They had this practice of throwing money after the coffin, it was their way of expressing sorry as well as helping with the burial expenses. That really pulled at the heart-strings.

The graveyard was simple, overcrowded with graves, tombs and people. The heat was intense.

He was placed in the simple, Redemptorist tomb-grave. Apparently, after some years his bones will be transferred to the tomb.

The parting was over with the brother I loved and grew up with – at least for the present.

Update: Olive, my brother Michael and I visited the grave again in 2008. There was a family living on the tomb. They had a small, plastic tent and were cooking. A goat was eating the grass on the graves. Michael was offended by this.

However, I knew Gerard would not mind. He was always concerned about the poor, and he would have love to know that, even in death, he was helping them.

Keats' Half in Love & Going Home

The evening of the funeral, that tough nun, Sr Evelyn Flanagan, took some of us to visit the 'tribe,' the ones who had the ceremony over Gerard's coffin.

The Badagio tribe, and the lived over the city sewer. They couldn't buy land as they had no money. They had been evicted from their original homeland to make way for 'development'.

The city sewer-outlet was their only home. It was the shantiest of shanty towns. I immediately saw the yellow skin, and gaunt figures and faces that TB brings. I had had it myself.

Here, Irish nuns and priests worked amid the dirt and disease to educate and help those poor people.

The main fight was, as usual, with bureaucracy. The people had no votes and were illiterate, so they did not count. They had no say in the ballot box or at all.

Now, I am now trying to help Sr Evelyn to get some of the tribe registered as voters. The registration cost $20 each! She meets much bureaucratic resistance. Here again, 'The Law' working against the people. There is no law which says everything must be fair and just. There is much corruption.

Perhaps it's all this death and tuberculosis that reminds me of the poet, John Keats, who died from tuberculosis. I think of one line in particular, from his melancholy poem, '*Ode to a Nightingale*'. He said of dying of TB, that one reaches a stage of 'being half in love with easeful death'. As I get older, I understand this line more and more. Keats died from TB aged 26.

I was glad I could afford to travel part of the journey home in business class. I didn't miss the Ryanair-type travel. BA does it better. I slept most of the journey.

We had done Gerard proud. He was surely with his Creator and our parents. I was going home to my wife and family, whom I love.

God is in his Heaven and surely Gerard is with him. And I know Gerard will be rooting for us, just like he did during his temporary stay in this transient place.

On the plane, I thought of the following words; from James Clarence Mangan's *The Nameless One*:

> Roll forth my song, like a rushing river,
> That sweeps along to the mighty sea;
> God will inspire me while I deliver,
> My soul to thee!

Wind Change & More Jokes?

My children, my severest critics still, will say I am writing too much Pauline and preachy stuff, and too much poetry stuff too. I like it, so I write it!

It was a good weekend on Iona, a place of peace. It was a pity it ended in shock.

That's a lot about my brother, but my audience here on the caye were very interested last night. I must take a few hours off to lighten my mood. Wind seems to be changing direction – is that a good sign?

I am back, so let's have a few jokes. Speaking of religion, (we were talking last night about religion), there are religious jokes I would love to have put in my Road Traffic Book.

As it happens, I hadn't the courage. Law books must be ponderous tomes to be considered useful; that is how the law sees itself. The joke, which should be in the intoxicated driving section, goes:

Fr O'Toole was driving down the main road, his destination; the Pro-Cathedral in Dublin. A garda signals him to stop. He did.

The garda smells alcohol on the priest's breath and then notices an empty wine bottle on the floor of the car. He says to Fr O'Toole:

'Father, I am of the opinion, under the Road Traffic Act 1961 as amended, that you have been drinking an intoxicant.'

'Just water,' replies the priest.

Garda: 'Then why do I smell wine?'

The priest looks at the bottle and says: 'Good Lord! You have done the miracle again.'

Don't get me wrong, I am not anti-clerical in any way. Some of the finest, the very finest, people I know are priests and nuns.

I do not go along with this tendency to blacken religion or clergy, just because of the few black sheep. Remember, Jesus himself picked a Judas.

Well, here is a parking joke I could not put in my book.

A solicitor was driving around the streets at the back of the Four Courts at 10:30 am. He was scheduled to meet his client and barrister at 10:30 – but inside the buildings.

He could not find a parking place, and he was sweating as it was a big case. He looked up to heaven and said: 'My learned Lord, take pity on me. If you find me a parking place I will henceforth go to Mass every Sunday and I will give up whiskey for good.'

Miraculously, a parking place appeared right in front of him. The solicitor looks up again and says: 'My learned Lord, never mind I have found one.'

Then there is this one, which I shouldn't tell at all – one has to be so 'politically correct' (in other words, be a non-entity) nowadays. However, here goes, I'm going to tell it anyway.

Paddy, an Irishman, was a little deaf and trying to cross a road in New York. He waited patiently. Then, the cop in the centre of the road stops the traffic and shouts, 'OK PEDESTRIANS'.

After the cop shouts this, the traffic stops. However, Paddy didn't move, he waited on the sidewalk.

Then, the cop shouts 'OK PEDESTRIANS' for the tenth time, and Paddy shouts at the cop: 'When are you going to let the Catholics cross?'

Politics, the Media & the EU

I just said to Olive that I will give the religious topic a rest, and move onto power and politics. She says that will really bore them; yawn!

Well, it was good for about a half hour last night, but the kids wanted to move onto romantic matters. What do you think?

I am just letting my thoughts come as they come. Of course, you have to the luxury of turning to the next page. I just want to have a hop-ball discussion with the youngsters.

Right now, I'm hoping there will be a tomorrow for this island. A good bit remains, especially at this end of the island. At the other end however, the island could get washed away or cut off.

I suppose we shouldn't worry, these Belize guys knew where to put the cabins, and where to leave space between the boards that make up the walls.

I am hoping we will not have to go under the bed tonight, as it has been pretty cramped down there for the past few nights. No head room to manoeuvre. Difficult to get out to go to the toilet, or, should I say, go down the steps and let fly in the wind.

I also like the matrimonial bed to be 'King-size', *a lá* Henry VIII. Oh! Is that a sexist remark? One has to be so politically correct, even when it comes to these domestic matters.

You know in Spain a double bed is called a *'cama matrimonial'*.

Anyway, I'm optimistic about the weather.

Now, to get back to politics, wasn't Olive's reaction fairly typical? Politics is a turn off for most women, probably many men too.

Well, that is what they say anyway, but in my experience women practise politics better than men. (Be careful now Robert, you are walking on eggshells!)

What did Helen of Troy or Cleopatra practise? They got the guys hyped up to kill other guys so that their guy, and by extension themselves, would have more power.

Women have power, but in a different way to men. They have power over men and their children. I remember a good-looking woman telling me once that she just loved the power of frustrating men. She claimed women were men's great weakness. She lost them all though, and ended up lonely with her cat.

Maggie Thatcher was a politician I admired for her singularity of purpose. She had the power to smash unions, to swing the handbag, or to say to her Irish colleague, 'out, out, out,' even if she took the teapot.

I believe she did a lot for England that is unacknowledged. Of course, the same is true of Tony Blair, who has done a lot for Irish peace and unity, and that will also go unacknowledged.

Why? The press, who are avid in their intent to pull people down. Wasn't it WB Yates who wrote:

> They must to keep their certainty accuse
> All that are different of a base intent,
> Pull down established honour, hawk for news,
> Whatever their loose fantasy invent.

I hope that quote is OK. Because, no doubt, if ever this book gets into a reviewer's hands he or she will slay me! But you get my drift – I am not gone on most of the media. I find the 'popular press' numbing in its stupidity, and it usually entails a mindless invasion of privacy.

Mugging by the media is their daily diet. They forgot about individual suffering. The so called broadsheet media are slowly descending to their level.

Well, just before I leave Tony Blair, it sickens me about these WMD's (weapons of mass destruction). Of course Saddam had them. He had used them on his own people.

Of course, they are well hidden and they may never be found. Iraq is a big place, lots of desert. In Northern Ireland, comparatively a much smaller area, the British Army, police and a huge section of the community never found all the IRA arms. The IRA arms should be much easier to find than Saddam's canisters, bottles of gas or anthrax.

I remember Carmel O'Donoghue, Olive's sister-in-law, telling me how, one night, while watching Gulf War footage on TV, she saw the Americans guide a big missile into Baghdad. She saw how the missile was guided down the street, and was directed through the third window, on the top floor of a post office. She saw death and destruction: war is an evil thing.

You might recall in the first Gulf War; how thousands of Iraqi soldiers hid under the sand. Their generals expected the coalition forces to pass without seeing these underground guys, and when they did pass the underground soldiers were to jump out and wham the 'invaders' in the back.

What the Iraqis didn't know then, but learnt the hard way, was that the US had satellite surveillance. The US bombs buried the underground soldiers as they passed by. I believe these satellites are so accurate they can photograph you leaving for work. I do not like all this 'Big Brother' stuff.

I do think many politicians are very good and committed people. They really have a difficult job in a democracy. And I believe our Irish multi-seat constituencies make the job even more difficult. The demands of constituents allow no time for the reflection and research necessary for making complex legislation, the legislation they are elected to make and pass.

Politicians love playing 'Big Brother' and love the power of the nanny state. Have you noticed that you are being watched in different ways?

You have a number, and they keep changing it from social welfare number to tax number, to PRSI number and so on. I cannot think of what it is called at present; o yes, it is PPS number.

The first 'P' stands for 'Personal', but do not be fooled, it's not anything you, as a person, have any say in. Of course, there is not much you can do anyway as the system is one big machine, of which you are a finite cog. No, I am being too gloomy – or am I? On this occasion, the kids seem to think I am not.

I hope these views, and the way I am expressing them, are not arrogant and patronising.

You should be stuck in politics, especially if you are young. The politicians are, or at least ought to be, movers and shakers, and the young are best at moving and shaking. Remember that it was an Irish man, Edmund Burke, who said: 'All that is necessary for evil to prosper is that good men do nothing.'

Burke was a very bright politician and you should read his writings. He was good on liberty, including liberty for women. His speeches are well crafted, logical and relevant to subjects today. He, along with another ex-Irishman, Richard Brinsley Sheridan, gave Warren Hastings a bad time. Those two Irish buckos didn't come out of that too well.

Fintan O'Toole has just published a good book on Richard Brinsley Sheridan. I was only starting it when I left for here. It is called *A Traitor's Kiss*. Seems well written by F O'T, even if he is very controversial at times, he is one of the *Irish Times'* columnists. I'm gone off the *Irish Times* – too liberal in a leftish sort of way. Gone so called 'pro-choice'.

That little quotation of Edmund Burke, plus some youthful idealism and family tradition, was what got me into Fine Gael Politics.

Of course, university politics was full of debate. Should we join the EEC (European Economic Community) or not was the ever growing and big topic at the end of 1950s and the 1960s.

There is no doubt that the formation of the EEC was a necessary miracle in post-World War II Europe.

What worried me was what will happen when the IRA realise what EEC membership entails? How each treaty has diminished our independence; the creeping usurpation of our sovereignty. What will they do?

The superpowers within the EEC, or EU now, will gradually gobble up the small states, with all the inevitability of gradualism.

It is just like with supermarkets and my small shopkeeper clients. One of my small village shopkeepers told me the other day that he cannot buy his goods wholesale at the price the town's supermarket sells them at. So, another local centre goes into history. It is such a pity, another decent man forced into idleness, and it's happening to many other clients also.

I can never understand farmers voting for EU enlargement – turkeys voting for Christmas. All the money they get from the Common Agricultural Policy will be shifted to Eastern Europe in the next thirty years.

Oh, and this new 'Celtic Tiger' is not for farmers or us country people. Tigers gobble! It's getting too big and complex: 'Ill fares the land where wealth accumulates and men decay.'

Since we joined the EEC in 1972, about 40% of Kerry farms have closed down. Decent hardworking families gone. Cities growing. I get it now in offices in Dublin: 'Ah, you are up from the country for the day, how nice!' I go out, smell the Liffey, and long for the Kingdom.

In the late 1950s, while I was at college, the 1957 Treaty of Rome established the six-nation economic union, designed to prevent the tensions that led to World War II. That was good. It will stay good as long as it does not become a political power struggle, with money instead of guns. Or money leading to guns!

The EU's leftish laws do not go down well with a lot of people. Its approach to law is different to our traditional system, which is the 'common law'.

Speaking of which, I have memories of that war: the ration book; no petrol for my father's car; my father in the LDF (Local Defence Forces); and more.

I think many Irish had ambivalent feelings about the war. I know that a republican group was preparing to welcome the Germans to North Kerry, and they trained in the sand dunes at Beale, at the mouth of the Shannon.

It really wasn't until after the war that the big, anti-German feeling grew. I remember the initial, absolute disbelief as pictures from the concentration camps emerged, where people were first dehumanised and then killed. It took a lot of these pictures and newsreels to convince the Irish that the German people could have allowed the gas chambers.

To this day, there seems to be a question as to whether the German people really knew what was going on. I believe they did but it was presented to them as 'good' and 'necessary'.

There is no doubt that the mass-media presented the mass removal to work camps as a way of providing workers. *Arbeit Macht Frei* (Work Makes you Free) was placed over the entrance to Auschwitz. Sending Jews, Gypsies and others to Auschwitz was seen as an eradication of evil and the 'unwanted', and so an unpleasant necessity.

As I mentioned before, I went myself, with some slight scepticism, to Dachau in 1996 (I think). It was undoubtedly an awful day – the ovens, the rules! It was appalling to see these rules, or 'laws' as they were called, in the camp. The place, even in that warm summer day, had me shivering and numb at the presentation of these rules as law, necessary for the good order of camp society.

At the wall where thousands were shot I said prayers out loud. The guide said she had never seen anyone do that before.

I have been to the even more terrible Auschwitz-Birkenau twice to remind myself of man's inhumanity towards man. Am I a masochist?

One of those visits was made while attending a legal seminar organised by the Law Society. We had a local guide who took us to see more horror than I had seen previously.

On our way back to Krakow the guide started crying as she had got the news, from her husband, that the Polish pope, John Paul II, was dying. I learned that John Paul, as a parish priest, had baptised her children, and, as a bishop, had confirmed them.

The law conference was abandoned by most of us. We went to the square in front of the bishop's palace, with a massive crowd of locals. We saw big men with children on their shoulders; the men and children crying, holding candles and praying for their 'Papa'. We stayed there among the tears and prayers until he died, RIP.

He was a great man.

What is also inexplicable to me was that the vast majority of Germans were Christians – Catholics mostly in the south, Protestants mostly in the north. They were all believers in the commandments inherited from the Jews, which were brought to new prominence 2000 years ago by a Jewish messiah. How was the fifth commandment 'thou shall not kill' forgotten? A much older law, ignored in the name of political power.

It shows the power of fear in the informer society, in the regulated conformist society.

Still, when one looks at this century from another angle, haven't the abortionists of USA, England and China wiped out far more children than the Nazis or the world wars killed? What a shocking indictment of law and people.

Enough said, but I think these dreadful events should be constantly brought before us. They did encourage me to get involved in politics, although I was never a successful politician.

I still believe that the price of our liberty, or what is left of it, is eternal vigilance. That is why I am still very suspicious about this emerging political unity in Europe.

I think my son Seán is the one of my children who is most interested in politics. He was involved in the discussion last night and seems to be Progressive Democrat inclined.

However, he would never succeed with the current Irish attitude to democracy. He would be for a balanced budget, live within your means Ireland. He would not be an 'auction' politician.

It's extraordinary that the electorate endlessly favours the soft option, not realising that they are being bribed by their own money.

Seán sees that. Interestingly enough Aislinn, his girlfriend, has an interest in politics too – her father Jim Gildea from Shankill, Dublin is a FG man.

Our Constitution

People forget, I think anyway, that we have enshrined good principles in our 1937 Constitution. Just the little bits I can remember as being very appropriate (and will check all these when I get a chance!) are:

The Preamble to the Constitution was described in 1960 in our Supreme Court as declaring the purpose of the people in, adopting, enacting and giving themselves the Constitution.

As it is cited in one of the law books I have here, I think it's worth writing it out, particularly the bit about our national purpose or ambition. It reads:

> In the name of the Most Holy Trinity, from whom is all authority
> and to whom, as our final end, all actions both of men and States
> must be referred,
> We the people of Eire,
> Humbly acknowledging all our obligations to our Divine Lord,
> Jesus Christ, who sustained our fathers through centuries of trial,
> Gratefully remembering their heroic and remitting struggle to
> regain
> The rightful independence of our Nation,
> And seeking to promote the common good, with due observance,
> Of prudence, Justice and Charity, so that the Dignity and

freedom of the individual may be assured, true social order attained

The unity of our Century restored, and concord established with other nations.

Do hereby adopt, enact, and give to ourselves this Constitution.

Did you ever read that before? Think about it objectively please.

2018: Will these principles survive the wave of humanism, self-gratification and pack-pressure?

Art 1.1. says:

The Irish Nation hereby affirms its inalienable, indefensible and sovereign right to choose its own form of Government, to determine its relations with other nations and to develop its life, political economic and cultural in accordance with its own genius and traditions.

These seem to me to be the laudable sentiments in 1937 of a sovereign nation and an independent sovereign state. In 1972, I believe we began, in a very dramatic way, to throw it all away – at least that is what I said at the time.

I said economic treaties or a treaty was essential, but the clause being put into the constitution would lead to political sovereignty becoming gradually eroded. We were re-enacting the Act of Union and doing it with a much more diverse Europe. Hidden in the provisions inserted into the Constitution in 1972 is the following sentence:

10. No provision of this Constitution invalidates laws enacted, acts done or measures adopted by the State which are necessitated by membership of the European Union or the Communities, or prevents laws enacted, Acts done, or measures adopted by the European Union, or by the Communities or by institutions thereof, or by bodies competent under the Treaties, establishing the Communities, from having the force of law in the State.

I find this provision, and others like it, incompatible with an independent, sovereign nation-state. At the very least it sets up two legislative systems.

Already, we are being swamped by EU directives, decisions and regulations. I think the new godless EU constitution that was being prepared would have made it worse. Have we left one empire, only to join another?

We were bought off and we continue to be bought off by a vision of wealth. In the words of the old song, 'money talks, it don't sing and dance, but it sure talks'.

What has happened in Ireland is that the words 'republicanism' and 'nationalism' have become categorised and debased because of what are termed the northern 'Troubles'.

90% of us down here cannot forget Enniskillen, Omagh and other examples of atrocities, assassinations and mayhem in the North. Nor should we ever forget. And the best way not to forget them is to join legitimate democratic parties.

Be aware of the PR that presents differing views on peace since the Good Friday Agreement. This whole island must be active, not mouthing polite meaningless political words and tutored phraseology by spin merchants. These 'sound bites' seem to overrule thought. Let's be careful.

Are We Trapped?

Look, I am getting worked up as I did last night, so I am going to go for a walk. There is nothing like a walk to calm me down.

I also must go looking for paper – a visit to the toilet maybe, or I'll see if anyone has finished a book with a few blank pages at the end.

We did have a lively discussion about the EU last night. Many expressed the popular view that it is good for Ireland at present. I agree, but still, I am very uneasy.

Everyone brought a few books for the trip. Amazing the diverse tastes in literature.

Maybe I bored you with my political views?

Olive has tabooed politics for the rest of our stay. We are getting worried now, as we were supposed to be gone yesterday. Will we miss our flight home? And the perpetual meals of fish is getting a bit much. Our oatmeal for porridge is gone; we ate the last bit this morning.

Look, I will go for a walk! Where is Scruffy? Yes, there he is and down at the tip of the caye. Harry the hare is washing his face with his paws near the cabin. He does not fear humans either. I think the caretaker must feed him.

Last night we had a more serious discussion than the night before. It's probably due to the oppressive nature around us, and the thought that we may be trapped on the island.

Will the storm ever go? Will we miss our plane back to that green and misty land of home? This storm cannot go on forever.

During all this, we talk about climate change and what is being done to stop it. But I can't help thinking of the old saying: 'What is everybody's business is nobody's business.'

Kevin told us about Belize. It has an informal but very supportive family structure, which I think is the basis of society.

There is an absence of taxation, something Donal finds most helpful. I do not understand why there aren't more USA tourists down here. It is so unusual and beautiful. I suppose it's the absence of mod cons.

Olive told stories about growing up in Killarney and Baraduff. Come to think of it, I wish Olive would write a book. Or, are books going out of fashion?

Isn't nature just wonderful? I have been studying the art of fishing here. Kevin and the lads are fishing still, and Aislinn and Caroline are doing a bit too.

The big fish are not biting. Something to do with atmospheric pressure Kevin says and, of course, light. He needs to use his gaff on the Big, Big One, but there is no hope of that today.

I was lying on my stomach under the cabin amid the stilts. The sand is dry here. The water has been brought up to the edge of the cabin by the storm. Now I can watch the fish from under the cabin.

They seem to ride the waves like these young people you see on TV, on those boards.

I would have thought fish would head away from the island and not stay at the edge of the beach. Some of them get washed up as the wave recedes quickly. Unthinking fish, but are they any different to us?

Yes, they are; at least I keep well back from the highest wave.

It did puzzle me why the fish stay at the windward side of the island,

"The Fisherman"

and not at the lee or the more shaded side. However, Kevin solved that puzzle for me as he is fishing, very successfully, for lunch at the lee side. He told me a few minutes ago that the big fish can be found on the leeside – so these brown sprats aren't such fools after all! The big guys are not gobbling them up. The lee side has deeper water for the big fish.

Is that a fear we all have? Being gobbled up by the big guys? At least that is how I feel when I think of Dublin, or Brussels, nowadays. What am I but a sprat in the eyes of these big institutions or organisations?

Uniforms have that effect on me, be they uniform roles or persons. The two types of uniformities go together a lot. I rarely meet a person in uniform, or someone who is part of what I call a uniformity institution, that hasn't some rule book that has become a set of absolute laws. You know the bureaucrat with the rulebook regards himself as a SUPERIOR just with a look.

'The wise have pitied the fool!' It was against this sort of thing that Padraig Pearse gave his life. He was a barrister you know. Also, did you know his girlfriend drowned in the White Strand off the Great Blasket?

Back to being a Robinson Crusoe! Kevin is up near the swaying trees and the dog is there eating the cleanings of the fish. I notice four birds with long beaks have arrived. Is that a good sign?

I see Kevin, who is a great nature man, recycles back into to the sea anything that is not eaten by the dog, or was not eaten last night by the humans.

'Won't the blood attract sharks?' I ask.

'So what? They are just big fish.' He responds.

'It's the big teeth I am afraid of,' I say.

It does seem that the sharks here are not man-eaters. But I am not going to trust them all the same.

It is too rough to go swimming anyway.

Last week, before we came down to this piece of Belize, we went to another tourist attraction. There we swam in a coral area.

Mind you don't cut yourself on coral, it's very, very nasty if you do. The area near us had one of these bottomless blue holes. We flew out there in a plane, an old propeller type, where I had to tie the door with a bit of rope. I had to keep the door open by holding the rope until we took off.

That was some experience. I tied my seatbelt very carefully, and Olive held on to my shirt. We took off OK with the help of my open door, so I hauled the door closed once we were airborne. Difficult job.

Staying low, we flew over miles of the most gorgeous green water, covering white and brown coral. It was greeny, rather than blue.

Then, we passed over this blue hole. The pilot shouted at us, over the noise of the engine, that it had no bottom. I said back, plug it fast or the Atlantic will disappear. He didn't seem to understand my attempted joke!

I do wonder at times what is underneath the known surface of the earth. Did you ever consider that? I did once before, while we were in Sicily, when Etna, the volcano, was belching furiously and lighting up the sky with lava. Speaking of which ...

Adventures in the Land of Mama Mia
Sicily is a glorious island. I went there by accident and because of an accident.

A Roman businessman was involved in an accident in Ireland. Like with all my clients it was the other driver's fault. Anyway, the client was shifted back by air ambulance to Italy, before I could get a proper statement from him.

Those doctors and nurses in the intensive care unit are a tough group of guardians who give no consideration to our legal concerns. You get mutterings of ambulance chasers, as we seek to get justice for our clients.

I therefore had to go out to Italy to get a proper statement from him, his passenger and doctors. I also wanted to look at the X-rays, or rather have the damage that they showed explained to me.

As he had no English and my old school Latin had little relevance to spoken Italian, I headed with my wife, Olive, and daughter Máire, to Rome. We decided to make a holiday out of it.

I was to discover the practice of law in Italy is different to Kerry. Odd people these Italians.

I had booked an interpreter and made an appointment to meet the client along with the interpreter the first morning, before interviewing the client's doctors that afternoon; after that, our holiday.

Alas, the best laid plans of Kerrymen and mice went a'glay! What I met next morning was not my young businessman client, but his formidable MAMA MIA and her lawyer.

My client, apparently, was away on business, and would not be back for four days. I did not believe it! I was furious, but what could I do, I was stuck with Mama Mia.

I did get, from Mama Mia's lawyers, up to date hospital and medical notes. I had his Irish ones and a garda report. I worried about client confidentiality, as really she was not my client.

Authority is produced for Mama Mia. Interpreter gets busy trying to interpret and translate the notes. Medical terms became confusing and so my wife-doctor proved a great help – wise of me to marry a doctor!

With Mama's lawyer we got down to sorting out possible damages. I explained the difference between what various judges award. There are those that are 'tight' (which I had to explain to the interpreter meant being mean) and those that are reasonable (explained as being good and generous). My Italian colleague told me, regretfully, that it was much the same in Italy. He said judges were always making life difficult for lawyers.

We discussed why it was that the most perfectly reasonable colleagues suddenly changed into unsympathetic judges as soon as they got their feet under the bench. Progress was slow until I produced a book of anatomical charts and a calculator. Then, Mama Mia seemed to think I might be genuine and not a complete fool. Went into calculation of:

General damages to date: how a judge turned pain and suffering since the accident into money. I estimated that the sum would be about £40,000 as the injuries were bad. That turned into a vast amount of Lira.

I remember going out to buy three ice creams later. There is good ice cream in Italy. I seemed to pay thousands of Liras in big notes for three ice creams.

The figure impressed Mama and the Lawyer, not the ice cream figure now, but the damages figure in Lira! Mama was relaxing and thinking of pots of Lira. Of course Lira is gone now, replaced by tiny Euro coins.

I tried to put Mama Mia in her place, pointing out that it was only her son who could help me in relation to his future. I needed to meet him, see how he had been affected physically; at work; socially, psychologically (at this stage, the dictionary and interpreter were working overtime). I needed to have a consultation with his doctors. I needed to look at all the X-rays from the radiologist, get reports, discuss arthritis, prognosis, future risks and so on.

She got tired and agreed, but it was going to be four days before she could organise for me to meet son and the doctors. And this was after an hour-long phone call to her son.

So, Olive and I could do nothing else but go out into the boiling hot streets of central Rome. We went to our hotel with Máire, our daughter. We decided in the taxi that we would go to Sicily, where, we hoped, there was sea and coolness.

I warn you about Roman taxi drivers. Downright thieves are mixed in with their (hopefully) honest members. The one we hired to take us on a 5 minute journey turned into a 15 minute journey, despite the easy traffic situation. I noticed we passed the railway station twice!

The driver then sought to charge me four times what the driver who took us to Mama Mia charged. I refused to pay and went in for the hotel manager, who spoke English.

Amid the torrent of excited Italian I conveyed that I would not pay taxi man No. 2 four times what I paid taxi man No. 1. The torrent got worse. I took out an appropriate bundle of Lira, and shoved it into the taxi man's hand. He threw it on the ground with disdain.

Your humble Kerryman, who had no disdain for money ever, picked it up, pocketed it and walked into the hotel. The manager gave me a knowing look thereafter and there were no extras on my bill.

So, off we went off to Sicily. We swam and I bought expensive ice creams. We watched Etna erupt from our hotel window. It was a lovely few days.

We did not meet any of the Mafia that are supposed to own the shoe of Italy. However, our guide on the bus tour around the island pointed to a square with a black hole in one of the streets. He calmly told us that a judge, who had been on his way to court, had been blown up there a few days earlier. He shrugged and muttered something like 'I hope he rests in peace' in Italian. Saddening! Shocking disrespect for the value of life.

We went to Mass there. The church was full of women. When we came out all the men were attending a communist meeting in the square

We nearly missed getting back to Mama Mia's son in Rome, as I got the plane times mixed up. We were back in the same hotel with a big welcome from the manager, who confided in me that he had never seen or heard of anyone getting the better of a taximan in Rome.

We remember going 'touristing' around Rome as well. My favourite place by far was the Villa Borghese.

I still have a clear picture of the face of David from the statue of David in my mind. How did Bernini, the sculptor, get that determined look onto the marble? No wonder Goliath bit the dust. Determination to win is a great plus in any battle.

You see the determination in football games often. The determination to win often motivates the underdog, and it makes them top dogs in the end.

We were back in the lawyer's office at 8 am the following morning. Mama Mia was there, but we quickly got past her false smile and heaving bosom.

The client was bright and had fairly good English. We got on well. We met the doctors in the nearby hospital at 11 am, looked at the X-rays and heard grave words about prognosis.

I asked that it all be put in writing, translated into English and diagrams included. Then, we had a quick lunch with the client and got more information out of him, how his injury, for example, was creating sexual difficulties for him.

These back injuries often do, but men are slow to give you that bit of info, and certainly not in the presence of Mama Mia. I told him to go back to the doctor and give him the details. I (in hope!) added another £20,000 to my damages calculation.

We headed to the Vatican, St Peter's, saw the Pieta and that wonderful museum – what treasures, what beauty! Only a wonderful Creator could create, through his or her creatures, such glory

Olive told them about our adventures in Italy last night in the cabin. She thought the concept of Mama Mia should be brought into Ireland.

I argued that it was there already, but the Irish women have a cuter way. The Irish colleens did not really tell the men they were the bosses and the men the boys.

Going back to the story, we met the son, the injured businessman, for a final chat. I came home and settled the case for a good bit above my estimates. Mama Mia was pleased; at least that is what her son told me on the phone after the settlement cheque was cashed.

Min Taking off the Caps

I came back to our min again last night, here in the *Seagull* cabin. The girls want to know more about them. They are a dying breed now.

The precise function of 'the min', or at least how they see it, is to give free advice about everything and anything.

They are great in the pub. In they go and off comes the cap to dust the barstool. The older members of this class will sit on the cap, because the shape of the rim resembles the lower end of their anatomy, and it enables them to be comfortable on a timber stool.

On the other hand, some of them will never take it off. Some of them will hold up by the outside wall the church rather than go into mass and take off the cap.

Funny, women do not wear headscarves in church anymore. That can be very distracting you know, those long blonde tresses when one is trying to concentrate on buying fire insurance. One must be prudent in risk-management for the next life.

Now, where was I? Yes, the 'min' who will not take off their cap.

I got a phone call from a local hospital one time. It was about a client for whom I had been making a will. The client was a bad example to the other patients, he would not take off his cap. The older 'min' were putting on theirs.

Worse still, the nurse had to give this 80 year-old client a bath. The clothes came off eventually, but not the cap, no way. I had never seen him with the cap off, not for as long as I knew him.

The only time I saw him without the cap was in the coffin, and I didn't recognise him. I said to his son: 'He'll be very cross if St Peter will not recognise him without the cap on. He might not get in.'

Sure enough, his son took my sound legal advice and the cap went on, plus a ten shilling note, a bit of shamrock and a small whiskey.

Do not tell me you do not know what they are for? You must be a city person. The ten shillings was for the boatman on the river Styx, to make sure he took him to the right side of the river. The shamrock was to call out St Patrick if St Peter was humming or hawing about letting a decent Irish man in.

I always thought St Peter was a bit of a weakling, whereas St Patrick was a toughie saint.

The whiskey was to keep him warm crossing the river. Go to Downpatrick, where I have so many friends, to learn about St Patrick. And when you come back, go to Fenit and learn about St Brendan. He was a great Kerryman.

If you are a Kerryman, and you are having trouble with St Peter, you can be sure St Brendan will get you inside the pearly gates.

Renouncing the Devil

The min with the caps would tell you all about piseógs and superstitious happenings, things unexplained by reason and forbidden by the religious. I suppose the modern horror movies have an element of superstition in the background to frighten people.

How it happened that my brother, Gerard, joined the Redemptorists I am not sure. The Redemptorists were a tough order and not my mother's choice. It may have been because of the tough retreats the Redemptorists gave.

One of their favourite sermons was about piseógs, a form of cursing and wishing bad luck on neighbours. This cursing entailed putting rotten eggs in the neighbour's hay. Farmers were terrified of this, as cattle aborting their calves and other major calamities were said to follow.

The Redemptorist came on a mission to Listowel, delivering great sermons about these evils and others – drink, dishonesty, and non-marital sexual relations figuring strongly.

The piseóg sermon came on Thursday night. Fire and brimstone would rain on those practitioners of such evils. We youngsters learnt a lot of things we never knew about, like spells and curses, and indeed sex.

The evil ones in the parish had to repent, and confessions would be held on Friday from 12 noon and all day Saturday. Saturday night there would have to be full-attendance to renounce the devil.

Then, something happened! That Friday at confessions, when the missionary went into the confession box, there was something there waiting for him. Right you guessed it – a box filled with a dozen rotten eggs.

The church shook with the terror that night. The parish was surely part of hell.

So, on Saturday night we all brought our candles to renounce the devil. The missionary shouted, 'DO YOU RENOUNCE THE DEVIL'? We said, rather quietly, 'we do'.

'LOUDER' cried the missionary: 'DO YOU RENOUNCE THE DEVIL?'

We said 'WE DO', with gusto.

'LOUDER, LOURDER, LOUDER,' the missionary cried. 'HE MUST HEAR YOU IN HELL.'

The church shook with our frenzied, 'WE DO'.

Then a lone, loud voice from the back of the church cried, 'THE BASTARD'.

Gosh, we loved it!

Flying Parents

I suppose all boys of the 1940s and 1950s were urged to think of the priesthood.

My mother was very religious and near to God. I thought in later life she had a personal telephone line to Himself. She felt she needed His help with 8 males to deal with.

My father was different, he had his own few religious practices but he was not immersed in the way my mother was.

Gerard went off to join the Redemptorists at an early age of fourteen, I think, off to the 'Reds' as my mother called them.

We visited him one day at their Novitiate in Esker, Co Galway. My mother ran into trouble with the Reds, who she claimed did not like women. I think they regard them as Eves.

Ma Pierse wanted to see where Gerard slept and so on. The rules of the house forbade women going into the dormitories, and they had a red rope barrier at a certain point to indicate no entry. Such a dust up – my mother won. Red rope barrier pulled aside.

Gerard went off then in 1959 to the Philippines with some other young novices to establish a new novitiate there and train local students. It took him a month by sea. He sent a postcard from every port, and I added to my stamp collection. He was ordained there in 1964.

My parents did a round the world trip, which included a stop off in the Philippines for the ordination. My mother got an awful shock when she saw her third son throw back a whiskey! Our 'flying parents' as they called themselves were great.

My father came back with interesting comments for his sons. Like, for instance, the finest looking women were in Australia, due to all the body-boarding (or did he say baring?) there. Apparently, the type of swimwear those women wore was bottom only! 'What were those hussies up to?' my mother said.

My father and mother had an interesting few days in Hawaii as they continued on their journey east.

When they got a taxi they started questioning the black taxi driver, who only wore shorts in the open vehicle. Eventually he said: 'You folk aren't English, as they do not ask questions. Are you folks Irish?'

They answered in the affirmative, and he told them his grandmother left Ireland to become a housemaid in New York. Then, she moved with the family she worked for to California, before following them to Hawaii. She eventually ended up marrying a Hawaiian. She had one daughter who married locally, and she in turn had one son, the taxi driver.

He said his grandmother loved the sea as she came from Kerry, leaving a brother behind on the small farm. Eventually, this was narrowed down to Ballybunion.

My father recognised the surname, which was an unusual one in the locality. He said to the taximan: 'I was on that small holding with your cousin 6 weeks ago as a vet, and I can tell you your cousin had sick pigs.'

The taximan gave them, my parents, a great few days on the island and refused all payment from his fellow Irish folk!

I love the joy on the young people's faces when they hear these stories

last night. I got to bed late, but not before giving them some Philippines stories.

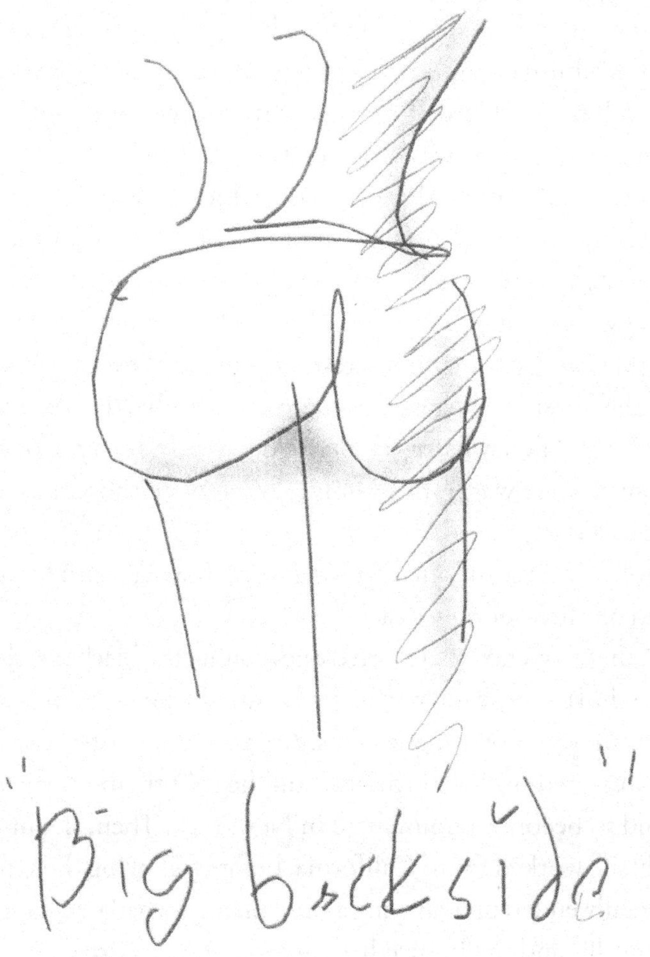

A Crucifixion

My brother Frank and I were part of an Irish Chinese Friendship tour in 1985. At the end of it we had a few days in Hong Kong. We had in fact booked to visit Gerard in the Philippines on Easter Saturday.

We were not keen on Hong Kong. It was too luxurious and expensive. We slipped out for McDonald's, rather than paying for the hotel's pricey food.

In the hotel, a man with white gloves showed us how to flush the toilets!

We decided we might go to the Philippines a day earlier.

We were fortunate to have in our group a Mrs Noreen Trota – her maiden name being Noreen Finucane – from Moyvane, Co Kerry. She was the honorary Irish consul to the Philippine islands at that time. She was a wonderful woman. She always offered a home to the many Irish in the Philippines – Redemptorists, Columbans, nuns and everyone else.

So, she arranged to get our (Frank and I) tickets transferred to Good Friday morning. When doing so, by some mysterious exchange of information, the airline got the impression that we were two important Irish ministers.

They reported back to Mrs Trota, in shocked tones:

> We are glad to tell you that we have changed the tickets to Good Friday. We also have corrected a dreadful mistake. We found these important people had been mistakenly booked in as economy class passengers. A dreadful mistake which we have corrected, of course. The tickets we are sending to the Mandarin Hotel for these honourable persons will be first class. We would like to know if they would wish to avail of the two sleeping compartments in the first-class area, as they have not been booked so far.

We did not book the beds, but we did enjoy the upgrade!

We arrived in the airport, in a stretch limo (we were ministers after all) and ushered into a sumptuous lounge peopled by lovely hostesses. Wine flowed freely.

As I do not drink alcohol Frank was getting double helpings. The same on the plane. We arrived in Manila at about 1 pm on Good Friday. We went looking for a taxi to Noreen Trota's home.

I exited the airport first, and saw a truck parked with a crucified, almost naked man on the large cross in the carpark just opposite. I found out that this crucifixion was done fairly regularly on Good Friday.

Frank came out, blinked, gave me a nudge and said, 'Robert, what do you see over there?' in a slurred voice and with narrowed eyes.

I said, 'a carpark'.

He replied, 'no, look there,' pointing.

I kept a totally straight face and said, 'a carpark'.

He clasped my arm and said: 'God, that wine was strong. I am as drunk as a coot as I see a crucified man on the back of the truck.'

Our hostess, Noreen Trotta, lived in a guarded diplomatic compound. She was a true friend to Gerard and all the many Irish priests. She welcomed us as neighbours' children.

That evening, I was struck by the tension in Malina (the capital of the Philippines). This was during the Marcos regime. When we went to the local supermarket for sun-cream, we passed armed guards with shotguns and pistols, who were guarding the gates of the diplomatic compound.

In the supermarket, I noticed soldiers patrolling metal walkways that were raised 15 feet above us. They had nasty looking guns.

The supermarket was owned by Mrs Marcos. The soldiers would shoot anyone caught pilfering anything. A considerable encouragement not to steal. You remember Mrs Imelda Marcos and her 400 pairs of shoes?

A mildly subversive joke, Gerard told me later, was that Mrs Marcos was in the mining business: 'THIS IS MINE, THIS IS MINE, ALL MINE.'

We ended up staying in the 'Reds' monastery in Cebu. It was a very male institution. I remember trying to get the dirt off the door of the fridge. I also remember, one night, an argument about liberation theology and religious colonialism from the west, although the Philippines was deeply Catholic.

The poverty was frightening there, 95% of the wealth was owned by 5% of the people, and boy were the wealthy wealthy. They had their own ranches guarded by what were effectively private armies.

Gerard had the gift of finding water by divining. Water was very valuable out there. My father had that gift too. When a rich rancher wanted him to find water, Gerard would do it in return for a community centre for the poor.

I went to his mass one day in an outside, open-air church. Suddenly, I found the ground shifting under me. I thought it was an earthquake, but, to my surprise, no one left the timber church.

Gerard told me later: 'It was only rats, as the church was built on the town's old dump.' The dump had been covered with earth and the church built on top of it.

I went up to the *barrios*, or mountain villages, with Gerard one day. We left the jeep at the end of the road and walked the last three miles; it was very hot. It was more of a mud-track really, as we had left tarmacadam 20 miles back.

He was going to a swearing in ceremony for new Catholic lay workers, but also to marry, baptise, hear confessions and say Mass.

His parish was so big that he only got to this village once every 4 months or so. Another official was to assist Gerard in the swearing in but he did not make it, so Gerard said to me: 'Aren't you a commissioner for oaths? Can't you do the job?'

I swore them in. I remember their lovely smiling, trusting faces. I remember their hospitality in the midst of their obvious poverty.

Gerard showed me one 'house' on the way down that night. It was a collection of bamboo poles covered by tattered black plastic, like the kind we used in silage bailing at home.

He told me the only asset they had was a single mango tree. Their sons were sent to work for the ranchers from the ages of 6 or 7. The eldest daughter, aged 14, was 'sold' to a soldier stationed in the American base in the next island. Gerard did not like the Americans in the Philippines.

One of Gerard's functions was to be a prison 'visitor'. I arranged to visit the prison where Fr O'Brien and others were being held for a long time on trumped-up charges. I was then a member of Amnesty International and so asked to inspect.

I could write a book about my experiences that day, but you would probably not be interested. However, I can sum the place up with the following few observations.

During the day, the prisoners were corralled into an open shed where they sat waiting for food. The prisoners fortunate enough to have relatives, got their food from their relatives through the barred window on the street-side of the prison.

I saw one prisoner get an egg. He remained in the shed, but went to the yard side. He then got a 6" piece of corrugated iron. Still in the shade, he carefully cracked the egg on the iron. Then, with even more care, he extended the iron out of the shade and into the sun. The egg fried quickly and, more quickly, he ate it.

The window through which his brother gave him the egg had a window sill of about 4 feet long. A man was sleeping on that window sill, and he had tied himself to the bars so he wouldn't fall off. There was nowhere else for the poor man to sleep.

The second observation was what had been Fr O'Brien's cell. It was a ghastly, swelteringly hot shed. We in our cushy, 'Emerald Isle' have no idea of how wonderfully courageous these priests and nuns are. They are Christ-like in their love, in their faith and as messengers of Hope.

In that hell-hole of a cell, in stifling temperatures, I found a man who should not have been in the prison at all. He could not get a trial as he had no relatives or money to get a lawyer.

He had been arrested a year earlier in another island. The army had come looking for a Mr AB. Apparently someone pointed out this man as being named AB. However, there were about ten other men in that town named AB also.

The army took this man, totally in the wrong. He was 'disappeared' to this prison 200 miles away. I got his name on a bit of paper.

After I left the prison, Gerard got me to meet a human rights lawyer. The lawyer told me his colleague, who was trying to expose police corruption, was shot dead outside the courthouse two months earlier. I gave him $50 to get Mr AB out of prison – it took him 6 months, but he did it.

Lawyers do good things. I hope you agree. There are a lot of good lawyers protecting freedom all over the world, as I learnt while in the International Bar Association. The trouble is fat-cat, city corporate lawyers give lawyers a bad name.

Fr O'Brien and four others had been wrongly arrested on trumped up charges. They were called the 'Negros 5'.

Amid all the abuse scandals by the religious now being revealed, remember they are a tiny minority. Think of the wonderful work done and still being done by the little-honoured majority.

I wonder how many remember the terrible ordeal of Fr O'Brien and the Negros 5? Just like the Birmingham 6. Fr O'Brien and four others had been wrongly arrested by the Marcos regime, on trumped up charges.

Abuse of the law. Just look at the new revelations about the Hillsborough disaster.

Back in Belize: things are better here now. I think it's the angle of the wind. I'll get some air. I think I'll be able to sit on the veranda of the cabin.

I'll look out at the brown tide of sprat. I suppose the predators will be there too. Such is nature.

The sun in warm. I'll take time out. I go. The Americans (new tourists) will be inside but it is agreed the shaded veranda is okay to anyone who wants to use it. Good international relations.

A West Cork Election

We discussed politics again last night, even though Olive did not approve. It was more light-hearted. I like to get people interested and involved, otherwise democracy fails. There certainly is a waning of patriotism. The EU is sterilising political thought.

I think one is either interested in politics or not. If one is interested in the affairs of the state then one should get more and more involved.

In my case my interest started while at university, where I joined the Fine Gael branch there. Initially, they told me to join another branch, which I refused to do. That was the branch I wanted to join. I eventually got in there but I was carefully monitored by the branch so my activities were of little use. The objection seemed to have been that I wasn't from the Dublin elite. Even though I had Collins pedigree, many of them were snobs. I was a country boy.

Back in the 1960s, as a fledgling lawyer gaining his wings in Dunmanway,

West Cork, I got involved with an uncle of mine, Seán Collins TD. This uncle was a bit of a wild man in many ways.

My mother said that the burning of their home by the Essex Regiment and the Black and Tans had a very bad effect on the children, and on Seán in particular. It made him insecure.

He was what would have been described at that time as a 'character'. His deeds and misdeeds were legendary.

When it came to the election, I, in a way, became a sub-office of his. He would never actually address the problems I sent his way, so I ended up having to invent solutions and attribute them to him.

Very often his constituents would call to me about a problem. I would tell them I would write to Seán, my uncle. After a suitable period of time, I would reply with my views on how they could solve the problem, with some accompanying letter from a department office that attributed the result of my labours to Seán. I got him some votes.

The election was memorable for two reasons.

The first was my maiden speech in a village called Drimoleague, my introduction as a political 'maestro'. I remember being half-way through my speech when, through an act of misfortune, I looked down at the people who were listening to me.

There planked in the middle of them were my two parents, who had heard about my political baptism. They had come down to West Cork to see my mother's father. The sight of them threw me off and I got totally confused. I think my mother, God rest her, was the only one who said I was great – mothers!

The second was a visit to Bantry with Seán Collins. I remember being collected by him on Sunday evening with a view to having an election meeting at 8 o'clock in Bantry.

When we arrived in Bantry he was somewhat worse for wear and I full of enthusiasm. We soon discovered that there were virtually no supporters present. We were told that organising the meeting had been a total failure because Seán had failed to look after his constituents. Everybody thought that he was going to lose the election.

Seán however, like all the Collins people, was never one to be easily beaten. He accepted the challenge and went around the street with a microphone. I was driving his car. He shouted things like: 'Hey Biddy are you gone to bed? Are you not going to come down to listen to me?'

The populous of Bantry were regaled by his personal remarks about the various sides and factions. They were told that they were getting lazy and that they weren't interested in their country.

The result was people thronged down to the square. Seán had this pied-piper effect on people. We had a ball of a meeting at which Seán spoke eloquently and everybody cheered. As for the election, he was elected.

No Free State Literature

When I starting practising in Listowel, I was careful not to get too involved in politics, although I kept in touch with Fine Gael for many years.

Eventually, in 1979, I stood for the Listowel Urban Council as a Fine Gael candidate.

Initially, it was difficult to get active in the local Fine Gael because they were controlled by a few families, whose main objective appeared to be to keep other people out. Not unusual for local politics.

My brother John, who had been a member of the Urban Council under the Fine Gael flag, was a victim of this carry-on. They forced him into a position where he had to either violate his conscience or get out of Fine Gael. He got out of Fine Gael. I remained in the party.

When John did not seek re-election, I was put forward. I was successful in being elected.

Last night in the cabin, Olive gave her version of that election night. Olive, being the loyal daughter of a Fianna Fail TD, kept her distance initially. Then Chris Walsh, a strong FF supporter, told her women always backed their husbands. Olive literally got on her bike to support me.

On polling day, she stood behind the table and canvassed people as they approached the booth. So much so that the saying around town after the election was: 'Poor old Robert was the candidate, Olive the Politician!'

I was second from the top in first preferences and top of the Fine Gael list. This of course caused instant jealousy, so I did not get much party support after that, and I didn't do as well in the next local election.

From then on, many within the party saw it as their role to 'down me'.

However, my interest continued. I got re-elected.

At that time, the fortunes of Fine Gael in North Kerry were very poor. That urban council election coincided with a bad county council election, and it precipitated a sharp decline in Fine Gael fortunes. Their County Council seats were reduced to two, and eventually we lost the one TD we had and two senators. We ended up without any Fine Gael Oireachtas member for the North Kerry constituency.

Which was quite extraordinary, as we were the only constituency in the whole of the Republic then that didn't have a Fine Gael representative in the Oireachtas.

1982, as it turned out, was a year of sharp developments in my political career. In June 1981 a coalition government was elected. It didn't have a proper majority and was therefore dependent on the support of independents, the most notable being one Jim Kemmy. He was a Democratic Socialist Party representative from Limerick.

The budget introduced by the coalition in the beginning of 1982 was a tough budget. Dr Garrett Fitzgerald, Taoiseach and leader of Fine Gael, felt that this was necessary and I think the country as a whole felt it was necessary. However, Mr Kemmy differed. He thought it was too tough. In hindsight, I think it was all a bit politically inept by the government, arguing about small items such as VAT on children's shoes.

In any event, Mr Kemmy brought down the government and there was an election. North Kerry Fine Gael believed that the contender from the Listowel area would be the man who had formerly held a seat. However, he didn't want to run and stated that he wasn't going to be a candidate.

That left the field wide open and I was told to go once more into the breach. I was the sole candidate for Fine Gael. I was selected as the sole candidate in the hope that factions within Fine Gael, which were legendary at that stage, (particularly in North Kerry) would get behind a single candidate. Everybody was fighting with everybody else. Alas, this unity of purpose did not happen, and North Kerry Fine Gael were also in debt.

For the election, I set up 2 offices, one in Listowel and one Tralee, as there was no structure or unity. I hired a driver. There were no funds in the constituency. The election cost me £3,500, which was a lot of money then. However, it was worth it, as I met so many good and helpful people.

Sadly, the disunity continued, and it is well known that factions within the group deprived me of the seat.

Despite this, I did reasonably well. I was only three votes behind a sitting TD, and I got 4,536 first preference votes. However, as I had no back up person with me I wasn't elected.

I wasn't eliminated though, which was some achievement I suppose – coming in fourth in the race for a three-seat constituency.

I had worked extremely hard. I remember getting up at 7 o'clock and ringing my director of elections. We made out our programme for the day, a draft preliminary programme for the following day and then set-off.

We were often at the factory gates at 8 o'clock in the morning, meeting shifts going in and coming out. It was an interesting and exhausting experience.

What struck me the most was the number of very good people in the country, but also the number of extremely selfish people in the country. There were people in the major political parties who were prepared to sacrifice themselves on behalf of the country. Unfortunately, there were a very large number of people whose sole interest in the election was what they could personally get out of it.

Without doubt, the most common question asked was: 'What will you do for me?' I rarely, if ever, was asked: 'What will you do for the country?'

Of course, electioneering is a very funny occupation.

Common answers I got included, 'of course we won't forget you Mr Pierse,' or 'certainly Mr Pierse, we will give you a scratch,' or 'sure, you can rely on us,' and perhaps the most common of all, 'we will do the best we can for you'.

One of the funnier incidents was going to a convent. I happened to meet a Fianna Fail rival candidate, with whom I was very friendly, as we approached the convent gates.

We decided, between us, that we would go in and count the number of nuns who promised us No. 1. We knew that there were about 40 nuns in the convent. He went in the front door and I went in the side door, and we were seated in two different parlours.

The nuns flitted from one parlour to the other. They discussed the issues with us, including contraception and abortion which were in the air at the time.

When these interviews were over the other candidate and myself met. Of the 40 nuns, he got 36 promises of first preferences and I got 33- you couldn't keep up to the nuns, could you?

There was of course great rivalry between the parties. Fortunately, it was friendly, most of the time anyway.

I spent a day canvassing in Lixnaw with the late Jimmy Conway, a diehard 'blueshirt,' as the Fine Gaelers were called. We would come to a house and he would say to me, 'waste of time going in there, black Fianna Fail,' or 'these were inoculated with Fianna Fail the day they were born'. However, I always told him I would go in, as I had said I would pass no door.

I remember coming to the top of a certain road outside Lixnaw. Jimmy said: 'Don't waste an hour going down there, there isn't a single FG vote in the road.'

However, I 'did' the road. I remember going into one house. The people in the house were clients of mine and my father was their vet. We had a nice handshake and chat. I tried not to stay too long, Jimmy had told me they would try to delay me so I would not get the canvassing done.

I remember putting my leaflet on the table and saying, 'I hope you will not forget me next Friday'. Then, as I was leaving, the man of the house delicately picked up the corner of my leaflet and handed it to me.

He said: 'Sorry Mr Pierse, we never took Free State literature in this house'.

The young people last night enjoyed these stories, but I had to explain what the Free State was, and civil war politics. They were amazed that the division was still there 60 years on. Then, they asked what happened to my career in Irish politics.

One tremendous positive I took from the election was the family help. The kids were all at an age where they could be realistic and enthusiastic, and they worked very hard for me. I think it was very good for the family and indeed for the staff in my office who worked very hard and were enthusiastic. Teamwork is a building exercise.

I also remember how all the family supported me in my defeat – that was wonderful!

After the Dáil election I didn't try the Senate. I was advised I wouldn't be elected, and I thought that was the right advice.

In any event, I did not have a whole lot of regard for the Senate, which I see as a political limbo. In the Senate, failed politicians, in the sense of those not being re-elected to the Dáil, suffered on until the next general election, when they would have another go. It was also a useful, if fairly meaningless, platform for aspiring politicians looking for publicity. It badly needs to be reformed, so it can be a meaningful part of the Oireachtas.

The eventual North Kerry nominee was well and truly beaten, as I would have been if I had gone forward. The electorate comprised only 900 electors and you were up against some extremely cute and committed politicians, so it was difficult to break in to the field.

Fianna Fail got in as a result of the February, 1982 election, but it was even more unstable than the previous one. It soon fell and there was a second election in November 1982.

I can safely say that in the intervening time I had worked extremely hard for the party.

I admired Dr Garret Fitzgerald. I had attended, as far as I could count, about 82 political meetings, which meant being out endlessly at night. I had attended all the new political clinics, which had been set up for the first time in North Kerry following the poor election result. I had written about 1,000 letters. The party had cleared its financial debts and we were in much better condition to fight the second election, which of course we had been expecting.

Then came the convention. I got an inkling a few days before the convention that there was a concerted move, organised by various factions, to unite against me. They did this successfully.

There are several religions in Kerry, and many of them have a stronger pull than politics. The Catholic Church religion was, at least at that time, much stronger than politics.

However, there was another religion that at certain times was, and in certain ways is, even stronger than Catholicism. That was the religion of GAA football.

The man who was proposed against me was a very decent young man called Jimmy Deenihan. However, the fact he was a Kerry footballer of considerable renown was one of the main reasons why he was being proposed.

This was unfair on him, because he was also a teacher and his family had been Fine Gael people. However, it emerged in the convention that football was the only thing that counted. During the convention, when the way things were going was becoming clear to me, I remember meeting my brother John and saying to him, 'Say a prayer that I am beaten because this crowd are crazy'.

Whether it was answered prayer or not, beaten I was, by the people who forwarded Jimmy Deenihan and of course a very nice, young lady candidate called Mrs Bernie Gannon.

We therefore entered the election with two candidates. I supported the two candidates. I worked hard for them, but unfortunately we were beaten again. Jimmy got elected to Senate and later became a minister in the Dáil.

I then had a decision to make, either to stay with or get out of substantial politics. I must confess I found the disruption it brought to my business and family life considerable.

I felt that going back to the law full-time, and rearing my family as best I could, was in my best interests. I always thought creating employment was very important. I had an office in Tralee as well, also in Kerry.

I wanted to build up the firm's services. Law was becoming more and more complicated. I think this, initially at least, disappointed my wife Olive, as she is a natural politician. I can't say that I am, a natural politician that is. I am probably a bit too abrasive and cranky for the job.

I found the internal dissensions within the party, and the implicit belief that politics was the art of promising something for nothing, difficult to stomach.

That is not to say that I did not admire a lot of the people in politics, some of whom are in it for the very best of reasons and are trying to do the very best they can.

It was often difficult to tell who were trying to be the bigger rogues, was it the public who were trying to make rogues out of politicians, or the politicians who were trying to mislead the public? It probably confirms the fact that democracy is, in some ways, the best form of government, and in other ways the worst.

I continued to hold my seat in the urban council. In many respects, I think that this was the best political forum for me, the one I could obtain the most satisfaction from.

My brother had told me this before I was elected to the urban council, but I hadn't really accepted it. I discovered urban councils were not hotbeds of contention, that all the nine people were doing their earnest best to regulate the affairs of the town for the benefit of the community as a whole, rather than for the purpose of gaining political fame.

This made me a great believer in local government and in local people handling local affairs. However, this handling must be done in public, because otherwise they would no longer be events of public involvement, in the sense of allowing the public scrutinise and judge the activities of the council.

One of the great failures of Irish politics is it has allowed bureaucracy to replace local representation in government. You see the same in the EU now – bureaucrats manipulating the law and politicians.

Update: Listowel Urban Council has been abolished and power has become more centralised. What a pity!

Update 2018: I have left Fine Gael over its promotion of abortion, which I found horrifying. How could the Irish people vote in abortion? The whole, dreadful decision offends my sense of shared humanity, my beliefs in equality, human rights and Christianity.

My Father

My father was not only a beloved father, but also a great friend.

His brilliant career as a vet began by getting first place in the British Isles in his final veterinary exams (and I think 9 medals).

My grandfather John had become a vet due to the determination of his mother and not that of his boozy father. You know the excusing sentence of the Irish, 'a great man but a martyr to the drink'! John, my grandfather, on qualifying moved to Listowel and then my father, Richard Robert (Dick), followed him into the veterinary profession in time, scoring mightily in exams.

An old pal of mine, Victor Ryan of Tralee, recently gave me a photocopy of the following extract from *The Kerryman*, which was found by James Walsh, his friend, when searching old microfilmed newspapers.

Brilliant Kerry Student
First place in Great Britain and Ireland at the recent examinations held by the Royal College of Veterinary Surgeons, went to Mr. R.R. Pierse, son of J.H. Pierse, M.R.C.V.S. Listowel. He passed his final examination with first class honours. He obtained first place in Great Britain and Ireland.

He has the unique distinction of being the first student from the Irish College to obtain first class honours in this examination. Furthermore, it is twelve years since first class honours have been awarded to any student in the British Isles.

Yes, my late father and friend to me was: 'A man, taking him for all in all, I shall not look upon his likes again.' All his life he loved his farmers. He said they were the salt of the earth. I remember their strong rough hands at his funeral, saying, 'the doc was a friend and advisor as well as my vet'.

It was at the Veterinary college in Ballsbridge he met my mother, Mary Collins. She was a poultry instructress, and therefore obliged to bring in dead or ill birds for examination.

One of the professors called her in one day and said, 'Mary, I want to introduce you to the most brilliant student I ever had here,' and added, 'Mary you could not do better than this Kerryman'.

My mother's most abiding memory of that first meeting was that of a shy, young man whose hands were holding a dissecting knife and who talked about bugs in a bird's liver, and his big boots.

She says she was not particularly impressed. Father, on the other hand, admitted he was very impressed and he pursued her his way. She had a car, which was most unusual for a woman then! He had a bike. He learnt her route home. My mother laughed at the number of times she saw his bike and big boots in front of her at a particular crossroads in Haddington Road, Dublin. So, it began!

My father took over his father's practice as soon as he qualified, as my grandfather Pierse was dying. My grandfather came late to the profession due to the fact that his father drank too much. However, he had a great mother, and she educated her one son to become a doctor in spite of her husband. Then she made the doctor son finance my grandfather's veterinary education.

My grandmother on the Pierse side was a sharp, flinty woman who had a hurtful tongue. We were all afraid of her, especially my mother. My father was her youngest child, so probably spoiled. Women are strange about their eldest son and their youngest child.

This grandmother's first son became a priest, which only made things worse for the family, and their youngest child was my father. I always regarded her as a bit of a hairpin, (a difficult woman in other words).

My father loved his wife, children, farmers, animals, and his profession – in that order. I adored him, and every chance I got I would be off with him out the country.

He worked 6½ days a week. My mother held sacrosanct Sunday mornings for him to rest, before 12 o'clock mass.

She very much ruled the roost at home, firmly with caring love.

He had his surgery, which would often have up to 20 farmers in there, especially on wet fair days. He used to urge them to improve themselves. Sometimes, he would spend an hour advising them on their family, farm and care of animals, as well as draining and putting fertilizer on the land. He had, of course, a farm in Meenogahane.

It is wonderful to me that our daughter Eilín has that great love for farming and animals.

I mentioned earlier about piseógs and how the min with the caps believed in them. My father was not a cap-revered man but he believed in piseógs or curses. He had a personal experience that convinced him of their existence.

He had a row with a widow once, a Mrs X, who refused to pay him for a lot of work. When he insisted on being paid she cursed him 3 times, wished that he may have bad luck.

He was a terrific surgeon and I witnessed him operating on horses, cows, dogs (greyhounds were his specialty) pigs, and many more. He rarely 'lost' an animal, (the term for when an animal died). However, after the curse he complained he lost some animals.

I remember one day being out with him in Florry Healy's farm. He was castrating colts. This was a big operation, and about 7 men were required to knock the colt and tie him down with very strong ropes.

My father was in the middle of this operation, when, at about 3 o'clock, he stood up and shook himself. He said 'something happened'. We all said, 'WHAT'. 'A great weight has been lifted off me,' he replied.

When we returned to Listowel a few hours later, we were greeted with the following news: Mrs X had died at 3 o'clock that day.

I was cursed once by a widow. I had been on the other side of a law case. In the early part of my career I can remember being solemnly cursed 3 times by her who I sued for my clients and won. I always laughed it off.

A priest psychologist told me once that laughing it off neutralised it.

Mary Pierse, My Mother

My mother was a more complex character than my father. At least I thought so.

I confess that I am not much good at sizing women up, even though I have been super-lucky with my mother, wife, and 3 daughters.

I suppose it is being the second of seven sons that causes me to be astounded at the differences between men and women. I always remember what the frustrated Rex Harrison said in the film *My Fair Lady*: 'Pickerington, why can't women be more like men?'

I was Rex Harrison, until I met my wonderful wife. I now say, like Brigette Bardot, *'vive la difference'*.

I believe my mother was very much affected by her troubled family upbringing. She was the eldest child of Seán (Johnny) Collins, who was the elder farmer brother of Michael Collins.

In fact, my mother never told us much about her beloved, the really tragically assassinated, Uncle Michael.

I first learnt about him really from my brother John, when I was 5 or so. He brought the news home from school one day – a Fine Gael teacher had mentioned it in class.

My mother's eyes welled in tears and we were told go out and clean the yard. She used to make novenas for her uncle. The events of 'Bloody Sunday' saddened her.

When I stood for the Fine Gael party 30 years later, she was not at all happy. She said to me they'll stab you in the back if they think you might get there. How right she was!

I remember the day President Hillary opened the Collins home in Woodfield, Clonakilty (14th October, 1990), where she, my grandfather and Michael were reared. My mother was a guest of honour, as she was a niece of the great man.

She was the eldest of her family present at the burning of Woodfield. She had been asked to identify the house's exact location before it was burnt down. She did that by locating the big stone at the front door.

Her brother Liam, who had been the baby in her arms at the time of the fire, had bought the site and, with the help of a good local committee, got it restored.

Liam was a great man.

That day of the opening of Woodfield was a dreadful day of rain. The guests of honour had lunch with the dignitaries. I parked my car just behind the president's and got near to the platform in the Collins' homestead.

I tried to get my then frail mother to stay in the car, from where she could see and hear everything. No such luck – out she got and sat in the rain with 'the family'.

It continued to pour rain. I went over and said, 'Nana have sense, you will get your death'. She looked at me and said, 'I'm a Collins, this is my place'.

The day cleared after the ceremony was over. My mother showed us where she had been standing when the Black and Tans, guarded by the crown's regular forces, the Essex Regiment, burnt down her home on 16/4/1921.

She was the eldest child. Her mother had died from TB shortly before that. Her father Seán was away in Cork at a county council meeting. He was a Sinn Fein councillor.

He was arrested that day on the way home and became a political prisoner in Spike Island, and later in Bere Island.

The Tans burnt her house and contents, including the baby's pen, and killed the goose and the bull in the outhouse. The only real item that they were allowed bring out of the house was a new Singer sewing machine – because it was English!

She remembered standing under a tree when Captain Percival of the regular forces came over and asked her what age she was and what age the other children were.

She had her baby brother Liam in her arms, who was delighted with the flames, the windows popping and the excitement.

My mother spoke to the captain. He said: 'My God, my children are the same age, what am I doing here?' He whistled up the soldiers and marched them away.

The 'Tans' however would not leave. They forced the neighbours to help burn Woodfield, saying to the neighbours who came with buckets to help put out the fire: 'We'll plug the first bloody Paddy who moves.'

The Captain who went away later became General Arthur Percival, the man who surrendered Singapore to the Japanese. The Japanese had invaded the city from the back during World War II. All the British guns were pointed towards the sea, but the Japs came by land, riding on bicycles.

When Tim Pat Coogan wrote his book *Michael Collins*, I got a copy of it for her. I asked her to write her own recollections of Uncle Michael.

That is all she wrote in her lovely writing.

The Day of my Uncle's Assassination
By Mary Pierse (nee Collins)
On the day of the ambush, Kitty and I went to Clon to buy clothes with our father. We met uncle Michael. He was very interested in our going to the convent in Wicklow. He was only two hours in Clonakilty. He gave me a kiss. Kitty said she was too big to be kissed even though she was younger.

We went home by the fields, because it was a shortcut, and because my father did not let us around the town late in the evening. The whole family and neighbours were sitting around. We asked what was wrong. My father said young uncle Michael was shot 2 hours after he left Clonakilty!

There are a number of mistakes towards the end of the little bit she wrote. My brother John, the family historian, thinks she got the day mixed up with the previous day. I'm not sure that John is right.

My father told me that she was crying so much at that stage and saying 'poor Michael, poor Michael,' that he simply took the book away and gave it back to me. I have it still. My mother was a victim of the Civil War too, as were so many others.

Everybody listened respectfully last night while I told the above story. I find it strange that Michael Collins' name is still so well-known and remembered.

I was urged last night to stay up late, something I hate doing, to recount what 'Nana,' my mother, remembered about her beloved uncle Michael.

It would take me many pages to record them all. Many were small incidents such as:

How Uncle Michael went with Papa, my grandfather Seán, up to a certain field where there was a high sheltering fence. There they discussed serious business.

On one such occasion, she remembered her Papa talking about the need for peace and a truce. They hadn't even one bullet for every gun in the hands of Irishmen and the British had their weapons and ammunition.

Also, that the English had thousands of soldiers demobbed after the 1914-18 war with nothing to do. They would let them loose in Ireland.

How Uncle Michael had hugged her when he came down to Woodfield after the Tans had burnt her and the children out of their home. He said to her: 'They knew how to hit me where it hurts most.'

She and the other children were divided out among relatives but kept out of school for some time for fear of reprisals.

How she had slept in the back of the house so she could take food to the 'lads' on the run. They had a small, secret room at the back of the bull's stall. The lads threw pebbles at her window and whistled to wake her.

She told me how she didn't like her Uncle Michael's moustache, which he had on one of his visits. However, he refused to shave it off, as he said they were reward posters up showing him without a moustache.

A Terrible Day: 22nd August 1922

There was her account of the morning of that day above. I'll give you a bit more she told below even if it's a bit repetitious.

My mother's account as it was confirmed to me by my aunt Kitty, my godmother. My mother was 13 years old and Kitty about 12. Young girls of that age are very perceptive. I did try to get more details later from Nana, my mother. This seems to be the story.

My grandfather Seán took his two oldest daughters, Mary and Kitty, into Clonakilty that morning. He had decided, because of all the reprisals that were happening, that they should go away to the Dominican nuns in Wicklow. They had to buy clothes for going away.

When she eventually got to that convent school, the nuns were so good to her. My brother John's second Christian name is Dominic.

Uncle Michael had been in Skibbereen overnight, and had sent word to Papa, his eldest brother, to meet him in Donovan's hotel in the morning.

They met and the two girls were there. My mother said there were a lot of solemn faces and solemn talk.

She did remember Michael telling her Papa that a secret meeting, to help bring the dreadful civil war to an end, was being planned.

She remembered it was a short stay, as Uncle Michael had to be off on a tour. Before he left, Michael picked up the two girls in his big, strong arms, and kissed them both. Kathy (aged 11) protested, saying she was too old to be kissed.

He told Mary and Kitty he would visit them. He said he was often in Wicklow. He got into the open vehicle, not the *Sliabh na mBan*, the armoured Rolls Royce used by high-ranking Free State defence personnel during the civil war. He thought his own West Cork people would never kill him – so my grandfather always said.

My grandfather and the girls continued their shopping. My grandfather had to stay in Clonakilty on business so kept the horse and cart. The girls headed home through the fields by a footpath, a 'short cut'.

On the way back, they called into the parson's wife, with whom they were friendly, for tea and scones and to admire her garden. They dallied there.

It was late afternoon before they got back to Woodfield, where they lived in a reconstructed outhouse and a cousin's house. My mother told me later she felt something was wrong when the dogs did not run out to meet them.

When they got into the house it was full of people. They overheard that

Uncle Michael had been killed. Lots of people were crying.

The days, weeks, month and years that followed were a nightmare. She always felt that Uncle Michael's death caused such a shock that it helped 'to bring the country to its senses'.

Update: Since we got home, my brother John told me about recordings made of my mother, where she discusses her uncle Michael. John has got transcripts of the recordings and gave them to me. Thanks John.

Find the transcript below. As you can see, it is a bit mixed up and on some points this account differs from what she told me.

When my father was dying, he warned us that Nana was suffering from Alzheimer's, which we didn't accept at the time.

We knew, of course, that she would get upset or distressed whenever 'Uncle Michael' was mentioned, or the burning of the house.

Side 2 Tape 1
Mrs Mary Pierse, daughter of Seán Collins.
My recollections of Woodfield as a child and the things that happened there in relation to Michael Collins.

My first memory of him is as fresh and I must not have been much more than 4 years old. We were on the road below the house, what we called North Road.

Uncle Michael was throwing a ball, and I have no further recollection of what happened, but I can see him still throwing it. He looked to me to be a grand sweeping fellow, and he threw the ball with great vigour. I expect he was on holidays and he seemed to be carefree and very happy indeed.

My next recollection is of sweeping the stairs. It must have been perhaps a year later, on his next holiday.

I got a contrary notion that I would go behind the dust instead of in front of it, but I was severely lectured on how a stairs should be brushed. I was seven.

Perhaps that same summer, or it may be the next one, I remember a very indignant mother rushing into the house protesting that she had nearly been shot. The two (Michael Collins and Seán Hurley) were target practising and very nearly got her. Though I don't remember seeing Seán Hurley, I am under the impression that he was staying there, but I distinctly remember Michael at all times.

Perhaps it was that same holiday too that he played with us in the garden in his new suit, prior to leaving for London. My mother, I think, was ill because nobody repaired the pants for him. He decided to repair it himself, saying he was very good at doing it and that he was quite good at needlework. But a photograph taken that day in Clonakilty showed that his attempts at physical mending where not all that he thought they would be.

I expect all these little recollections are of different holidays because there isn't anything fixed in my mind about anything. All is just peaceful ordinary living until the burning of the house.

That morning my father left home and I looked out the window, I peeped out through the curtains to see him going, and I thought he looked very nice in a bowler hat. That was the last I saw of him for a long time.

About two hours later: We had at the time living with us a grandaunt and she asked me to clean a brass lamp belonging to her sister, who was my grandmother. In cleaning the glass of it, which was a very odd shape, I drove a knife through it, and the only thing on the evening when everything had gone up in flames was my recollection that I wouldn't get into any trouble now over this glass, which shows how very young I was.

Some officer or Black and Tan called on my aunt, and told her that the house was to be emptied, or at least we were to get out of it, and we went out to see all the neighbours under arrest, a long line of men, lined up against the ditch opposite the house. We were all ordered out and we rushed in every direction.

All of us were there, the 8 children, my grandaunt and Peg of course (my mother was dead at this stage, she had died on the 4th February and this was the 16th April). We all got out smartly.

I rushed to take a hen that was hatching chickens to safety and in my flight I met an officer who helped me. I said to him, were they going to burn the bull. All I can remember is that the bull was roaring in the stall, so he assured me not and he said he felt a monster because it was dreadful to have to do this because he had a family of children in England the very same age as we *were* and he just could not picture how dreadful it would be if anybody went in and burned their home.

There was quite a battalion of them. To a child, I suppose, it seemed that there were a lot there, but I suppose there were probably about 20. I can't really recollect seeing lorries or anything.

We were so eager to save what we could, especially any animals that were around, and get them out of the farm. We rushed to a neighbour's house, who was also a cousin, Annie Collins. We could stay there, especially the baby. I took Liam in my arms first, before I went to rescue the hens, over to her place and left him there.

Any recollections of the rest of the day aren't very clear, except to see the house burning, which I saw for months and months afterwards. We didn't feel too badly about things that day until the evening, when a cousin Maurice Collins went to the train to meet my father and came back to say that he had been arrested and was taken to Cork jail.

That was a very unpleasant day and we went to live then in the neighbour's house, Annie Collins. I don't know really how long we remained there, but I remember a visit shortly after the burning from Uncle Michael, who gave us the first and only demonstration of affection I ever remember.

He put his arms around Kitty and myself and hugged and kissed us and said he was so sorry that we should be the victims of all this trouble so young, that it was dreadful.

Later then, in a way I suppose making up to us, he sent Auntie Hannie to bring us to Dublin, where he gave us a most wonderful holiday.

She was living in London and only home on holidays – he gave us this wonderful holiday. He hired a taxi and put it at our disposal, it seemed to me for about a fortnight. We did tours through Wicklow, Dublin, Kildare, every beauty spot in the vicinity of Dublin, we did them all.

I can't remember the driver, but I know he was a very close friend of his. He was very, very nice to us and he minded us as if we were his own.

Then at night we returned to go to the theatre. This was always the Queens or some theatre of this kind where very exciting plays were enacted. I am sure that was in the Queens, but it was the very much cloak and dagger type of stuff that we loved. This holiday for two children from the country, who had hardly ever been in a motorcar and certainly not in a theatre, was paradise.

He also took us out to dinner. One in particular I remember was to Eamon Davin's house in Leeson Street. There we got on very well with all our knives and forks and he was very amused at our eager eyes looking around for information.

We went to Ring after that and we were in Ring for the following year and went back home then to Clonakilty, at least what bit of a home was there, for our holidays.

It was that summer that we got ready to go away to boarding school and my father took us to town one day to meet Michael and to get our clothes for school.

Before Michael came to Clonakilty most of the purchasing was done, so we saw our uncle that day for the last time. We thought he was just super in his uniform. He was in full uniform and he promised faithfully that he wouldn't neglect us when we went to school

We intended to go to school in Wicklow and he promised he would see us very often there, which I am certain he would have, had he lived.

He was in very good form. Somebody said something to him about the split that had occurred, and he said: 'Oh, with God's help, this will only be very temporary and we will all be together again.'

Not an Informer

Another story that comes to mind is from my grandfather's time as a judge in the Sinn Fein courts. I'm not sure who told me this story. On one occasion, he apparently ordered a man to be shot as he was suspected as being 'an informer'.

My grandfather retired with his second wife, Nancy (née O'Brien), to Clonakilty many years later. He learned then that the man who had been executed was not an informer. The man had been involved in a bitter land dispute, and the accusation was a form of perjured revenge.

My grandfather, Seán Collins, was a very religious man and he suffered, as did my mother, from scruples. He visited the family of the executed man, sought and received forgiveness.

Sometime after this, while Nancy and Seán were leaving mass in Clonakilty, Nancy was approached, as my grandfather, at this stage, was getting deaf.

She was asked to arrange for three men to come visit my grandfather, and have a private meeting about Michael's death – if Seán agreed.

Seán agreed to meet them alone a weekend later, at about 7 pm, while his wife Nancy was at Benediction.

Afterwards, he said they told him the full-story behind the ambush.

My father and mother were never told what was said. I mention my father as he and my grandfather were very close, but they were very much men's men. Gosh! Will I get into trouble for writing that?

Later, I thought the only person Papa was likely to tell was his son, Liam, his youngest child and special confidant. When Liam was dying, I went to see him. We were more than uncle and nephew in many ways, as we were both solicitors and interested in the law.

Liam told me Papa never said anything, except that these things were best left buried and forgotten.

I hope 2019–2023 will not open deep wounds in Irish society.

Mrs Dev

My grandfather left West Cork after the burning of his homestead in Woodfield. He bought a farm in Kildare, but due to health problems he was forced to sell it and go first to Donnybrook, and then to Booterstown, the Dublin suburb.

While in Booterstown, Nancy became acquainted with Sinead de Valera, Dev's wife, as they were both daily mass goers.

Mrs Dev was a gentle woman who wrote children's books, and she always remembered that while Dev was in prison, in Lincoln jail, England, Michael Collins arranged the taking of food to Dev's family. She was also aware that Michael was behind Dev's escape.

During this time, my Grandfather applied for a job in the Land Commission. There was a lot of work being done by the Commission, including the compulsory purchase of big estates, which were paid for in land bonds. The commissioners were the people who divided this purchased land. I'm not sure whether Seán was a commissioner or an officer.

Sineád De Valera heard of Seán Collins' application. He was a farmer and therefore qualified for the job. My mother credited her, Mrs Dev, with getting my grandfather the job.

She could also have been the reason why my grandfather was permitted to stay on as land commissioner after retirement age.

Nancy, my step grandmother, always believed Dev had a guilty conscience when it came to Michael Collins' family.

I remember, at my grandfather's funeral, a big, old man from Tipperary saying how 'fair and just' my grandfather was as a commissioner. Apparently, this Tipperary man's family were all anti-treaty, Dev-men. They didn't expect to get a thing if Michael Collins' brother was in charge of the division of local estates. However, he said they got their fair and just share.

'Who Shall I Say is Calling?'

Some years later, my grandfather Seán was at St Vincent's hospital Dublin for an operation.

He always had difficulty with his hand. And the hand got worse during his time in Spike Island, where he was interred.

While interred in Spike Island, my grandfather shared a cell with Alfred O'Rahilly, a very famous Listowel man. My mother wrote to her father and got replies written by Alfred O'Rahilly, as my grandfather was unable to write, due to his damaged right hand. He claimed he received excellent treatment for his hand on Spike Island, from an English doctor.

Alfred also, like my father, was not afraid to stand up the clergy. Fr Anthony Gaughan, in his book on Alfred O'Rahilly, describes one such confrontation: 'In a letter to his wife Alfred was dismissive of the parish priest as "a timid, pious, little man, no use whatever to me". It seems Alfred's unfavourable opinion of Father Walsh was partly based on the latter's refusal, because of a promise made to the British O.C., to smuggle in or out letters or messages for him.' Father Walsh was a Listowel man. Apparently, the altar boy had so such qualms.

I must ask my brother John, who is the family historian, about that when I go home. It is a real pity John doesn't write a family history, he has a fabulous amount of knowledge!

Update: John tells me my grandfather damaged his hand in a farm accident.

While my grandfather was in hospital, Dev, who was the Taoiseach at the time, arrived with his bodyguards to visit one of his ministers, who was also a patient in St Vincent's.

After visiting the minister, apparently with instructions from Sinead his wife, he sought to visit Seán Collins.

He and his guards were directed to go down the stairs to the male surgical ward, named after some saint, as was the custom at the time.

They were met there by the ward's sister – and we all know how austere nurses can be about their patients, and territorial!

This particular ward sister was a Hurley from west Cork and very much a Fine Gaeler. She was related to my grandmother's people.

Dev asked where Seán was. Nurse Hurley said, 'I will have to see if he is allowed to see visitors'.

She turned to go away, only to turn back and say sharply: 'Who will I say is calling?'

Dev Helps a Collins
I have another interesting story that illustrates the complex Collins/de Valera relationship.

As I mentioned above, my step grandmother, Nancy Collins (née O'Brien), became close friends with Mrs Sineád de Valera. The ladies shared a love of the Irish language. Nancy visited Mrs de Valera's home on a regular basis, and they would talk Irish and discuss the Gaelic League.

Nancy and my grandfather had children. One of these was named Nancy, after her mother. Later, she married Michael Hurley. It is their son Kyron who told me this story.

Nancy was attending Sion Hill, a girls' secondary school in Blackrock. She wanted to do honours maths, but Sion Hill didn't teach honours maths.

During one of her visits to the de Valera home, Nancy mentioned this to Mrs de Valera. Mrs de Valera thought this was ridiculous and thought girls should have the opportunity to do honours maths. She promised to talk to Dev about it. She did.

Dev had been a mathematics teacher in Blackrock College, which was located near Sion Hill. Dev personally helped Nancy Jr to do honours maths.

What is curious is the way Dev tutored Nancy. Dev would attend early mass in Booterstown, so he arranged for Nancy to meet him after mass so they could walk together. They discussed the mathematical exercises Dev set up for her, and Nancy had completed the previous night. All the while the state car, with Dev's bodyguards inside, drove beside them. Nancy went on to get honours maths thanks to Dev. They are all gone to their God.

The Female Spy

My grandfather's second wife, Nancy O'Brien, who I mentioned above, worked in the civil service in London and Dublin's GPO. Like so many young Irish people, she got employment in the civil service in England or the colonial service.

Michael Collins worked in London until conscription arose. He worked in an accountant's office, where a number of his colleagues were leaving to join the British army.

Michael told his employers he was leaving, but not to where. The firm gave a send-off and a few bob to each. Michael headed to Dublin, not the front.

Nancy became one of his spies. Nancy always said that she and other Irish girls were half in love with the handsome west Cork boyo, and half afraid of him.

He had a bad temper at times, even my mother remembered that; his eyes would go black and his jaws tighten. She remembered his rage when Woodfield, their home, was burned.

Through her job, Nancy got hold of some sensitive papers. She was appointed a decoder in 1918, by the British. This fact startled Michael Collins. On one occasion, she had copied, in a toilet, a lot of these coded messages.

She wanted to make quick contact with Michael Collins, who, incidentally, was a cousin of hers. She took the late ferry to Dublin and stayed in a friend's house in Booterstown. It was also a 'safe house'.

She had the papers hidden in a hat, which she had put into a hatbox. Going to bed, she put the hatbox on top of a wardrobe.

At about 2 am, British troops raided the house.

Nancy was a super intelligent woman and a great character, had a lovely smile, and to me, forty years later, a natural flirt. She was also very good looking.

Out of bed she gets, and puts on a very revealing nightie. The soldiers come up the stairs and were carefully searching every room. Her door was open and the light was turned on.

Suddenly, Nancy sat up in bed and started screeching that she was going to be raped.

When an officer appeared, Nancy was crying and shouting. The officer said, 'calm down madam', with his eyes only half averted from her ample bosom.

Nancy kept saying, 'I'm going to be raped,' and the officer replied, 'madam, British soldiers don't do that'.

Nancy kept crying and shouting, and the officer kept saying, 'calm down madam'.

Eventually, he ordered the soldiers out of the room and he left closing the door after him. They left empty handed. How Nancy laughed about that incident.

Another memorable incident happened when she was a younger woman, and was asked, along with another woman, to transport guns from Dublin to Cork by train. She didn't tell me this herself, someone in the family did.

They were placed in a chest – you know the type, the ones with the brassy handle. They were called trousseau chests, I think. Women will know what they are!

While Nancy was on the train, it was held up by British forces at Limerick Junction.

Everyone was ordered off of the train and forced to identify their luggage. The luggage was pulled out onto the platform, and each owner had to stand beside his/her luggage as it was searched.

The officer in charge was an older man with a large, bushy moustache. Nancy went up to him and, with her sweetest, demure smile, said:

'Sir, I trust you are not going to allow these young soldiers to lay their hands on me. My bridal clothes and wedding gifts are in my chest. I'm going to Cork to get married next Saturday. If I am to be searched, can it be done personally by you in the privacy of the waiting room here?'

'You remind me of my father with that lovely moustache and that manly, figure that fits your uniform so well. Could you tell me what that coloured bar stands for?'

The officer blushed and spluttered, eventually saying it was a service decoration.

'Madam,' he began, 'I wish you a happy marriage. My own daughter is getting married next month. Of course, there is no need to search you, or your sweet sister or the bridal luggage.'

She began asking him about his daughter's wedding, and, to escape her, he lifted her case back into the train.

Nancy's eyes would twinkle when she told these stories; everybody loved her.

A Spy in Brompton Oratory
One other story I recounted last night was prompted by Paul's questions about Michael Collins.

My mother had a great story about how Michael and Churchill clashed during the negotiations. I think that's a well-known fact.

My mother's story was about how her uncle accused Churchill of spying on him. Collins said to Churchill: 'We are here as full plenipotentiaries and you should not be spying on us.'

Churchill replied: 'Nonsense, we are doing no such thing.' Collins said: 'Well you had better watch out as your spy who sits four seats behind me at mass in Brompton Oratory each morning will become a Catholic.'

No one sat behind Michael Collins in Brompton Oratory after that. It seems that Collins and Churchill thereafter had a considerable respect for each other.

Interestingly, according to my step-grandmother Nancy, Michael Collins had very old-fashioned views about marriage.

She attended a wedding where Michael was bestman; I think it was Seán McKeon's, the blacksmith from Ballina.

In his after-dinner speech, according to Nancy, Michael said a woman's place was in the home, the heart of the family, and if the bride was blessed with children it was so important to rear them to be good citizens of Ireland, and to build up the country.

There are echoes of that in Dev's constitution of 1937, article 41.

No Escape

This is my afternoon session at the 'book', and my notes are out again.

Lunch was good. Scruffy was satisfied too. No sign of Harry the Hare.

I suppose I am making a lot of notes and writing other bits and pieces. I will write a bit on the plane, as I never sleep much on planes.

The wind still blows 5 days on, or, worse still, 4 nights on. I find the nights longer than the days, even though we have 12 hours of each here.

We are now in bed for about eight hours and of that I would say we sleep four. The noise! The worry!

Yes, it is Wednesday; no, hold on, I think it is Thursday. I do not know the date or time as I deliberately didn't wear a watch today, just to 'get away from it all'.

I am glad of that, as time, except day or night, is fortunately pretty meaningless on this diminishing island.

Yes, the island is now down to about 3/4 of the size it was on Sunday, before the big, bad weather-wolf of the storm came along and gobbled up some of it.

The past 24 hours have been the worst. What happened yesterday was pretty traumatic in a small, unnoticed way.

Donal felt under pressure to get back to work, as apparently accounts were to go to Fyffes this week. The group accounts cannot go out until all branches put theirs through. HQ Fyffes will have to, instead of forwarding figures, notify everyone that: 'Our accountant in Belize is marooned on an island with 10 others and his boat sank last night.'

Yes, Donal's borrowed boat sank last night, pulled out into deeper water from the lagoon at the end. It must have been a rogue wave. That was after he persuaded us all to try and sail to Big Creek. We were mad to try. The boat was later rescued from the lagoon. Kevin had tied it to a palm tree – strong, long rope.

So, I guess you are wondering how did the boat sink? Well, it was like this.

We had no dry clothes, so we wrapped ourselves in blankets. Then, Olive found a bag of dry panties – my son Paul insisted I include this useless piece of information!

I had a very wide blanket, so I was told wear one! A panty! Well, thank God I got my shorts dry overnight. However, amid the distribution of these unmentionables, the wind, now in the late evening, changes. Kevin sensed it. He shouted, 'THE BOAT, THE BOAT'.

Out into the dark with re-donned wet shorts the four men go to find Donal's boat sunk. Fortunately for us, it was not fully sunk; the long rope held, preventing it from going out to sea. Two hours later they were back, having hauled it out. They partially filled the boat with sand to hold it down. We then sat down to rice and fish. Never more welcome.

The rain pelted down as the boat was being rescued, but we kept at it. The rain quietened the wind. Kevin said we should go to Big Creek. The forecast on the radio was better, they were now saying the storm was gone!

We also knew Kevin really wanted to get to Placencia, near Big Creek, so he could show off the 40 lb. tuna he caught earlier. It is the 'Big One'.

What a battle to land that tuna. We spectators shouted for 90 minutes. That reminds me, I must get Spencer Tracy's film about the big fish, an adaptation of Hemingway's *The Old Man and the Sea*.

I also promised Kevin last night I would send him Tim Severin's book, *The Brendan Voyage*. Like Tim Severin, Kevin is a man of courage and many skills.

So, the time came, we donned all our clothes as we knew it was going to be rough and tough. Donal's boat was loaded and Kevin's boat was loaded.

Hold on, I forget to tell you about the policemen – they are part of the story.

Last night, the four, patrolling policemen in their big oilskins and big boat visited us again. They came late, said nothing to us and left early. Their going encouraged us to try and leave too.

Boy, what we learnt about drugs and the cruelty and wealth of the drug barons in Central America. Huge profits apparently – and who uses all these drugs? The American middle classes so it seems, but it is spreading rapidly in Europe. Wealthy westerners should not be buying drugs.

Apparently, the drug barons have bigger boats than the police and move drugs during storms with virtual impunity. No mention was made of the earlier boat. A shut mouth catches no flies, or bullets!

Going back to the matter at hand, the idea this morning was for three boats to head in convoy to Big Creek, so the first two boats would make it a little easier for the third, the one with Caroline (expecting mother) and Olive and I (expecting grandparents) on board. I was worried but kept quiet. Kevin was the boss and I was not going to be left behind.

The take-off was delayed by electrical trouble in Donal's engine – electricity and salt water are real enemies.

Then suddenly, with a burst of engine life, we were running down the coral beach and into the sea.

The 'policemen', in their big, rubber and fibreglass boats, had disappeared into the still angry sea. They wouldn't help. Donal followed their direction and we followed Donal's boat.

It was bad, worse than it appeared after the initial launch. We were hitting the waves with a nasty slap. Suddenly, we took water over the bow. Our boats are too small for this weather. Not right for a pregnant woman.

Then Kevin made the very difficult (for him at least), but philosophical decision to abandon the mission.

He said saving his crew and boat was the important thing. Showing off the 40 lbs. tuna to his pals in Placencia came a very distant second.

So, back we came to our island, to Jean, the caretaker, to her unseen husband and son, to the dog who had been renamed 'Crappy' again (no longer Scruffy), and to Harry the hare. I renamed the hare George, as, for some reason, he reminded me of George Bush.

Then, strangely, a boat with two Yanks arrived from the mainland.

I immediately changed the hare's name back to Harry. I thought the Americans would not like the fact I named the hare after their president – although Harry is unusually hairy for a hare.

They, the Yanks, had the bad fortune of coming the previous night, when the extent of the storm would not have been evident inland.

When they met the storm, they could not turn back, it was too late. They were intending to leave again by this morning, but, like ourselves, are still here. Although they were wise enough not to try. The whole thing is getting mixed up.

❧

The direction of the wind suddenly changed to west, and the men parked the boats on the other side of the island. And eight wet (thoroughly wet) figures tramped the 50 yards to the *Man of War* and *Seagull* cabins, and the 'outhouse' in which Olive and I now reside.

We had to give up the *Laughing Bird* to the two Yanks, and the only place left for us was the outhouse.

It is called the *Flying Fish Store*, where there are two trestle beds amid the provisions. It is warm despite the storm.

The *Flying Fish* outhouse was even more windy, shaky and leaky than the *Laughing Bird*. We survived in it, although Olive says it is a good job her mother is not around to see where I have her now!

Natural Law

I return to my legal reading wrapped in a blanket. I read an interesting article on natural law. This is a good place to read it, even though the dissection of that profound subject by lawyers has really not being developed.

The basis of natural law is that man, by virtue of his/her nature, has to comply with certain laws to be properly human. This law comes from the essence of human nature. I suppose it is too simple and indefinite a concept for people in power.

The concept of power in law and for lawmakers has produced much verbiage, much of which few understand.

I would say there are more laws in existence than there are grains of sand on this island.

I just went back to the *Seagull* cabin to get a legal book I left there last night. In it, there was a very interesting quote about natural law from an Irish adoption case of 1982 *Northants Co. Co. -v- ABF*, where Judge Hamilton said:

The natural law is of universal application and applies to all human persons, be they citizens of the State or not, and it would be inconceivable that the father of the infant child would not be entitled to rely on the recognition of the family contained in Article 41.

Article 41 of the 1937 Constitution acknowledges the inalienable rights of the family. It seems to me that much modern legislation does not even pay lip service to Article 41. Politicians seem to be hell-bent on taking control of families – imposing their own unusual views of what a family is. And these politicians pretend that they are the authors of rights. They are not.

The corruption of language and thought in much modern legislation, particularly EU based, is frightening.

Bureaucrats and politicians are like Humpty Dumpty, who said: 'Words mean what I want them to mean.'

As I read more of the Irish constitution, I come to believe courts have not acknowledged its flavour of natural law sufficiently.

Judges are afraid of being seen as Christian philosophers, and therefore they don't expand or develop the constitution's natural law tenets.

The late, great judge Brian Walsh, whose mother was a Kerry neighbour, was a noteworthy exception. Indeed, the recently retired Judge Rory O'Hanlon had scorn poured on him for his similarly valiant efforts.

What is called secular modernism, with vague European and American roots, seem to be the basis for current legal and academic thinking, and it is undermining Irish people's view on religion.

What an extraordinary lack of thought there is about our nature and the meaning of each human being, the value of life and our duties towards others.

The principles of true human values, it is claimed, are not to be found in man's nature. It appears they are to be found in 'modernism', even in Ireland!

I suppose this 'humanism' algorithm stems from the belief that people, either as individuals or as a group, are entitled to do whatever they feel is best for them to do for themselves.

Thoughts on Law in an Outhouse
Before I go out to the howling, battering wet night and my misgivings, I should mention where I am as I write.

I am sitting by the side of the outhouse, where there is a makeshift line. My job; getting the clothes dry.

So, I sit out here in the open. If a drop of rain gets the page, it's ruined, as it is only toilet paper.

Hold on, rain! I jump up and dash out to salvage the sopping T-shirts and unmentionables.

I am to sit here writing until they dry. Later, I will hang them up on the line again, and continue to sit here in the wind.

The windy gales have increased very much in the past hour. We are lucky we came back!

I was wondering there, amid my legal musings, how tidal waves are formed. I have addressed that question to the dog, Scruffy, who sits here alongside me. Oops! It's raining again, up I get! I dash.

OK, with that out of the way, let's continue as the rain continues.

I'm in the shed writing, my material is four blank pages at the back of my current reading – the life of Lord Mansfield, a great lawyer and judge.

I bought it recently while on a trip to Scotland to visit my gorgeous daughter, Carina, a physio student.

We visited Scone Palace when up there. This was Mansfield's seat, yet it had no book on this great lawyer. Strange people, the Scots.

Mansfield's successors have all been lawyers, an unbroken line since his death in 1793.

He himself was one of the great activist judges – the ones who are not afraid to develop the common law in line with developing society.

Scone was the home of the famous 'Stone of Scone', which represented Scottish sovereignty.

Well anyway, where did my thoughts drift to as I lay awake in the shaking, leaking and battered outhouse last night?

I use an interesting photo as a bookmark while reading through the *Life of Lord Mansfield*. It is of a sign on a gate in the Highlands. This wise sign reads:

> Be ye man or be ye woman,
> Be ye going or be ye comin,
> Be ye early or be ye late,
> Aye take time to shut the gate.

That is good legal advice too.

My master early in my legal apprenticeship, the late James Raymond, told me: 'Robert, drains and rights-of-way are the curse of the Irish countryside. Rights of Way = ROWS.'

He told me that after he asked me to attend a case in Dublin between two neighbours. These two families had fought, for two generations, over the drains, rights of way and boundaries with great gusto. They were experts in the laws of easements. They still fight on.

When I worked in Dunmanway, the first office I worked in, I was shown a legal opinion from the Great Liberator himself, Daniel O'Connell, about a commonage and right of way dispute. What I remember most about it was the fee £6-6-0, six guineas.

I suppose most of you never heard of a guinea. I forget the date, but it must have been a century old then.

For comparative purposes, the wage I was earning then was £9 a week, which amounted to about £462 a year. In modern money (Euro) that is about €15,000 a year.

I paid £6 a week for full board, and thirteen shillings & four pence for my social welfare and income tax PAYE, which had just been introduced.

In the end, I had £2.6.8 to fund my lavish lifestyle. In fact, my main expenditure in the week was 9d for the once a week film.

The Dunmanway office had a 72 year-old office clerk. He had been a fixture there for 50 years. He told me about the Skibbereen and Bantry sessions in the early 1900s.

His job was to keep Mr Powell's (his boss) witnesses sober, if possible; as well as encouraging the other side's witnesses to get drunk.

Apparently, each side attended court with a good supply of poitín (or poteen). This was to aid the victory celebration if their attorneys won, or help drown the sorrows and damn the attorneys if they lost.

A thought has just struck me! Why has no one made a film about the Liberator? He was a truly extraordinary man.

Dunmanway Potín

One of my first Dunmanway cases concerned potín. Actually, hold on! It was in Macroom court.

The defendant, my client, came from near Kilmichael, the site of Tom Barry's famous ambush of the Tans.

My client, Sam, brought me a sheaf of summonses under the Illicit Distillation Acts. He told me a sheaf of lies too.

He said he had no potín, which is a raw alcoholic drink, in the house and the guards had it in for him, Sam, my man.

And why did they have it in for him? Sam was a 'Collins man,' or a follower of Michael Collins/Fine Gael, and all the guards were Fianna Fáil! They had found potín under a bridge and 'pinned' it on Sam.

In law, if found under a bridge it was on public property, and therefore not in the possession of Sam, my man.

On the way to Macroom, my driver, the district court clerk, Denis McCarthy RIP, stopped his car at a crossroads. (I didn't have any car of my own – not on £2.6.8 a week net!) The clerk, also a very strong Collins man, showed me, pointing towards a faraway white house, where the 'Long Fellow', Dev, stayed the night before my granduncle was ambushed and shot dead.

I do not know if this was true – my Collins relations seem to think Dev did not order or approve the assassination. However, 38 years after the event, my friend the district court clerk believed it. He told me the shooting of Collins by his own countrymen was a mortal sin.

Feelings were still bitter after what is the worst type of war, a civil war. Returning to Sam's case, it was heard just after 12 o'clock.

The sergeant gets into the box. On the day in question he had, with two other guards, visited Sam's farm 'on information received'.

Mrs Sam was alone in the house, so she went to locate Sam, who she found out with the sheep. While waiting, the sergeant saw a bottle of Lucozade on the kitchen dresser.

After inspecting this suspicious object, he noticed four tea leaves at the bottom of the bottle. He then suspected the bottle contained illicitly distilled liquor, and proceeded to take off the cork. The purpose of so doing was to smell the contents thereof.

Alas, dear reader, the sergeant smelled and pronounced, in a definite tone, that it was the illicitly distilled liquor known as potín. He even took the smallest sip to make sure of his findings – and yes, definitely it was the aforesaid illicitly distilled liquor.

I was sinking in my seat. The sergeant continued:

Justice, we then proceeded towards the yard as Mr and Mrs Sam had not come back yet. There, I noticed the cattle-trough was full of water and there was a cork floating on it.

We proceeded to search the trough with sticks and soon ascertained there were a large number of bottles therein. We emptied the trough and found 30 more bottles. Upon examination, I concluded that they also contained illicitly distilled liquor. My examination, which was assisted by my two accompanying guards, entailed smelling and tasting the contents of all such bottles. At this stage, we loaded these into the car for further analysis and probably destruction, before returning to the house.

Shortly afterwards Mr and Mrs Sam arrived. I took down the bottle of Lucozade from the dresser and asked Mr Sam to account for same. Sam said a friend of his gave it to him for a sick calf with white scour.

The sergeant said he then cautioned Sam, telling him he had the right to remain silent but anything he might say would be taken down in writing and may be given in evidence.

What a relief to me it was when Justice Crotty looked at the clock. It was one o'clock, so we adjourned until two.

I shot out with Sam and Mrs Sam. I pulled Mr Sam to one side and escorted Mrs Sam into the street.

I asked Mrs Sam: 'How much of that was true?' Her reply was: 'Most of it, but the guards had drunk half a bottle of potín by the time I got back from the mountain with Sam. He was hiding the still!'

I went for Sam – I was not going to put him into the box with a cock and bull story about the potín being found under a bridge. He took a bit of persuading, but I told him I had a duty not to assist perjury.

At 2 o'clock, we go in and he pleads guilty. I humbly said: 'Sam had just made these bottles for relatives for Christmas.' They were all small farmers, and they could not afford any other drink.

Justice Crotty looked very sceptical. I referred to Mr and Mrs Sam's six children. I kept Sam out of prison, not easy as it turned out he had a previous conviction.

We later petitioned the Minister and got the fine reduced. The fact there was an election in the offing helped.

Mrs Sam brought me a fine bottle of potín as a Christmas present, as I was a Collins by blood. I then took the bottle home to my father, a vet. He used it for embrocation, and he would rub it on greyhounds before a race – he claimed it put great life in them.

By the way, I discovered the tea leaves were to change the potín's colour, make it look more like Lucozade. I also learned it was impossible to get a conviction for potín found under a public bridge, as it was on public property and owned by the county council.

There was another Dunmanway potín-story. Apparently, if you were friends with a certain guard around Christmas time, he could supply potín at 10/- (ten shilling) a bottle.

His job was to get rid of seized potín by pouring it down the drain. According to the shocking rumour, there was another barrel under the drain.

See the interesting things I was learning about the law through clients. Be cautious about totally believing a client!

Gosh, I have wandered. I cannot find any order in my toilet sheets.

I am going to go for a walk with Scruffy in the wind. We have become real friends again. He thought he had lost me. Olive is above with the girls in the *Seagull* cabin. I might check in for a chat.

Back soon, as I have to go!

I Wonder about Computers

I am writing this just for myself. I have stopped talking religion with my fellow 'marooners' on the island.

In this storm, it is natural to wonder about fundamentals. This piece of island was 'created' by coral – there are millions, probably even billions, of pieces.

Thousands of sand grains are being eroded by each wave, and because this process is so regular, I wonder have we enough of these millions?

In time, ourselves and this island, millions of us, indeed billions of us, now on earth will be gone, going in each wave of a year.

Coral is created from dead fish bones and shell, but where did these fish come from? Where did we (you and I) and the billions of others ultimately come from? Where, and very soon, are we going to?

It is time for me to wonder about creation and the Omega here on this windswept island. I have this time.

I think it was Aristotle, (or was it Sophocles?) who said the secret of wisdom was 'to know thyself'. Hold on, it was Socrates in fact, I'm sure of it.

Do you ever wonder at yourself and the marvellous creation that you are and that is around you? Stop and wonder, and do be pleased with what you find. You are a wonderful creation.

It is not necessary to get 'lost' here off the shore of Belize to wonder and try to know yourself. Indeed, this point is phrased much better by St Augustine of Hippo, when he wrote:

> People travel to wonder
> At the height of the mountains
> At the huge waves of the sea
> At the long courses of rivers,
> At the vast compass of the ocean,
> At the circular motion of the stars
> And pass by themselves without wondering.

My wondering about our creation and the creation of this coral island is tinged with apprehension, but maybe we are in constant subliminal apprehension about death?

Is death the end of our personal creation? I think that is unlikely. Of course, you may disagree.

People disagree, especially in this technological age of personal computers. However, is there not a Creator creating the people who created these computers? I wonder very much about computers.

What is it that Longfellow wrote about our footprints in the sands of time?

> Footprints, that perhaps another
> Sailing o're life's solemn main,
> A forlorn and shipwrecked brother
> Seeing, shall take heart again.

No footprints on the sand of time here, not on this wet, windy caye, but I do take heart from Longfellow.

Some years ago, I was asked to fill in on Radio Kerry for some guest who could not make it.

During the interview, I said I found death a very interesting subject. The rest of the interview turned into a discussion about death.

People phoned in and asked why did I find death so interesting, rather than simply frightening?

As it happens, I cannot remember much of what I said, or how I continued talking cheerfully about this interesting subject for 30 mins.

One story I do remember was from growing up. A neighbour had died in Meenogahane. Full of curiosity, Gerard and I headed across the field to the wake house.

Gerard wanted to see a dead person. The corpse was upstairs. Up we went, got a fright at the sight of it, and came down the stairs quickly.

On our way down the stairs, I met a man with a bucket. I glanced into the bucket and saw movement. I looked further in. It was a bucket of brown porter, and there was a mouse swimming inside. We fled. I think that was one of the reasons I never drank alcohol.

You see, I believe everything we do or create, even if it's just a loaf of bread, is done for a purpose. Therefore, I assume the great Creator has created me with some purpose in mind. Simple, isn't it?

I do remember saying that my views on death centred on HOPE and JUSTICE, two difficult values or virtues, and their two opposing vices, despair and injustice.

I remember discussing this with Jack McKenna, a family friend, once, on one of our St Vincent de Paul rounds. I told him that life seemed to be very unjust for so many people: Why was their poverty? Why could some people not cope with the vile blows of the world? Why did the rich get richer and the poor poorer?

Jack's argument was that the absence of justice in this world meant there would be justice in the next life. The very nature of the concepts of justice and a just Creator demanded accountability at some stage of our continued existence.

It was all a bit Jesuitical for me – but then Jack had spent time in a seminary, and his brother Liam is a Jesuit priest.

I often wonder why the Jesuits are so feared by the enemies of the Catholic Church? I suppose it is because they deal in fundamental ideas and therefore challenge others.

It is easier not to think, easier to criticise than to think.

Enough of Robert's speculations! I am going to go out to the wind and surfing sea – to change my mood level! Am I right to not discuss this with the others? We'll see tonight.

DAY SEVEN: SHIPWRECKED PORRIDGE

Another Storm!!
We awoke at about seven this morning, on this our sixth day on the island
– actually the seventh for the juniors, Aislinn, Séan and Paul.

This is D-Day for us, as we were to fly to Miami, and then onto Ireland,
the day after tomorrow – going from Placencia to Belize Airport for a
2:30 pm flight to Miami.

I had thought, on Thursday night, that the wind wasn't quite as noisy
as previously, and that Wednesday had shown some signs of a break in
the weather.

However, Jean (the caretaker), who listens to the radio regularly, has
picked up some disturbing news; 294 people have died in Mexico, just
north of Belize, in a bad bout of weather, and this weather is heading south
towards us now, as I write!

Kevin's view is that if this weather does come our way, we could be
imprisoned on the island for a week or 10 days.

We are, of course, running into food problems; we are down to two
meals a day; Aisling and Séan are worried about their jobs (occupational
therapist and accountant).

Personally, I am happy to let the world get on without me for another
while. I know it will do OK without me.

I was reading articles about the law on health and safety recently, on
the doctrine of proportionality in particular, which is a sort of new craze
in Irish law, a new notion for the measurement of justice.

I am also delving into the thoughts of Lord Mansfield. I discovered
a very informative judgement of his about slavery – given a little more
than 200 years ago. He emphasised the supremacy the natural law, and
its allowance of personal and natural freedom for all, against positive or

manmade law's principle of freedom of contract. This contract principle regarded slaves as the property of their owner. Mansfield freed a slave, and the author claimed it was the first real triumph for the abolitionists.

We are sleeping better. Initially, the wind seemed to be calmer, but this morning, all of a sudden, the hut shook.

I was worried. Was this the tidal wave I feared? This radio news from Mexico had that crazy wind hitting us from another direction, like a whirlwind.

However, it didn't seem as bad as I thought when I looked at the sea. Apparently, as Kevin told me later, the original storm wasn't able to escape out of the big bay we were in. This was because it could not get over the high mountains of Honduras to the west – it got thrown back and went around the bay again.

Kevin warns the storm can return again. Something to do with temperature apparently. I hope it won't!

So, I lay here thinking about when we might get off this diminishing island. It got about 10 yards shorter yesterday.

We are now only eating fish and rice and coconuts, although the rice may be gone. I wonder do we have to go to New York, in order to get back to Shannon. Have I enough money, or Olive enough in her visa card, to cover 5 tickets?

Olive just went off to see who was up. She arrived back with a bowl of 'poor man's porridge', more like shipwrecked porridge here. This was made from flour and coconut (to sweeten it).

It looked like famine soup, but the hungry cannot be choosy. That was my breakfast. It tasted better than it looked. It was Kevin, who made it, that called it the poor man's porridge.

James Bond to the Rescue

Donal and I went up to Jean's cabin, where there was a ship-to-shore radio. We could not get on in touch with Brian, Donal's friend, who had the biggest boat on the mainland at Big Creek.

We raised Mark, who was very competent. The shipping forecast was that today would not be too bad, but trouble was coming fast from Mexico, in about 8-10 hours.

"the Patrol Boat"

Between us, we decided we should make a second attempt at getting to the mainland. Mark got Vernon, his friend, to come out from Big Creek in the big boat – a James Bond-like, heavy and fast boat, about 18 feet in length, and with twin Yamaha engines.

When I saw Vernon and his boat, I immediately rechristened him James Bond. He came out very fast as he had the wind and the tide with him. It meant both wind and tide were against us going back. The tide is not such a big factor here.

We loaded up all of Kevin's fish, a huge, heavy box. We packed our books and clothes. Then all of us donned our lifejackets and we headed out.

BANG, BANG and SMASH! Vernon was shooting out into the waves. The boat shudders. He slowed and began to pace her slowly on the waves. Less waves, less vibration. We had to protect Caroline and her precious cargo.

It was a good boat, but still, we had a bad hour. We made the last 4 miles quickly enough, as we got shelter from the land. The sea calmed and the spirits rose.

We came into land at Big Creek's Placencia, which was pleasant, peaceful and sunny. What an extraordinary difference 8 miles can make. *Terra firma* was nice.

We were all wet and we spent the entire morning trying to dry out. All is well that ends well.

Update: Months later, Caroline and Donal's baby, Benedict, died just after birth. However, they now have four wonderful children.

Getting Teeth Pulled in India and Japan

So, what thoughts and stories did I share last night? I thought of stories to tell in the *Seagull* cabin. I was a coward. I did not go into the philosophical stuff. Olive said I would turn the kids off, so I told stories instead.

I have a theory that flying affects your teeth. Two recent long-haul flights resulted in my losing a filling within 12 hours of hitting the runaway.

The first occasion was on a visit to a legal conference in India. It was the IBA (International Bar Association) – heavy legal stuff.

Out pops the filling at breakfast, so Robert has to pop off to the dentist, although it wasn't that easy.

The Hotel rang a dentist. For some reason, the dentist insisted on picking me up at the hotel in his chauffeur driven car, and take me to the dental hospital. Then, I was driven around all of New Delhi. I was lost. I had a big hole in my tooth, and I was being told by this man that he was a wonderful, professor-dentist and he worked in a wonderful university hospital.

We stopped at one crossing, and I remember spotting a backstreet dentist at work – one man drilled, while another cycled furiously on a machine to supply power.

Eventually, we arrived at this man's surgery and not at 'his' hospital. The surgery looked unimpressive from the outside. However, he did have a good deal of equipment and big, bright lights. I refused an anaesthetic for fear of Aids.

Admittedly, he turned out to be a good dentist. He gave me very reassuring advice, as well as doing a good job on my tooth.

He explained that my old metal fillings were heavy, and were getting slightly loose. This allowed bacteria in and so forth, which resulted in decay. Apparently, I needed a big job. He did it quickly. I still have that bit of Indian handiwork.

He charged me $100 US dollars, which was a fortune in India.

I meekly paid up, as I didn't know where I was and I didn't like the look of his two tough-looking bodyguards. The other place I remember seeing a lot of tough bodyguards guarding the rich was the Philippines.

I bought a lot of legal books in India at about a quarter of their English price – I am a bookaholic! They were shipped back to me.

Interestingly, Mahatma Gandhi used the Irish constitution as a base document when drafting aspects of the Indian constitution. He corresponded with de Valera.

India is such a massive place, it was startling. It's beginning to become an economic power, but it has a long way to go. Its population is similar to China's, which is another emerging power. Europe and USA lookout!

The visit to the dentist in Tokyo happened in a similar same way. Off the plane and out pops the filling, so off pops Robert to the dental clinic.

It took 36 hours to get it arranged! I entered the clinic at 8:45 am.

My first difficulty was they insisted I take off my shoes. I didn't want to as I have fallen arches. I was forced to take out my arch supporters in order to demonstrate that I needed my shoes on to get around. No good; no English on their side, and no Japanese by me. And no slippers with arch supports.

Eventually, in order to get inside the door, I relent, off comes my shoes and I cramp my feet into tiny slippers and shuffle in. Oddly, they allowed me bring in shoes on my hands, but not my feet!

Then I'm presented with a form I couldn't understand, as it was in Japanese! Being a lawyer is very inhibiting in these circumstances. I won't sign a document I can't read. You shouldn't either – free legal advice.

After 15 minutes of looking through a phrase book and dictionary, they find a form in English.

It asked me all sorts of embarrassing questions, such as: 'Are you constipated?'

Again, I relented, I filled it up in an answers to questions way. I was directed towards a tiny dentist chair.

I remember my head hanging over one end, my legs over the other. Eventually, there was something put under my head. It didn't work, so I was moved to another room and a bigger chair. The room was festooned with lots of high-tech equipment.

They gave all kinds of instructions, and the phrase book had to come out again.

Eventually, I opened my mouth wide and pointed to the offending molar. Great progress – target identified!

With the aid of the phrase book, I conveyed to them I wanted it without injection.

After some drilling, I was led off for an X-ray. More discussion and dissection of the X-ray film. Out comes the phrase book, and it transpires he would only do a temporary job.

OK, I said. More drilling; plastic in and Robert out – job cost £30.

I sit by the door, extract my feet from the tiny leather slipper, and place them, one by one, into my size 10 shoes, arch supports included. Relief!

❦

Two other very memorable things happened to me in Tokyo.

Firstly, I remember looking out a window and seeing that the large roof of the nearby building, it was adjacent but lower than the one I was in, was being used as a driving school. There were 4 cars reversing and turning on the roof top.

Secondly, I will never forget the translation of the toilet sign: 'Please flash strongly as our water is weak.' Yes. It was an 'a' ('flash') and not a 'u' ('flush').

Also, the sign near the phone in our skyscraper hotel. Our bedroom was on the 40th floor and it said: 'In case of an earthquake: If the building is falling ring the reception for instruction.' That did not seem to me to be very useful information; or maybe I was suffering from cultural misunderstanding, the dreadful smog! And the masks people have to wear.

The smog was a blanket above the street. What attracts people to these cities? I know of course, more money! 'Money talks, it don't sing and dance, but it sure talks.'

I am glad I had no fillings popping out now on the caye. We had enough to contend with.

❦

You know they have 6 million drivers in Tokyo? Seriously! They have failed to reduce the number or cars.

Drivers have to graduate through a series of lessons to earn a licence and a car permit – it costs about £2,000.

Lorries have outside and visible speed-indicators.

Also, if you can show you own a parking space within 1 km of your home it helps in getting a permit

And the reason they drive on the left? I discovered it comes from the trains. The British engineers who put in the train-system used the left-sided platforms for entrance and exit, and this spread to the roads.

The left-side also suited the horse-mounted warriors, the Samurai, who kept their swords on the left and fought with their right hand.

There is often a three-tiered road system; a main street, a road under the street, a railway system, and underneath that, a metro system.

A highly efficient way to move masses of people, although most people live within a mile of their work. They really do not need a car, but, like the Yanks, a big car is a status symbol.

We can't talk, the Irish are becoming like that too. They work for the car and pay taxes and tolls for the roads.

In Japan, most males work in the one job in the same corporation all their lives. When I was there, they claimed every male employee was expected to, and was glad to, work an extra 10 hours a week free to help his company survive the recession.

They had 4.6% unemployment, it is usually 2%, so it felt that their economy was shot to pieces.

Remember when we had 16% in Ireland?

I don't think they bother with figures in Belize – they are too busy enjoying their fishing and their natural abundance of fruit.

Travel in Japan is usually best done by trains. We even travelled on the 'bullet train', which has a speed of 120 mph. It was super, and I was surprised to learn the first one was commissioned in 1964.

We saw Mount Fuji, which was almost perfectly concealed by clouds and was snow-capped from half-way up.

The word Fuji derives from two Chinese characters: 'fu' means 'wealthy', and 'ji' means 'warrior'. Whether there was anything further behind those two words, I never found out.

At the base of that mountain is steam billowing out of sulphurous hot-springs, huge clouds of it. Lower down again, are cherry blossom and magnolia trees – and we were lucky to be there when they were in bloom.

Even in Tokyo, they did a little to alleviate the concrete horrors. Extraordinary place to live in – the tiny flats!

In railway stations you can rent a 'room' for a night in train station buildings. It is like a coffin, and you crawl into it on your hands and knees.

During the cherry blossom season, CEOs and company big-shots take their lunch out of doors. As space is limited, it is not uncommon for office boys to go out early and sit on seats under the cherry trees. As soon as the bosses appear, the office boys vacate the seats and head back inside.

Pedestrians have clear lights and get the right-of-way – unlike in Dublin. In Dublin, one needs to be a kangaroo to get across the street.

In Tokyo, when you arrive at a crossing, if the little man isn't green there is a sign next to the red man which tells you that, through slowly extinguishing figures, the number of seconds you will have to wait for the green man. It helps to keep the blood pressure down.

Driving in the city was a nightmare. It took 2 ½ hours to get from the hotel to the airport (a distance of 6 miles), in a bright, air-conditioned bus with lots of anti-pollution filters in the air system. No speeding there!

No traffic-lights or speed-lights here on the caye.

I'm Not Perry Mason
This reminds me of the following:

> The law
> What is your attitude to the law?
> Is it something you hold in awe?
> Or is it something for idle chatter
> When you speak of things that do not matter.
> There was my friend called Joe
> Of his Lady Betty he had spoken so,
> Then he was caught doing seventy
> So suddenly he fears a very stiff penalty.
> Said the Judge to Joe – your speed,
> What seventy, was there any need?
> Joe spoke up 'My Judge, your lady
> My wife was about to have a baby'
> The Judge pondered: Joe worriedly wondered.
> The Judge said 'In view of that fact
> I will apply the Probation Act.'

Joe got away with it, but here is what I am assured by a US law book is a true story.

Perry Mason, Rumpole and Judge Judy are the bane of all practising lawyers. Clients read books, see films and watch TV shows by the dozen. They see these lawyers, like Perry, pulling legal rabbits out of a non-existent legal hat and winning all his cases.

So, Robert *et al* are told, 'do a Perry Mason for me' on a no motor-tax summons!

The actor who played Perry Mason is called Raymond Burr. Well, in 1964 Mr Burr decided to be his own lawyer when a man sued him for $1085, a debt allegedly dating from 1960.

Mr Burr should have answered the claim through a lawyer, as any wise man would, who would have no doubt argued the money was statute barred – there is a three-year limit there.

Then, to make matters worse, Mr Burr failed to turn up at court to make a deposition. Result: the judge ordered Mr Burr pay up. Costly error!

To Hong Kong, Guilin and Back
This is a note I found on a plane heading to Shannon. I cannot identify what night it was written. This is what it said:

> *On a night such as this it is good to listen to other messages in the wind.*

However, the problem is, which direction does it blow from. It seems to come from the east. I think of our son Gearóid and a visit to China.

Hong Kong is an interesting place for those driver maniacs among you who wish to study road traffic law.

Beijing is a city with lots of Chinese driving lots of bikes, lots of trains, lots of lorries and trucks, and lots and lots of cars.

Now, how has Beijing come into this note? I want to say something about Belize.

Belize and Hong Kong share a few things. Both are smaller than Ireland in area. Both are tropical. It ends there however. Belize is underdeveloped and under populated. Hong Kong is overdeveloped and overpopulated.

The best way to see both of these aspects of Hong Kong is to take the tram. The tram is so cheap it is wonderful, you get on it and it runs for miles. The plastic seats are simple but, provided the windows are open, it's comfortable.

It takes about an hour to get from one end of the city to the other. There are skyscrapers everywhere. The streets and the bridges, which are walkways over the streets, are thronged.

The problem with Hong Kong depends on whether you are a shopper or not. If you are, you stay, if you are not (and I am not), you go. I went.

I couldn't stick the place, despite its wonderful modern architecture along the waterfront. Then there were the stacked-small, box-type high rise buildings behind the sea front. Those dreadful and impersonal buildings!

In one of them, the entire population of a big Belize town could sleep and watch TV together. Indeed, all the people of my home town of Listowel could live in one. Perish the thought, as we would lose our individualism. Our son's small flat was on the 26th floor, and that was only about half way up the building.

Giving in to my peculiar addiction, I bought a very expensive book on Hong Kong road traffic law – British-based like ours.

So, we left. We went first to Guilin, on a wonderful packet tour with Dragon Air.

On the drive to the Sheraton hotel, I noticed how warm and wealthy a place it was compared to the considerable poverty I saw in the streets and countryside before. I saw so much poverty in the Chinese countryside, when I visited there some years ago. There was still poverty.

However, I did see remarkable improvements since I was there last, fifteen years previous. They had brought back colour and art – along with free enterprise.

Mao's blue or green jacket and cap are gone. That was *de rigour dress* when I was there first. Now, the cyclists are multi-coloured. You could also see some motorcars.

All the same, you also did get the feeling you were under constant surveillance. The people are always friendly, but less on guard than before. However, prices had increased enormously.

Guilin boasts that tourists have been visiting for 1500 years, and I believe it. It has 20,000 peculiar geological items, all of which are really impressive.

You can take a boat trip up the Li River, and see startling limestone peaks that tower in the mist.

On the boat, I remember seeing what appeared to me to be these odd, unreal and massive rocks. They were real and startlingly so.

If you saw the James Bond 007 film *The Man with the Golden Gun,* you would have seen, towards the end of the film, the unusual and startling scenery of Thailand. Well, Guilin is even more unusual and a lot more impressive.

And all of this is just an hour's flying time from Hong Kong, so visit it.

The countryside had not changed as much as the towns. There were oxen in the fields ploughing the rice paddies, although I did see one tractor. The men and women worked the fields by hand. Up in the mountains, they cultivated areas as small as a square yard, nestled there among the rocks. They carried material in buckets, hanging from poles balanced on their shoulders. Their houses were the small, shanty-type.

I found the change in the clothes unusual. Young women were now dressed in bright colours, although they were still carrying four buckets on a pole. At times it looked more like India than China!

Then, there were the duck farms. I saw about a thousand white ducks swimming in a field, about 2 acres in size, rented from the government by a farmer. I did not eat duck that night. I do not know why, as I like duck. It was probably the colour of the water. I eat fish, but then a fish does not seem as presentable as a duck swimming. The fish came from the adjoining two-acre field, which happened to be a state-run fish-farm.

The first time I was there, as part of a group of Irish lawyers, we visited prisons inter alia.

One prison for young people had a large fish farm. Before breakfast at 6 am, each juvenile inmate had to catch, with his bare hands, a bucket full of fish.

I remember the governor telling us, with the lovely, patient smile of the Chinese, that if a young person was forced to fish in the ice and snow for a few months he or she was unlikely to want to come back to prison!

Well, urban Guilin is a hive of rebuilding.

At the airport, they are obsessed with form filling – 3 per person. When we finally got beyond the bureaucrats, who were dressed in army uniform, we saw a poster which said: 'Be Just and Honest – Guard the Pass with Good Manners.' Figure it out for yourself!

The airport was 25 miles from the city. We went in by bus via the dual carriageway. I saw only 4 cars, but there were a good lot of trucks, probably about 50. Many of these were army trucks, as soldiers provide many services, even to the extent of picking up rubbish!

However, we met hundreds of cyclists and these hundreds quickly became thousands when we reached the city itself.

Olive, (Doctor), Carina (Physiotherapist) and I had an interesting experience in a genuine massage parlour. As a man, I felt protected by having my wife with me in these institutions. I suppose a man should not say he feels threatened by these places, but I do.

Anyway, we had great giggles as well as an interesting time. Three young Chinese girls manipulated our legs for an hour first.

Then, they did a body massage, a fully-clothed body massage, on the three of us. I remember them giggling at the size of our big legs and toes.

The foot massage was, by far and away, the most interesting. They gave us a card, in English, which explained how the various pressure points in the foot were connected to almost all other parts of the body.

It certainly made me interested in reflexology. My girls, Olive and Carina, because of their respective professions, were comparing medical notes at a great rate, and all while we drank our green tea.

All that cost us 200 yuan each. One púnt was about 13 yuan. Yuan is the People's Republic of China money, which is different to Hong Kong dollars, which are again different from US dollars.

However, they all want US dollars. A tip of one US dollar brings a smile to the face of the person being tipped, so I always come armed with a wallet full of Abraham Lincolns!

The Chinese appeared to have little interest in Europe. Indeed, no one knew anything about Ireland – good for our humility!

The few in Hong Kong who did, spoke only of 'The Troubles'. It is a pity that the media make our squabbles appear important and the participants appear important. They are of no importance in world terms. If we only realised that, we might start behaving like two groups of Christians. We might even cut out the political posturing and platitudes.

In China, you are among a quarter of the world's populations – if .0001% of them ever heard of Ireland they have forgotten it.

The same sort of statistics apply to India – another quarter of the world's population, where very few knew where Ireland was, at least when I was there in 1998 – 'somewhere near London'!

About 5% of the population in China had heard of England, and about 50% of the population in India, where English is an official language, had heard of it. India had been under British rule.

So, we have an inflated sense of our own importance when it comes to our green and misty island.

Still, I do love getting back to it and the Kingdom of Kerry.

It is easy to see how the People's Republic of China, or communist China, is puzzled by capitalist China, Hong Kong.

Returning to Hong Kong from Guilin is quite the culture shock, as great as returning to Knocknagoshel from New York.

The massive new airport in Hong Kong, still only in the first of four phases, is something else. It is a gigantic, engineering feat, and an architectural feat as well.

I think one will need an aeroplane to get around it, it is so, so big. There is a spectacularly efficient airport express-train in the centre of Hong Kong, but the airport bus is one third of the price and you have a better view. I dislike being dashed into tunnels like a worm.

I suppose you have to accept the toothpaste travel system – you know what I mean? Funnelled into a plane, and then squeezed into a seat where there is no room for your legs, your hands or your head. Then, you are squeezed out of the tube, through a narrow hole and into another funnel or series of funnels, before being squeezed into another tube, be it a bus, a train or whatever.

Still it is all very interesting, isn't it? It makes you appreciate the value of space at home. We really are lucky.

The relative poverty of Guilin compared to the obvious wealth of Hong Kong summed it up for me. I remember seeing a sign which read 'poverty is wrong'. However, they do not like being wrong in Hong Kong. They like being right and rich.

I wrote to a number of business friends when I got back: Get into China. It is going to be the country of the 21st century!

Guilin

F.P

Going to Mass in China

Before we leave China, let me tell you about a very interesting experience I had there; attending mass!

I was in China years before on what we called Kinlen Tours, organised by Dermot Kinlen SC. It was officially called Ireland China Friendship Exchange Tour. We were a group of lawyers sharing legal knowledge.

The whole visit would take almost all night to talk about, and would probably take days to write about. I might do it sometime.

However, here in the *Seagull* cabin I'm going to stick to the highlight of going to a mass.

I had said to our Chinese guide, Mr Wong, that, on what was Holy Thursday evening in our Christian calendar, I would like to attend some sort of Christian religious event over Easter if available.

Mr Wong said he would ring people in the big city we were planning to go to. It is a pity I do not remember the name of it. Many of these names were unpronounceable.

Eventually, our guide called us to say there would be a religious service in the People's Republic of China Catholic Church, on Easter Sunday morning.

So, off we all went to the People's Republic of China Catholic Church on Sunday morning. The church was old-fashioned, dark and with about 100 souls. As usual, they were mostly women! Men in China, like in Ireland, are often lukewarm about religion and thinking about life and death.

As we went up the aisle, the parish priest came down to meet us. He had an old-fashioned black soutane and biretta with three spikes. He reminded me of the old parish priest in Causeway that I knew.

We all bowed to each other and shook hands. Mass began. The priest, dressed in mostly white vestments for Easter, was accompanied by two altar boys.

To our utter delight, the mass began with *intro ito ad altar dei* (I will go to the altar of God). Yes, the priest said mass in Latin. As many of us had been altar boys, we answered the mass in Latin. This was much to the amazement of the priest and the congregation.

Dermot Kinlen would not allow us to go to communion, as Rome did not recognise the People's Republic of China's Catholic Church. In fact, they were excommunicated.

2019: Pope Francis is trying to reverse that. I hope he succeeds!

I would have gone to communion, but obeyed our leader. I have always gone to communion in the Church of Ireland's churches in Downpartick, and indeed Tralee.

I am not sure whether this is grounds for excommunication or not, Olive thinks it may be and therefore doesn't take communion at these non-Catholic events.

After mass, the priest hurried around to meet us. He asked would we like to meet the bishop.

We said of course we would like to meet the bishop. However, this caused our learned guide some consternation. He was a learned man who quoted Yeats and Robert Frost. The problem was, the bishop was under house arrest, as he was 'a Rome man'.

However, we dug in our heels, and eventually our guide agreed to ring the police. The police agreed we could meet the bishop, but insisted an English-speaking note-taker accompany us, as everything that was to be said at the meeting had to be written down and examined.

We took it that we were being spied on. So, we went into a huddle and put together what we were going to say in Latin.

The note-taker arrives an hour later. In we go to meet the bishop – note-taker following. When we get inside, and out comes the note-taker's notebook.

Dermot begins conversing with the bishop in Latin. The note-taker sat there with his pen poised, and a shocked look on his face. He didn't record one word of what was said.

The Bishop knew all about Ireland, Maynooth, the Vatican Council and everything else.

As we were leaving, just after receiving the bishop's blessing, I said to him: '*Vide tu in Maynooth, deo volente* (I will see you in Maynooth, God willing).'

Later, Dermot told me another story about China. The Chinese 'guardians' all claimed to know no English. However, when Dermot and Martin, his driver, began to tell simple, funny stories, the Chinese 'guardians' all laughed.

I knew the great Dermot Kinlen was trying to get bishops out of China, and was trying to establish whether they could go abroad.

To my utter amazement, about two years later I got a call from Dermot to attend a meeting. Apparently, 'our' Chinese bishop had arrived in Killarney.

I hastened down to meet 'our' Chinese bishop in the bishop's house in Killarney. Our Kerry bishop at the time was The Very Rev. Diarmuid O'Sullivan. He didn't approve of us meeting the bishop at all, but was polite.

I have always said that the fact Christians don't get together more, don't come under the one umbrella of Christ, is a failing on our part. It is a failure to understand the central message of Christ, love; which is something to be shared.

Going Home, AT LAST!
Well, yesterday's tomorrow is today. Finally!

When we arrived, we eat in a restaurant here in Big Creek. Like all seaside places, there are good fish restaurants here – not fancy ones, but good. The food here is good and good value.

It rained all afternoon and all night. We got the tip of that Mexican weather, but, thankfully, not the full storm.

I finished reading the life of Lord Mansfield. I was just reading about his slavery case when we left the island.

I was shocked to learn that between 10 and 15 million slaves were taken to the Americas from Africa. The British king, or more accurately the Crown, owned slaves. They cost £30 each, if delivered in saleable condition.

Another case Mansfield dealt with was the case of the slave ship Zong in 1781.

Zong was sailing to Jamaica with 470 black slaves and 17 whites, when a sickness broke out. The slaves were shackled. The whites had guns and whips. 60 slaves and 7 whites died. Many of the slaves were ill.

The captain concluded that, while the cost of a slave who died from natural death fell on the owners of Zong, if they were thrown overboard, and therefore lost cargo, the insurance company was liable. He had 133 slaves thrown into the sea.

When the Zong returned to England, the owners sued the insurers. The matter came before a jury, who held that the insurers must pay the owners for lost property.

The insurers appealed it to Mansfield's court, the Court of the King's Bench, and won. The judgement: throwing a slave overboard had been a crime, and therefore the issue of insurance did not arise.

I came across an interesting connection between Tralee, the capital of Kerry, and the anti-slavery movement.

How? Through its connection with James Stephens (1759-1832), a barrister, who wrote an important law book on international law called *War in Disguise*. To further, *inter alia*, his abolition of slavery aims, he won a seat in parliament. He initially took a seat for Tralee, which was, I believe, a 'rotten borough' at the time (1808). I must follow up that when I get home!

I also finished my 500-page *Irish Jurist* last night. I was so busy talking, writing and reading on the caye, that I did not get it finished there.

I read a diverse range of legal articles, including *The Trial of Jesus as a Conflict of Laws*, *Nonconsensual Sterilization of Mentally Disabled People*, *The Third Branch and the Fourth Estate* (the 'third branch' being the courts, and the 'fourth estate' being the press).

I hope you get a flavour of how fascinating and diverse the subject of law is. I love it even if it frustrates me at times.

So, this am:

> We will arise and go now and to Inish Ireland,
> We have left our small island and huts of timber made
> For we had little peace there
> Where peace should have come dropping slow.

(Apologies to WBY)

We plane hop: Placencia to Belize City, Belize to Miami, & Miami to Shannon.

In Shannon, we are surprised at the cold. Fortunately, I anticipated this and made sure to put my long underwear on.

Putting on long underwear in those small, airplane toilets is actually quite a feat, but I got it on just in time, just as we approached Ireland.

Then, I looked out lovingly at Kerry Head and Loop Head. We were home.

I hope you have enjoyed my ramblings dear readers.

I love you all – well, almost all.

Robert.

AFTERWORD

Olive and our family are doing well thanks be to God. There are far more ups than downs.

I hope that you dear reader, have enjoyed this book which started with thoughts under the bed.

As I mentioned, when I turned eighty, on the 31st of December 2017, real pressure came on me to put it all together. When you have your ten children, their ten spouses and your thirty -two grandchildren at your party, you yield.

I'm still trying to retire as a lawyer, not easy.

You must not be too hard on yourself. Do not pass by yourself without wondering. You are a wonderful part of creation. You have a meaning by living.

I have thought a lot about Ireland. It has lost its moral compass. That needs to be rebuilt and improved. We owe 200 billion euros, a legacy we should not be leaving to future generations.

We need to rethink Ireland's position on abortion and the environment. We are told that Ireland is a very wealthy country. All the more reason for young educated people to get involved in rational politics.

Do not be complacent or afraid. I can't help repeating those wonderful words on Longfellow's:

> Let us then be up and doing,
> With a heart for any fate,
> Still achieving still pursuing,
> Learn to labour and to wait,

I hope you have enjoyed my ramblings.

Warm regards,
Robert
17/03/2019

Robert Pierse grew up and lives in Kerry, Ireland. He is one of the county's best-known lawyers. He is also husband to Olive and father of ten children. As well as being a storyteller, legal author and avid adventurer, he is a strong social campaigner.

In *Under the Bed: Stories & Thoughts from a Desert Island*, Robert describes how he and his family survived a tropical storm off the coast of Belize, Central America. In the book, he also recounts many events from his life and travels:

Visiting Downpatrick during the troubles, where he helped twin Listowel to the unionist stronghold; helping political prisoners in the Philippines; how a Russian prostitute came to his aid while on the other side of the iron curtain; and attending mass deep in communist China.

Made in the USA
Monee, IL
07 March 2026